Mental Content

Colin McGinn

Basil Blackwell

Copyright © Colin McGinn 1989

First published 1989
First published in paperback 1991

Basil Blackwell Ltd
108 Cowley Road, Oxford, OX4 1JF, UK

Basil Blackwell Inc.
3 Cambridge Center,
Cambridge, Massachusetts 02142, USA

British Library Cataloguing in Publication Data
A CIP catalogue record for this book is available from the British Library.

Library of Congress Cataloging in Publication Data
McGinn, Colin, 1950–
Mental content / Colin McGinn.
p. cm.
Bibliography: p.
Includes index.
1. Consciousness.   2. Mind and body.   I. Title.
BF311.M428   1991
128'.2—dc19
ISBN 0–631–18029–X

Typeset in 11/13 Caslon by Hope Services (Abingdon) Ltd.
Printed in Great Britain by T.J. Press Ltd, Padstow, Cornwall

Table of Content

Preface

Philosophy is a wonderful subject but it does not make a human life. I wrote this book after coming to see that. Philosophy is too spare and exacting for single-minded devotion. There is something heartless about it, and withering too. Too much of it is not good for a person. (Then there is the phenomenon of philosophical fatigue.) So after ten years of philosophical concentration I spent some time sabbatically writing fiction. It probably shows.

This book has three parts. The first, and longest, part is a more or less comprehensive treatment of the thesis that the nature of mental states is governed by relations between the subject of those states and the world beyond the subject ('externalism'). Here my aim is to expose the presuppositions and consequences of that thesis, and to determine the scope and limits of its applicability. This part continues work that I have been engaged on, intermittently, since I started doing philosophy. The second part addresses the question how the ascription of content to states of mind aids our understanding of persons – what the *point* of such ascriptions is. After rejecting a number of possible suggestions, I go for the idea that teleological conceptions provide the rationale for content. Eliminativism about content is thus avoided. The third part enquires into the structural basis of content, the shape of the enabling cognitive mechanism. I defend the hypothesis that the basis consists in analogue structures ('mental models'), not in sentential forms. The book becomes less purely philosophical, and more speculative, as it progresses; empirical psychologists might prefer to skip the first part altogether, while some analytic philosophers might not see the point of the third part at all.

I am not being modest when I say that the bulk of the book falls far short of definitiveness. The topic of content has been central in the philosophy of mind for some time now, and the ferment shows no sign of abating. And it *is* a hard topic. I would not be surprised if I come to think quite differently about it in ten years' time. I have done the best I can with the subject in this book, but I am only too painfully aware of the limitations of what I have achieved. Still I hope, at the very least, to have focused some of the issues in a helpful way. And it *does* seem to *me* that a lot of what I say is *true*.

I have been influenced over the years by a number of philosophers working on issues to do with content: chiefly, Tyler Burge, Hartry Field, Jerry Fodor, John McDowell, Hilary Putnam – and others whose influence is less easily detectable. We have our various disagreements, yes, but that's just the way it is with philosophy (right?). Anyway, thanks. Other people I enjoyed discussing these matters with include: Anita Avramides, Ernie Lepore, Esa Saarinen.

When I first thought of going into philosophy I pictured the life of a philosopher as stationary and garret-bound. In the event philosophy has dragged me all over the place. The text of this book I wrote in Oxford, the footnotes in New York, some of the ideas I had in Lapland. So philosophy has at least helped cure me of a mild case of travel-phobia.

Colin McGinn

1

The Location of Content

1 *Introduction*   Recent philosophy of mind has been much exercised with the question whether mental states are 'in the head'.[1] *Internalism* is the thesis that they are; *externalism* is the thesis that they are not. The central disagreement between these two theses concerns their differing conceptions of the relation between the mind and the world: internalism takes the contents of mind to be essentially independent of the surrounding world, while externalism supposes there to be a deep connection between states of mind and conditions in the nonmental world. Is the mind fundamentally autonomous with respect to the world, or does the world enter into the very nature of the mind?

The classic and pivotal argument for externalism proceeds as follows. Consider a pair of subjects whose internal properties are supposed the same but whose external environments are different. Now ask whether this is consistent with supposing that the two subjects' mental states are the same. The externalist claims that this is not consistent – the mind varies with variations in the environment. Imagine that the two subjects are surrounded by numerically distinct material objects and natural kinds, to which they refer by their words.[2] Then, despite the identity of their internal constitution, we should say (according to the externalist) that they express different thoughts by their words: their thoughts are *about* different objects and natural kinds. This kind of thought experiment can be conducted either by imagining subjects in different parts of the actual universe (the original so-called twin earth cases) or by considering a counterfactual situation in which a given subject's environment is varied.[3] And, of course, the thought experiment can be applied to entire communities as well as

[1] The phrase is Hilary Putnam's, from 'The Meaning of "Meaning"'. This paper effectively began the debate I am about to prolong, though there were other straws in the wind around 1975.

[2] In a sense of 'refer' that does not beg the question: they *apply* their words to the things in their environment.

[3] Putnam originally proceeded in the first way, but the second way is needed if we want to consider the determination of mental states of a *given* individual or community.

to isolated individuals. The externalist thus concludes that the contents of mind
are not (wholly) determined by what lies within the subject. When we pull the
environment apart from a subject's internal properties we pull his mind with us.
Mental facts can vary while internal facts are held constant.

The internal facts that are held constant in such thought experiments divide
into three basic sorts: internal states of the body and brain; behavioural
dispositions; and proximate stimulations at the sensory receptors. These must not,
of course, be specified by reference to the subject's environment. What varies are
the causal and other relations which these internal facts bear to the actual
environment of the subject. It is important to notice that 'internal' is being used
as a term of art here; for internal facts are here taken to include overtly
behavioural facts, as well as facts that lie hidden beneath the subject's skin. A
behaviourist could thus qualify as an internalist in the intended sense of the term –
he could take mental states to be 'in the head'. So internalists, in the intended
sense, do not literally locate the mind inside the head (though they may do); they
assert, rather, that mental states are determined by facts relating to the subject
considered in isolation from his environment – by facts about *him*.[4] For this
reason, 'internalism' is not the ideal label for the position it names, but I shall
stick with it in what follows, urging the reader to bear in mind the sense I have
given to it. It would be quite wrong to reject internalism simply because one
disliked the idea that the mind is lodged in the skull. Internalism is, indeed, best
seen negatively as the denial of externalism; it is the role of the environment in
fixing the nature of mind that is centrally at issue.[5]

In this chapter I want to take up three questions about externalism. First, how
precisely it should be formulated – what kind of thesis it is. Second, what its

---

[4] This assumes that the person is not himself environmentally determined – that we should be
internalists of some kind about persons. Such internalism comes naturally in these discussions, though
it can be questioned; I shall be addressing the matter later.

[5] By the 'environment' I mean the nonconceptual environment, i.e. I am not including the
thoughts and words of an individual's community. We should distinguish what I call internalism
from what Tyler Burge calls 'individualism': see, e.g., 'Individualism and the Mental'.
Individualism, in his sense, asserts that an individual's mental states are independent both of the
mental states (and language) of others in his community *and* of the surrounding nonmental world.
Internalism, in my sense, asserts only that the mental states of subjects, either individuals or
communities, are independent of the nonmental world; so my internalist could allow that what one
believes depends upon facts about one's community. The issue I am concerned with here focuses on
the relation between minds and the nonmental world, not the relation between an individual's mind
and whatever lies outside that individual. It is the subject–object relation I am interested in here, not
the subject–other relation. I want to know how the world outside of persons in general contributes to
the determination of those persons' mental states. Unfortunately, the formulation in terms of
individualism has tended to blur this distinction of interests. The question whether minds can fix the
content of other minds is really a very different question from the question whether the extramental
world can fix what holds of minds: different 'interfaces' are being considered in the two cases.

philosophical significance might be – what it would show about the mind if it were true. Third, whether it is in fact true – in particular, what kinds of mental phenomena it is true of. Despite the vast amount of attention that has been devoted to externalism in recent years, I think that there is still much that remains unclear and much that needs to be investigated.

2 *Formulating externalism*   Externalism (like internalism) is best construed as a thesis about the *individuation* of mental states: a thesis, that is, about the existence and identity conditions of mental states. It places conditions on the existence of a mental state in a possible situation, and it tells us what kinds of change preserve the identity of a mental state – these being a matter of relations to the environment. The environment is thus held to be constitutive of the very nature of mental states, determining what they *are*. Externalism is therefore analogous to other individuation theses in philosophy. Discovering the principles of individuation for persons, for example, is a matter of finding the existence and identity conditions of persons, and hence understanding the essential nature of persons. In both cases we typically proceed by devising thought experiments in which we vary certain facts while keeping others constant, and then ask whether we still have the same thing – mental state or person. We might vary the body (say) of a person to see whether it is constitutive of the person; similarly, we vary the environment of a subject to see whether it is constitutive of his mental states – in both cases keeping all else fixed. A bodily criterion of personal identity (say) would make the body individuative of persons in the same sort of way that externalism makes the world individuative of mental states. Both are metaphysical theses about the essential nature of the entities in question.

But there is also an important difference between these two individuation claims. For persons are naturally *identified* with whatever it is that individuates them: a person will be said to *be* a particular body or brain or Cartesian ego or logical construction out of mental states. But the externalist is not in this way identifying mental states with worldly states of affairs; rather, he is individuating mental states (to put it intuitively) by reference to something *other* than mental states. (The form of the internalist's claim, by contrast, is analogous to that of the theorist of persons: the items in terms of which the internalist individuates mental states – say, behavioural dispositions of a certain sort – are naturally taken to *be* the mental states themselves.) Externalism offers to tell us the identity *conditions* of mental states, but it does not literally identify mental states *with* those conditions – how could it given that external states of affairs are not even properties of the *subjects* of mental states? In the thesis of externalism what we have is a claim of the derivative or dependent individuation of one class of items on a distinct class of items, not a straightforward identification between one class of items and another. Now can we make this intuitive idea a little more precise?

We can begin by recalling Strawson's notion of 'identification-dependence', as introduced in *Individuals*.[6] Strawson there develops the idea of one class of particulars 'owing their identity' to particulars of another class (but not vice versa), in such a way that the principles of individuation of one class are systematically dependent upon those of another class. The existence and identity of Fs is dependent upon the existence and identity of Gs, though the Fs are not identical with the Gs. Thus whatever it is that individuates Gs is transferred to the individuation of Fs: we have an asymmetrical dependence of individuation conditions. A hierarchy of principles of individuation is thus set up, with individuation conditions being transmitted upwards to the dependent particulars from the individuatively more basic particulars. Such an ordering would, Strawson supposes, reveal itself in our linguistic practices: we would refer to the dependent particulars *by* referring to the independent particulars – terms for Fs would embed terms for Gs (though not vice versa). As examples of this general pattern of relationship, Strawson cites events and substances, and sensations and persons: the former items in these pairs owe their existence and identity to the latter items.[7] This individuative dependence goes via a particular relation in which the items stand to one another: events have the relation 'occurring in' to substances, sensations have the relation 'enjoyed by' to persons. (In fact, I would say that the latter pair is a special case of the former, since sensations are events and persons are substances; 'enjoying' is one kind of 'occurring in'.) Neither of these cases is exactly analogous to the case of personal identity – again, events are not said to *be* substances.

Strawson himself concentrates upon the linguistic expression of relations of identity-dependence, but I think the notion can be extended beyond its original linguistic formulation. We can, I suggest, separate out four aspects to a claim of individuation-dependence: linguistic, epistemological, metaphysical, conceptual. Suppose Fs are individuation-dependent on Gs. Then we can say the following: (i) reference to Fs requires prior reference to Gs; (ii) knowledge of the properties of Fs requires prior knowledge of the properties of Gs; (iii) the essence of Fs is (partly) constituted by that of Gs; (iv) possessing the concept of an F requires prior possession of the concept of a G. Thus, taking the example of sensations and persons, we might want to say the following (assuming that this is an instance of the general notion): (i) reference to sensations requires prior reference to persons;

---

[6] See chapter 1 of that book, esp. 30ff.

[7] He is, however, properly cautious about how pure these cases are; and, indeed, they can be questioned. Donald Davidson challenges the event case (and by implication the sensation case) in 'The Individuation of Events', on the score of asymmetry.

(ii) knowledge about sensations requires prior knowledge about persons; (iii) it is part of the essence of a (token) sensation that it be enjoyed by a particular person; (iv) one could only possess concepts of sensation if one already possessed the concept of a person. These four subtheses would then express one's conviction of the individuation-dependence of sensations on persons.

Note that a claim of this form need not be a claim of *total* individuation-dependence: we need not suppose that there is nothing more to the individuation of *Fs* than their being *R* to some *G*; other factors may also contribute to the individuation of *Fs*. Thus the time of a sensation and its phenomenological character may also enter into its individuation conditions – as well as the person who has it. Individuation-dependence can be – and typically will be – *partial* individuation-dependence, a necessary but not a sufficient condition of identity for *Fs* in terms of *Gs*.

Now how does this general schema fit the case of externalism? How well does it capture the purport of that thesis? I think it fits it rather neatly. Let the *Fs* be beliefs and the *Gs* the objects and properties environmentally related to these beliefs, as it might be causally. Then, in holding that these beliefs are individuated by the environment, the externalist is advancing the following four subtheses. (i) Reference to beliefs embeds reference to the appropriate worldly entities: there is no way to specify what beliefs a subject has save by specifying the worldly entities the belief concerns – hence 'that'-clauses serve precisely to pick out the nonmental entities upon which beliefs are individuation-dependent. (ii) We cannot come to know what someone believes without prior knowledge of the nature of his environment, since that is what determines what it is he believes. Radical interpretation of another's beliefs must therefore be based upon antecedent knowledge of the subject's environment and can go forward in no other way.[8] In twin earth cases, for example, we can only make judgements of the distinctness of the beliefs held if we already know that the two environments are differently constituted. (iii) It is of the essence of a particular belief that it be environmentally related to certain entities; indeed, its very *constituents* are such worldly entities. It is simply not *possible* for the belief to be held by a subject unless his environment contains the appropriate entities, those the belief purports to be about. (iv) One could not master the concept of belief without having already mastered concepts for the worldly entities beliefs are about: one could not, for example, master the concept *belief that snow is white* without having mastered the concepts *snow* and *white*, since the former (complex) concept *embeds* the latter (simple) concepts. Moreover, the externalist will say, these dependencies

are not symmetrical; the world is not also individuation-dependent on the mind –
it could not consistently be.

Interestingly enough, Strawson was himself in a position to cite externalism as
an instance of individuation-dependence, since his own doctrine in 'On
Referring' is in effect externalist: the existence and identity of singular
propositions is held to depend upon the existence and identity of the objects of
singular reference.[9] Indeed, this alleged dependence of propositions on
particulars seems a rather clearer example of asymmetrical identification-
dependence than the examples Strawson actually gives in *Individuals*. But he does
not in fact give this as an example of his general notion – possibly because his
official concern is with particulars, which propositions are not.

Can we find another case of individuation-dependence that is intuitively closer
to the case of externalism than the examples Strawson himself provides? For those
examples seem not to contain any real analogue to the externalist idea that worldly
items are 'constituents' of mental states such as beliefs. Well, the obvious parallel
here is with the case of sets (or sequences). A set owes its identity to its members:
if they vary, it varies; if they fail to exist, it does too. Yet a set is not to be literally
identified with its members or with the sum of them. It is natural to think of the
members of a set as its 'constituents', and of the set as 'containing' its members –
though the spatial overtones of these expressions should not be taken at face value.
The membership relation is thus analogous to the aboutness or intentional
relation: both relations transmit a very intimate kind of individuation-
dependence – the kind that encourages talk of constituents and containment. The
externalist wants to think of the belief/world relation as formally like the set/
member relation. The case of sets conforms to the general Strawsonian schema
perfectly. And both cases exhibit what might protentously be called 'cross-
categorial' individuation-dependence: that is to say, in the case of sets, the
dependence of the abstract on the concrete (assuming concrete members); and, in
the case of beliefs, the dependence of the mental on the physical (assuming beliefs
about physical things). Such cross-categorial kinds of dependence, in contrast to
the kinds Strawson himself cites, are apt to generate philosophical perplexity: and
indeed both sorts of claim have attracted their share of puzzlement; for how, it is
felt, can items drawn from one metaphysical category depend for their very
individuation (their essential nature) on items belonging to some quite different

---

[9] This is made somewhat clearer in later work, e.g. *Subject and Predicate in Logic and Grammar*.
Essentially this is the idea of a singular proposition as developed by David Kaplan and others: see
'Dthat'. It is the idea of a kind of propositional content that is parasitic on the existence and identity of
objects, so that truth-evaluability (and hence propositionality) presupposes reference. And this is
tantamount to rejecting Russell's theory of descriptions for some singular terms (and concepts). From
small logical doctrines about singular terms large metaphysical thesis about the mind may grow: not
all singular expressions are analysable as quantifiers, *so* the mind is not located in the head!

metaphysical category? Thus the thesis that sets depend for their existence upon the (possibly contingent) existence of their concrete members can seem as problematic as the thesis that thoughts depend for their existence upon the (possibly contingent) existence of the nonmental items they are about.[10] Remembering this analogy will help us later when we come to enquire into the philosophical significance of externalism. For the moment, however, I am still trying to work up an articulate sense of what the doctrine of externalism says; and my suggestion so far, to summarize, is that externalism is a thesis of individuation-dependence which is most closely paralleled by an analogous thesis concerning sets and their members.[11]

I must now admit that this formulation slides over a crucial distinction of theses, a distinction that will prove of central importance in what follows. This is the distinction between what I shall call *weak* and *strong* externalism. So far I have spoken of worldly and environmental dependence more or less interchangeably, as if the former kind of dependence implied the latter. But it is vital to see that whether this is so is a substantive question – a question I shall be answering negatively. Weak externalism, as I define it, is the thesis that a given mental state requires the *existence* of some item belonging to the nonmental world, and that its identity turns on that item. Strong externalism, as I define it, is the thesis that a given mental state requires the existence *in the environment of the subject* of some item belonging to the nonmental world, and that its identity turns on that item. The latter thesis is stronger than the former because the former does *not* entail that the subject of the mental state in question should be environmentally related to the extramental item in question – as it might be, causally. Crudely put, strong

[10] Thus we can define the notion of a 'singular set', or a 'Russellian set' in Gareth Evans's terminology: see *The Varieties of Reference*. This is the idea of a set that would not exist but for the existence of its members: *all* sets are 'singular' or 'Russellian' in this sense. This can seem problematic if one insists on a sharp separation between the abstract and the concrete, between the platonic and the sublunary. If we represent the propositional content of a thought as a set (a sequence), in the style of Kaplan, then we are implicitly recognizing the close analogy between sets and contents in respect of world-involvement: they both trap worldly items in the same kind of way. Such entrapment can seem offensive if we are gripped by the idea of big ontological dualities, by a doctrine of metaphysical encapsulation. Or it can look attractive if we want to break down certain kinds of ontological barrier. More on such repulsion and attraction later.

[11] Another close analogy for externalism is provided by relationalism about space (also time). This thesis individuates spatial entities and their properties and relations in terms of the disposition of material objects in space; it holds that spatial facts are fundamentally constituted by facts about the occupants of space. Absolutism about space is then the analogue of internalism about the mind: just as space is intrinsically independent of the world of material objects, having its constitutive structure fixed by its autonomous nature, so the mind is held to have *its* 'configuration' determined independently of contingent external relations to items in the world. Thus relationalism makes places individuation-dependent on objects, as externalism makes mental contents individuation-dependent upon objects. Externalism is indeed a kind of relationalism about psychological structure: it conceives the mind as a system of relations among nonmental items and the subject.

externalism ties mental states to a particular *part* of the world – the part the subject himself inhabits – while weak externalism ties mental states to the world *at large*, whether or not the required nonmental entity is where the subject himself is located.[12] This distinction becomes obvious when we apply it to twin earth cases: for it takes strong environmental externalism to deliver a difference of mental states in these cases; weak externalism is quite consistent with taking the mental states in question to be the same, since the existence condition is met *somewhere* in the universe. Weak externalism says only that water must exist (in a possible world) if subjects are to have beliefs involving the concept *water* (in that world), that the identity of natural kind concepts if fixed by the identity of the natural kinds there are; it does not require that the subjects be (or have been) environmentally connected to water – seen it, tasted it, etc. So nothing in weak externalism rules out the possibility of a brain in a vat having the same mental states as we normally placed subjects do, so long as the right entities exist somewhere in the world; whereas strong externalism, which insists on a contextual relation, excludes that possibility, since the envatted brain will not have been environmentally connected to the same entities as us. The distinction between the two sorts of externalism arises out of the simple point that something can exist or be instantiated without existing or being instantiated in a given subject's environment, where the notion of environment is taken causally or contextually, thus making people on twin earth occupy a different environment from us. Co-existence in a possible world is not the same as co-presence in an environmental niche. These two conditions coalesce only for the case of God: because of his omniscience and omnipresence the whole of reality is his environment – which is why you cannot run a twin earth case for God. As we shall see later, there are kinds of mental state for which only weak externalism is true, and we will be prevented from seeing this if we confusedly assume that only

---

[12] We could say that strong externalism makes content a function of the subject's path through the world, while weak externalism ties content only to the world through which the subject traces a path. There is room in this general characterization of the distinction for various intermediate views, but these will not prove theoretically important in what follows. The important distinction is going to be between contextual and existential theses of world-dependence. This distinction is neatly illustrated by Kaplan's suggestion that there are two distinct ways of trapping an object in a singular proposition: either the thinker gets to be 'en rapport' with the object (strong externalism) or he exploits the 'dthat' operator to convert a definite description into a quasi-demonstrative (weak externalism). Consider the twin earth expression 'dthat (the liquid they drink on earth)': according to Kaplan, this traps water (that very stuff) into the expressed proposition, but the twin earthians are environmentally unrelated to what is so trapped. (I use this idea to illustrate what I intend by the distinction, not necessarily to endorse Kaplan's view of what it takes to have an externally determined content. In fact, as will emerge later, the chief significance of the distinction concerns the conditions under which *properties* can enter mental contents, not objects.) Note that the strong/weak terminology does not mark a difference in the degree of externalism being claimed; the distinction concerns the conditions under which externally determined contents got to be in the mind, not the degree of their externality.

one kind of externalism is available, viz. the strong variety. The formulation given above in terms of individuation-dependence does not by itself register this distinction; it is, as stated hitherto, neutral between the two strengths or kinds of externalism. We can, however, qualify that formulation by speaking of weak and strong individuation-dependence, and this is how I would wish to be construed in operating with the two notions of externalism. Strawson's examples are, in effect, cases of strong individuation-dependence, since the relation of 'occurring in' is a kind of environmental relation; it is certainly not supposed that the substances upon which events are dependent can exist just anywhere with respect to those events, that their *some*where existence is all that is necessary in order that particular events may exist. By contrast, weak individuation-dependence seems the appropriate notion for the case of sets: the members of a set do not need to exist in the environment of the set (whatever that may mean) in order that they should fix its identity – mere existence suffices. In the case of mental states with representational content, I shall be advocating a divided view – some are strongly external, others only weakly so – and it will be important then to keep the distinction firmly in mind. We need to allow room for the possibility, which is actual in a number of cases, of externalism without environment-dependence.[13] But more of this later; for now it suffices to have introduced the distinction and given it a name.

In the next section I shall work with this preliminary formulation of externalism in an effort to get clear about the general philosophical significance of the thesis. And the formulation may be further tested by seeing how far it helps in that effort.

3 *The philosophical significance of externalism*   Externalism, weak or strong, is a thesis about the relation between the mind and the world: it says that the world enters constitutively into the individuation of states of mind; mind and world are not, according to externalism, metaphysically independent categories, sliding smoothly past each other. To regard them so is to commit oneself to an 'untenable

---

[13] Methodological solipsism is commonly defined so as to be the negation of weak externalism: it says that mental states can be identified without reference to any individual save the subject of the mental state (see Putnam, 'The Meaning of "Meaning"'). But then it understates the case to express the upshot of twin earth reflections as inconsistent with methodological solipsism, since those reflections imply strong externalism, not just weak. Such understatement can be misleading if it encourages the idea that the inapplicability of twin earth arguments to certain cases shows that internalism is true in those cases. You can be a weak externalist about a certain kind of content, and so reject methodological solipsism, and yet deny vehemently that a twin earth case can be given for the content at issue: that is in fact my position about certain kinds of content, as will become apparent.

dualism', to marking a metaphysical boundary that does not exist. Internalism, for its part, insists upon such a duality, drawing a sharp line between mind and world; but the externalist holds that the mind is penetrated by the world, configured by it. I want now to investigate a pair of questions that arise out of this general externalist conception: (a) what it presupposes about the world side of the intentional relation; and (b) what it presupposes about the mind side of that relation. What is the significance of externalism for our view of the world and the mind? I begin with the world.

(a) *Externalism and the world*   Externalism holds that mental distinctions (distinctions of content) are grounded in worldly distinctions, that the former depend upon the latter, that mental individuation is to be explained by reference to worldly conditions. It thus regards the direction of individuation as running from the world to the mind. Accordingly, this individuation-dependence is deemed asymmetrical: the world is not likewise individuation-dependent upon the mind. For what serves to individuate a mental state cannot itself be individuated *by* that mental state. The world is individuatively basic with respect to the mind. It is in *virtue* of environmental differences that mental differences are established.

Now this asymmetry has the following consequence: that philosophical doctrines that make the mind individuatively basic with respect to the world are incompatible with externalism. For such doctrines attempt to *explain* the nature of worldly facts by reference to mental facts – they thus reverse the direction of metaphysical dependence. So externalism is incompatible with the likes of idealism and phenomenalism and projectivism. In other words, externalism presupposes (a form of) *realism* about the external world: it takes worldly facts to be fixed mind-independently, so that these can then be exploited in the fixing of mental facts.[14] Suppose a phenomenalist tries to define worldly states of affairs in terms of dispositions in perceivers to have experiences as of those very states of affairs. Such a phenomenalist would be taking the content of those experiences for granted and using it to tell us what the obtaining of a worldly state of affairs consists in. He could not then turn round and offer to explain the possession of that experiential content in terms of the states of affairs in the world that (say) cause such experiences. In general, theses of mind-dependence assume that mental distinctions are antecedently fixed, and then use mental states to explain various distinctions in the world. Idealism thus presupposes some form of

[14] The picture here is that the world is antecedently given and that the mind gets to have its content by being suitably 'situated' in that world; it is not that the *mind* is antecedently given and that the world (so-called) gets to be the way it is by virtue of the mind's representing it in a certain way. Externalism takes the world to be anterior to the mind in its intrinsic nature; it takes reality to be *objective*. So, in a sense, it takes objective facts to individuate subjective facts.

internalism.[15] Externalism precisely inverts the direction of individuation assumed by idealism. Equally we cannot consistently combine externalism with projectivism: if colours or moral values, say, are taken to be projected onto the world by the mind, then there can be no explaining the relevant distinctions of mental content by reference to prior worldly distinctions. If an object's being red consists in its looking red (crudely), then it cannot also be true that its looking red consists in being brought about by red things. What the mind projects it cannot also introject. What it spreads cannot also be spread on it. If we took natural kind taxonomy to be a (mere) projection of the mind, not determined antecedently to the operations of mind, then we could not *also* suppose that our system of natural kind concepts is structured by what natural kinds the world we live in actually and objectively contains. Hence if we have reason to believe externalism (about some class of mental states), then we thereby have reason to favour realism about the subject matter of those states. The truth of externalism about a class of mental contents would entail that the relevant sector of reality is not mentally constituted. Equally the truth of projectivist subjectivism about a class of 'worldly' facts would rule out an externalist account of how the appropriate contents are determined. This then is the significance of externalism for the metaphysical character of the world.

I think it is illuminating to see both externalism and projectivism (including phenomenalism) as responses to what we might call the *matching problem*. There are properties of objects in the world, and there are concepts in the minds of persons: how do these get to match up? How do our concepts come to have extensions that coincide with the instantiation classes of real properties? How do our subjective mental acts manage to latch onto the objective properties of things? By what miracle is the taxonomy of concepts in a mind not hopelessly mismatched with the taxonomy of properties in the world? Suppose for a moment that concepts and properties were individuated quite independently of each other, so that nothing in the individuation conditions of the one bore any essential relation to the individuation conditions of the other. For example, suppose that what

[15] We might expect, therefore, that anti-realists will be internalists of some sort, while externalists will be realists. A quick survey of philosophers confirms this expectation, I think. Someone, like Putnam, who rejects 'metaphysical' realism but accepts 'internal' realism, while subscribing to externalism, will have to devise some notion of 'internal externalism', i.e. will need a notion of externality that does not go all the way to full-blooded metaphysical realism. (See Putnam's *Realism and Reason* for his brand of diluted internal realism.) Kantian forms of 'empirical realism', which involve some kind of ultimate mind-dependence, will not deliver full-strength externalism. I am in effect speaking of 'transcendental externalism' in the text, the kind that requires full or transcendental realism (I mean the kind that involves *no* sort of dependence of the world on the mind). I very much doubt whether it is finally intelligible to try to combine externalism with anything short of such realism: you will just end up trying to explain the mind's content in terms of itself. But I won't pursue the question.

makes an object square and what confers the concept *square* on a person had nothing in common, with no path from one to the other. Then how *could* the two mesh – what could make the concept a concept *of* that very property? After all, the concept is a creature of the mind, while the property belongs yonder in the nonmental world: why should these metaphysically very different kinds of thing succeed in meeting up at all? Independent individuation thus leads to puzzled scepticism about the matching of concepts and properties. The matching could be at best accidental.

But suppose that the individuation conditions of concepts and properties were *not* independent; suppose that the individuation of one side of the divide made essential reference to items from the other side, so that the identity of the one could not be wrenched apart from the identity of the other. Then the requisite matching or correspondence or alignment would be satisfyingly secured. Concepts and properties would be firmly yoked to one another, variations in the one being matched or tracked by variations in the other. This yoking could come about in one of two ways: either the property is defined by reference to the concept, or contrariwise. The former way is, in effect, what happens with projectivist doctrines such as phenomenalism: for an object to be square is for it to produce experiences in which the concept *square* enters, so that the property is individuated by whatever it is that individuates the entering concept – thus securing a match between them. The latter way is the way of externalism: the individuation of the concept is made to depend upon that of the property, so that what makes a property the property it is serves to make the corresponding concept the concept *it* is.[16] The gap is bridged by crossing it from the opposite direction; or rather by not allowing it to open up in the first place. Both sorts of doctrine solve the matching problem by invoking the idea of individuation dependence, but they solve it in exactly opposite (indeed contradictory) ways. I would say that it is a condition of adequacy upon any account of content that it show how the matching problem can be solved. Anyone who rejects externalism for a kind of content, but also denies projectivism for the subject matter of that content, needs to face up to the threat that no acceptable link can be found between thought and fact. (The matching problem will crop up again later when I come to question the universality of the strong externalist thesis.)

[16] Suppose we follow Sydney Shoemaker in individuating properties in terms of their causal powers: see his 'On Properties'. Then the associated concepts will themselves be individuated in this way: concepts will be the same if they are concepts of causally equivalent properties. Clearly, to avoid circularity the externalist who accepts this view of property identity will have to exclude mention of contentful states in his specification of the causal powers of the properties in question. Specifically, he cannot mention the perceptual experiences instances of the property cause, since these are held to be fixed by the property that causes them. Still, there seems no *need* to include causal powers with respect to mental states in the individuation of the property, so there is no real problem about this. I am simply pointing out the logical commitments of the doctrines in question.

I have said that externalism and projectivism are incompatible: but did I mean weak or strong externalism? Are *both* kinds of externalism inconsistent with a phenomenalist thesis about some range of properties? I think that on the most natural formulation of phenomenalism it is only strong externalism that directly contradicts that doctrine; a clear-headed phenomenalist can therefore be a weak externalist. Let us define phenomenalism with respect to a kind of property P as follows: an object x can instantiate P only if, and in virtue of the fact that, x is disposed to produce in perceivers experiences as of the instantiation of P; to say that x has P is covertly to say that x is apt to look P to suitable perceivers. That is, this phenomenalist claims that x has P in virtue of the fact that x typically causes experiences as of P in suitably placed perceivers. Now this claim is plainly incompatible with the strong externalist thesis that perceivers have experiences as of P in virtue of the fact that those experiences are typically caused by instantiations of P in objects: for the 'in virtue of' relation in asymmetrical (it is a kind of explanatory relation). But it is not incompatible with weak externalism, since that thesis does not undertake to explain perceptual content by means of the *instantiation* of properties in the perceiver's environment – it does not require any causal relation between experiences and instances of the property in question. Weak externalism requires only that contentful experiences be identified by reference to properties that exist outside the head (wherever it is outside the head that properties exist – suppose for the sake of argument that it is in Platonic heaven), not that the perceiver have those properties instantiated in his environment. This means that the weak externalist phenomenalist does not have to appeal to the notion of an object's instantiating P in order to tell us what it is for an experience to have that content – and so he does not have to appeal to what, as a committed phenomenalist, he is trying to explain. Notice that this phenomenalist is not trying to explain what the property P *is* – he is not saying that squareness (say) is a mental entity – rather he is offering to explain what it is for this property to be *instantiated* by an object in mental terms. He is analysing this by making reference to a certain mental fact, but he is not saying that what is instantiated is *itself* mental: he is not committing himself to mentalism or conceptualism about universals. [17] So to commit himself would indeed be to give

---

[17] The same distinction applies with respect to materialism. We can undertake to account for the instantiation of all properties in terms of the instantiation of physical properties without also claiming that properties themselves are physical things: that is, we can combine platonic realism about properties (they are abstract nonphysical entities) with the thesis that all properties are instantiated in virtue of the instantiation of physical properties. Thus the property of being an electron might itself be a nonphysical abstract entity, yet its being instantiated is a straightforward physical fact – it obtains in virtue of the instantiation of a physical property, viz. itself. So we have to be careful when we express materialism as the claim that everything is physical; as we do when we express idealism as the claim that everything is mental. (I say nothing here about how well-motivated these kinds of restricted doctrine might be.)

up on even weak externalism, since mental states would then be identifiable without making reference to anything nonmental; but that would be to go beyond the phenomenalist claim we started out with. A phenomenalist can clearly be a realist about universals (and so not locate them within the head). There is thus no vicious circularity in explaining the instantiation of P in objects by reference to mental states in the identification of which the property P requires to be mentioned: presupposing the existence of the property (and locating it outside the head) is not the same as presupposing its instantiation. It is only the strong externalist who builds the notion of P-instantiation into his account of what it is for a perceiver to have experiences as of P. What this implies is that a phenomenalist can embrace a robust conception of the representational content of experience: he can suppose experiences to be genuinely as of real properties which things may have; he does not need to retreat to a thin subjectivist conception of experience on which experience does not succeed in representing states of affairs. Weak externalism ensures that experiences be genuinely world-directed (fully representational) without forcing the phenomenalist (local or global) to rescind his claim that states of affairs *obtain* in virtue only of mental facts. Here, then, we see one merit in making the strong/weak distinction: it gives the phenomenalist a fairer run for his money. Strong externalism blocks phenomenalism as defined, but weak externalism does not (though it does preclude mentalism about universals).[18] So the significance of externalism for the world side of the intentional relation is rather more complex than it might initially appear.

(b) *Externalism and the mind*   I believe it is correct to say that externalism, once it is forcefully and vividly stated, strikes many people as a strange and bizarre theory – a theory that simply couldn't be true. It seems to these people to fly in the face of some deeply rooted conception or picture of the mind and its states. The mind, it is felt, just *could* not be such as to satisfy externalism; it is simply not the *kind* of thing that externalism represents it as being. My suspicion, listening to such people, is that some quite fundamental assumption about the mind is being threatened by externalism, an assumption which has yet to be properly articulated. We need to unearth this source of visceral resistance to externalism if we are to understand its significance for the nature of mind. I shall

---

[18]   Can we formulate a strong/weak distinction for phenomenalism? We can: the strong causal kind requires actual episodes of perception for the property to be instantiated; the weak kind asks only that perceivers with the right experiences exist – along perhaps with the condition that the objects *would* produce those experiences if they ever were perceived. This kind of weak phenomenalism might be of interest to a phenomenalist who allows that certain kinds of property can be instantiated without being perceptible (he takes the above subjunctive to have an unrealizable antecedent) – as, say, with conditions inside the sun. This weak phenomenalism is also incompatible with strong externalism, however, since it takes the experiences to be possible without causal-perceptual contact with the property.

try then in what follows to offer a diagnosis of the basis of this felt resistance. What underlying picture of the mind is it that externalism comes into direct collision with?

We should reject the idea that it is some unreconstructed brand of materialism that gives off a reluctance to countenance externalism. It is true that identifying the mind with the brain, and mental states with brain states, conflicts with externalism, since the brain really does lie literally within the head. So it is a consequence of externalism that this simple kind of materialism is false.[19] But this cannot be what moves people to jib at externalism, at least pretheoretically. For the same resistance would be felt, I think, by an instinctive Cartesian dualist; she too would bridle at the suggestion that the mind is world-determined, shaped on the inside by what lies beyond the subject. The idea that the mind has its own proprietary internal landscape, in splendid metaphysical isolation from the (n.b.) external world, is surely not a peculiarly materialist conviction. Some more general conception must be at work, of which this kind of internalist materialism is merely a special case. It does not seem plausible that it is a decided position on the mind–body problem that lurks behind people's resistance to externalism; certainly the resistance can be felt by people who have no such decided position. Such materialism might be sustained in place by a tacit acceptance of an underlying conception that clashes with externalism, but it is not the *origin* of that submerged conception. And this becomes especially evident when we notice that not all versions of materialism conflict with externalism anyway: the materialist is at liberty to call upon physical facts that extend beyond the body and brain – he can appeal to physical relations to a physical environment. So it could only be the internalist version of materialism that generated a conflict to begin with, and there seems no plausibility in the idea that it is this doctrine that lies buried but active in the philosophical subconscious.[20]

What then is the more general conception of which internal materialism is a special case? I want to suggest, putting it crudely at first, that it is the idea that the mind is a *substance*, that mental states are states of a mental substance. The paradigms of the notion of substance are, of course, continuant material particulars – cats, trees, brains, and the like. My suggestion is that it is the tendency – the temptation – to model the mind upon such material substances that comes into conflict with externalism. To model it, not to identify it – that would be the materialist diagnosis just rejected. That is, it is the tendency to conceive the

---

[19] See my later discussion of externalism and materialism (section 5 (ii)) for more on this.

[20] So it is not the conviction that mental states supervene on brain states that causes the intuitive resistance people feel to externalism: this is far too arcane an idea to jerk horrified hands into the air when externalism is candidly proclaimed. It is one way to *explain* the autonomy that is under threat, but it is not what the naive belief in autonomy *consists in*.

mind as logically or metaphysically *analogous* to a physical substance that is at stake.[21] This is, of course, a familiar claim about our naive way of thinking about the mind – that we are prone to think of it as a rarefied material thing – but it is not, I believe, common to locate the resistance to externalism in this naive idea. In fact, I believe that this idea – or something like it – is more deeply entrenched than is often allowed; it is protean in its forms and surprisingly tenacious in its grip on the philosophical imagination. It is not an idea that can be instantly and comfortably dispensed with – root it out in one form and it will come back to haunt you in another. Nor do I think it is just a transparently erroneous conception of mind, an obvious pathology to be excised (or exorcized). We should be alive to the possibility that we simply have no other colourable way of thinking about the kind of thing the mind is. Externalism *may* thus prove in the end to be unacceptable if it undermines this idea too radically.[22] For the moment, however, my concern is not with the truth either of externalism or substantialism but with the relation between these two conceptions. If we are to succeed in staging an outright confrontation between them, then we shall need to have a sharper articulation of the substance conception than we have yet given. Let me try then to tease out the defining strands in the general notion of a substance.

There are, I believe, two central components in the idea of substance. First, substances are conceived as ontologically autonomous or self-subsistent: they do not depend for their existence or their intrinsic nature upon other substances – indeed all other substances could cease to exist (or never have existed) without (logically) a given substance going out of existence or changing its intrinsic nature. Second, substances have boundaries, determined by their intrinsic properties, which exclude other substances from their place: they are thus impenetrable or solid in the region determined by that boundary.[23] This second

---

[21] Just so an absolutist about space does not conceive space *as* a material object; rather, he conceives it as in certain crucial respects analogous to a material object. So my diagnostic suggestion has the form of a like diagnosis of resistance to relationalism about space: someone who recoils from *that* thesis also finds it hard to see how space could be other than substancelike. See Lawrence Sklar, *Space, Time and Spacetime*, for a discussion of substantival absolutism about space.

[22] It may be that we can think of the mind in no other way but that it isn't in fact that way. Our conceptions of things may be dominated by ways of thinking that are inappropriate to those things – and these erroneous conceptions may be ineliminable for us. Nevertheless, reality goes its own way. So we might find that we know externalism to be true, and hence substantialism to be false, and yet we cannot get ourselves to form a satisfying alternative conception of how we know the mind to be. In fact, though, I think we *can* form a conception of mind as the externalist represents it – so long as we don't try to imagine it. A certain abstractness in our conception of mind is the only way to keep it in line with how the mind really is. We have to radically divorce our conception of the mind from our ways of representing the objects of sense.

[23] Space, for an absolutist, has the former property but not the latter: it has its structure independently of what it contains, but it does not compete with material objects for location – on the

feature is closely linked to the idea of primary qualities, specifically shape: the shape of a substance fixes its impermeable boundaries. Substances essentially compete with each other for spatial location; two substances (with disjoint material parts) cannot share the same region of space. A cat, for example, plainly exhibits these categorial features of autonomy and exclusivity. Now there is, of course, much more that could be said in elucidation and qualification of these general remarks, but I hope I have said enough for my present purposes, namely to identify the metaphysical conception that externalism challenges.

Suppose, then, that we tried, with full explicitness, to conceive of the mind according to these two defining characteristics of substance; we take the mind to be both autonomous and exclusive with respect to other substances. Then it is hard to see how externalism *could* be true of it: for, first, it would have to be ontologically independent of other substances, contrary to externalism; and, second, it would have to exclude other substances from within its boundaries, having no substantial constituents other than its own enclosed parts. Externalism involves ontological dependence and breached boundaries (or no viable notion of boundary at all) – exactly contrary to substantialism. Suppose the mind were metaphysically akin to the body or brain, autonomous and exclusive like them; then externalism could not be true of it – for it would have its own world-independent intrinsic nature determined by its (quasi-) primary qualities. So, contraposing, if externalism were true of the mind, then it could not have the substantial nature of the body or brain; it could not have that sort of metaphysical

contrary, places are cut out to be coincident with objects. This is one respect in which even the most ardent substantivalist about space will agree that space is disanalogous to material objects. It might be worth asking whether a substantialist about the mind could adopt this kind of partial analogy view: could he hold that the mind genuinely contains objects (it is not exclusive) but that these objects do not individuate mental contents? Such a view would regard the mind's relation to its objects as logically just like space's relation to its objects: containment without constitution. Is this view externalist or internalist? In so far as it is intelligible, I would say it is internalist, for it holds that the identity of a concept is quite independent of the identity of what it is a concept of – as the identity of a place is quite independent of the identity of what occupies it for an absolutist. So this partially substantial view is still incompatible with the basic thrust of externalism. I suspect, in fact, that dependent individuation without containment is the more natural view for most people – externalism without worldly 'constituents'. I discuss this view later, arguing that if you admit the former there is no point in denying the latter.

Locke emphasizes solidity in his account of 'body': see the *Essay*, Book II, Chapter IV. Philosophers have not been apt to think of the mind as like empty space, i.e. as a nonexclusive receptacle for external objects. The constituents of mind *do* compete with other objects for 'location'.

On the autonomy of substances, Descartes says: 'By substance, we can understand nothing else than a thing which so exists that it needs no other thing in order to exist' ('Principles of Philosophy', First Part, Principle LI). Since he holds that the mind is precisely a (thinking) substance, this immediately delivers the autonomy of minds. Thoughts, for Descartes, can be present in a mind and yet nothing outside that mind exists (except for God); and thinking is the essence of mind.

structure.[24] Internalism feels pretheoretically attractive – there is a strong gut undertow towards it – precisely because (I am suggesting) it respects the implicit substantialist presumption; it is not merely an arbitrary prejudice plucked from nowhere with no philosophical underpinning. Giving up internalism would therefore be giving up more than some optional and confined philosophical *theory*; it involves completely rethinking the underlying metaphysics of mind – what kind of Being the mind is. Externalism removes our most natural way of thinking of what kind of thing the mind is, leaving us (as yet) with nothing to put in its place.[25] So something pretty deep and serious and far-reaching is going on here.

I can perhaps clarify this diagnosis by asking which specific externalist theses provoke the greatest resistance. If I am right, then these should be the theses that most directly challenge substantialism. The more problematic a putative thought constituent is felt to be, the sharper will its anti-substantialist implications be; and the more innocent-seeming, the more comfortable with substantialism.

There is an enormous range of contents to consider: in addition to spatio-temporal particulars in huge profusion, we have all the kinds of properties there are, as well as selves (one's own and others'), mental states (ditto), logical operators (truth-functions, modalities, quantifiers, etc.), mathematical entities, values, and so forth. Let me focus on particulars and their properties, as these will I think suffice to illustrate the general case. I should emphasize that the point of the exercise is not to argue that the felt-to-be problematic constituents really are

---

[24] Relationalism conflicts with substantivalism about space in essentially the same way, and it suggests a positive conception of the nature of mind according to externalism. Space, for a relationalist, is not an autonomous object, to be counted along with the other substances there are; rather, it is a 'mode of organization' of material objects, a 'pattern of relationships' between them. Similarly, an externalist will not think that minds are extra substances in the world, to be counted along with material substances; rather, minds are to be conceived as systems of relations between subjects and the worldly items mentally represented – minds have their being in the obtaining of these relations. There is no conceiving of space independently of its occupants for a relationalist, and there is no conceiving of minds without their external objects (those real objective things) for an externalist. (I am not here agreeing with relationalism about space – I tend towards absolutism myself; I am just using it to hit off the externalist thought, namely that the mind has its being only in relation to external things. Since I incline towards spatial absolutism but accept externalism, I am disinclined to think of the mind on analogy with actual space. But I can still think of it on analogy with how a relationalist *wants* to think about space.)

[25] I distinguish between a natural philosophical way of thinking and a commonsense way. I do not think substantialism is part of common sense, i.e. our ordinary scheme of psychological concepts; rather, it is a philosophical conception naively imposed on that scheme. What *is* part of common sense, I think, is precisely the externalism that conflicts with substantialism: but, I am suggesting, this is not part of our natural primitive *philosophy* of mind. The distinction is, of course, Wittgenstein's (cf. his idea that we naively take meaning something to consist in something queer that comes before the mind).

unfit candidates for externalism; my question is rather a diagnostic one – which have *struck* people as problematic and why.

It is clear straight off that material objects in one's environment – the objects of sensory perception – are the prime suspects: inserting these into the content of mental states has always seemed highly counterintuitive to many. This may suggest that the appropriate criterion is mentality: material objects are problematic and nonmental, while one's own mental states seem unproblematic (nobody jibs at sense-data and the like being regarded as constituents of content). But this cannot be right because properties (universals) have also not been supposed problematic, and they are not mental. Russell had no trouble populating his propositions with universals and he was a realist about universals.[26] And description-theorists adopt essentially the same view: they sense no difficulty in the idea (in effect) that the reference of general terms should feature as constituents of thought.[27] I doubt that it is tacit commitment to some form of conceptualism or nominalism about universals that smooths the way to this sanguine acceptance. Happily embracing logical operators, such as negation, as constituents of thoughts does not seem to depend upon the (false) thesis that negation is a mental phenomenon.

One might now suggest that it is contingent existence that is crucial. Universals exist necessarily, material objects exist only contingently; so there is no possibility of unfulfilled existence-dependence in the former case, unlike the latter. With universals, therefore, it is *as if* the mind were autonomous, because its ontological dependence upon the world will never, as it were, have the occasion to show up. But this cannot be right either, since Russellian sense-data are unproblematic too and yet they exist contingently. Besides, even if some material object did exist necessarily (say the matter of the universe), it would *still* seem problematic that it could enter into mental content.

It may now seem that the correct criterion is staring us in the face: the putative constituents should not be spatio-temporal particulars – as universals and sense-data are not and perceptual objects are. But I do not think this is the correct diagnosis either. In the first place, we experience no especial difficulty in the idea that our thoughts depend for their existence upon our body and brain; so it is not *simply* existence-dependence upon the spatio-temporal that poses the intuitive problem, creates the discomfort. And, in the second place, regarding the

[26] See Russell, *The Problems of Philosophy*, esp. V and IX.

[27] See, e.g., John Searle, *Intentionality*. The question arises, however, whether this divided view is well-motivated, since it cannot really be the inclusion of nonmental items in propositions that offends such theorists. Why are objective properties thought perfectly eligible for entrapment in belief contents but the particulars that instantiate these properties are not? Is it just because realism about universals is less obvious than realism about particulars? I myself find no principled distinction here. (We shall return to this alleged asymmetry.)

innocent-seeming constituents as themselves physical particulars does not seem to shift them into the problematic class. Thus suppose we are identity theorists about selves and sense-data: the self is identical with the body (or the brain) and mental states (including sense-data) are identical with brain states. Do we then feel that selves and sense-data can no longer feature comfortably as constituents of content? Does the ready acceptance of such constituents rest upon a prior rejection of materialism? Would it make any difference if you were a Cartesian dualist? I suggest that the answer to these questions is No: there would still be an asymmetry between the material objects outside us and these internal material items with respect to the shock-value of externalism. So we need to find some distinction *within* the class of material particulars.

I think the essential distinction concerns, not the intrinsic character of the items in question, but their relation to the subject — specifically, their spatial relation. The unshocking Russellian particulars, even when construed physically, are spatially within the subject and not at a distance from him, while the objects of sight (say) are spatially removed from the subject. The intuition here is that my mental states are (roughly) where I am, so their constituents must also be – at any rate, they must not be spatially distant from me.[28] This criterion seems at least extensionally correct: what groups universals (including logical operators and mathematical entities) together with Russellian mental particulars is the fact that neither are *spatially separated* from the subject who thinks about them. And this for two reasons: either the entities are not spatially located at all, or they are located where the subject is. But perceptual objects are spatially 'out there', distant, separate, removed. It is this spatial separation or fissure that seems to require that the mind be able to reach out (across space) and incorporate into itself what lies outside it (because outside the subject). Where the object is not spatially remote no such reaching out is called for; then the mind does not need to incorporate external space itself into its inner constitution. If we think of mental constituency as requiring spatial proximity or propinquity or overlap, then distant objects will have big trouble qualifying as mental constituents – they just have too far to travel – while objects which are not similarly distant will slide into place quite smoothly, no such journey being necessary. Thinking of the mind as spatially located, we naturally maintain a differential attitude towards remote and nonremote putative mental constituents. Locating the mind roughly where the subject is, we have trouble with the idea that it might be configured by what resides *over there*. This point applies as much to the mental states of others as it

---

[28] It is this that produces a sense of contradiction in the externalist's position: how can something be both within the mind and yet outside the person? It cannot be both inside and outside at the same time! The answer to this is that the mind is not where the person is, or not completely; we must distinguish persons from their minds.

does to the material objects of perception. Whether or not we construe other minds physically, it is a strain to suppose that their mental states might feature as constituents of my mental states. Why? – because theirs are where they are and mine are where I am, and they are at a distance from me (even if the distance is agreeably small). Intrinsic nature is not what matters; spatial relation is what matters.[29] (Note that there is no analogous discomfort in the case of sets. The members of a set may be spatially remote from each other, but they are not remote from the set – because we do not think of sets as having a location. Or if we do, the location automatically follows that of the set's members. But in the case of minds we are inclined to grant them a spatial location – that of the subject – which is distinct from that of the objects of thought. Sets do not have to traverse space – reach out across it – in order to have spatially located constituents. Minds, it seems, do.)

How does this criterion confirm my substantialist diagnosis? Well, it is precisely the spatial separateness of ordinary physical substances that constitutes their autonomy and exclusivity. A rock, say, is independent ontologically of spatially distant substances (though not of its own substantial parts), and it occupies a unique region of space that other substances do not and cannot (simultaneously) occupy. Substances are spatial beings whose configuration is independent of what lies beyond them; they do not incorporate constituents from *elsewhere*. That is essentially what their self-subsistence consists in. Their primary qualities, themselves spatial, constitute their intrinsic nature – relations to other substances are then as may be. Told of some putative entity that had spatially remote constituents upon which it was ontologically dependent, we would conclude that the entity in question could not be a substance – that it could not be of the same metaphysical category as rocks and cats and kidneys. But this is precisely what externalism affirms about the mind: it is constituted by its relations to distant objects. The characteristic properties of mind – its contentful states – are therefore not like intrinsic primary qualities of material substances, but are rather extrinsic relations that may take as their relata items from elsewhere in space. Neither does the mind seem to have clear (or clearly intelligible) boundaries, according to externalism. Do the distant constituents come within its boundaries, or is it that the boundaries are set somehow by the closer boundaries of the subject? We seem pulled in two directions here. Extend the boundaries out to the remotest constituents (some galaxy, say) and you have the mind spread

---

[29] Temporal relation also matters, if not quite so much: past and future constituents can also seem problematic, even if they are one's own sense-data. We get the idea of the mind as precariously suspended between the person and these spatio-temporally removed entities – as itself spatio-temporally distributed. This, in turn, leads to the idea that mental topography and physical space somehow overlap, itself a difficult idea (cf. John McDowell, 'Singular Thought and the Extent of Inner Space').

thinly out over deep space, its boundary pulled away from the limits of the subject. Restrict the boundary to that of the subject and then you have the puzzle of how remote objects could be constituents of mind. Either boundary line seems problematic and perverse. Indeed, the whole idea of a mental boundary begins to look misguided and incoherent – at best a misleading metaphor.[30] So externalism appears to undermine the idea of a mental boundary (a contour line) in anything like the sense in which physical substances have boundaries (or contour lines). And it is externalism about distant content constituents that does this most radically. Similarly, and connectedly, the notion of soilidity or impenetrability seems to have no clear mental analogue if externalism is true: the walls of the mind seem, on the contrary, built to be breached by other substances; the mind is only too willing to share is domicile with other substances (it keeps the front door always open). It is no wonder, then, that assuming a substance model of the mind makes externalism look magical and impossible: for no *substance* could do what externalism says the mind can do. The proper conclusion, for an externalist, had better not be that the mind is a special kind of miraculous and incomprehensible substance, capable of tricks no regular substance could contrive; it should be, rather, that the mind is *no* sort of substance at all – metaphysically, minds are not a *bit* like rocks and cats and kidneys. Minds should be seen as metaphysically sui generis, if externalism is true.[31]

These points can, I think, be made vivid by borrowing Wittgenstein's image of the beetle in the box.[32] Wittgenstein, of course, presents this image as representing a mistaken way of thinking about the phenomena of mind, as hidden and private and incommunicable. He is not concerned with externalism in the sense under consideration here. Nevertheless, I think his image can help expose the anti-substantialist consequences of externalism, whether or not Wittgenstein himself would approve of this use of his celebrated image. Think of the beetle as modelling the mind, the box as modelling the body, and what lies outside the box as modelling the environment. In my terms, the beetle is a substance, as is the box (with a hollow in the centre). If the box can vary independently of the

[30] The idea of a boundary to space is also dubiously coherent, and this is one respect in which space is genuinely disanalogous to material substances.

[31] Cf. Jean-Paul Sartre, *Being and Nothingness*. Sartre distinguishes the for-itself (consciousness), which is characterized by 'nothingness', from the in-itself, which consists essentially in substantial objects. The nothingness of intentional consciousness, as Sartre understands it, makes consciousness a radically different kind of 'being' from the world of objects; in effect, he is an anti-substantialist about the mind. His view is, indeed, strongly analogous to relationalism about space, since he conceives mental states as nothing (n.b.) over and above intentional relations to things in the world. Sartre is probably the most extreme externalist in philosophy, and his anti-substantialism stems directly from his externalism: consciousness is characterized by Nothingness precisely because its essence is to be directed onto things in the world.

[32] See *Philosophical Investigations*, section 293.

environment – if it is autonomous with respect to the environment – then so, a fortiori, can the beetle. The beetle could be of another species without there being any change in what is going on outside the box, and it could stay the same species however much the box's environment were to vary: the beetle's existence and identity are environment-independent. In this sense the nature of the beetle is intrinsic to it. Now if we are tempted to think of mind and body and environment on this model, then we will recoil from the very idea of externalism: for how could an entity like *this* ever be individuated by something bearing *that* kind of relation to it? What has the extra-box world got to do with the essential character of the beetle? The beetle, being a substance, is individuated as other substances are, not by what spatially surrounds it on the other side of an opaque solid barrier. Of course, the beetle stands in various relations to what is outside the box; but these relations are wholly extrinsic to it – they do not in any way constitute the beetle as the kind of substance it is. Similarly, the mind, understood on this model, will not (could not) have its nature fixed by the environment. So, contraposing, if the mind *does* have its nature environmentally determined, then it cannot be anything like the boxed beetle – it cannot be an autonomous substance.[33]

Wittgenstein's focus (in effect) is upon the relationship between the beetle and the box; and his target is the idea that the identity of the beetle is not reflected in the shape or colour of the box (to put it crudely). That is, he is concerned with the image of the mind as a hidden or private substance – an internal substance ensconsed within another public substance, viz. the body. Someone could object to this picture and not reject the substance model itself. A straightforward reductive behaviourist, say, could merge the beetle with the box (as it were) and still take the mind to be substantial – since the box (the body) is itself substantial. Yet this would still be a form of internalism in my sense, since it cuts the mind off from what *surrounds* the body. If the contours of the mind are those of the (behaving) body, then the mind is still being conceived as a substance, though not as a substance confined secretly within another substance. But externalism makes a more radical critique of this kind of picture, for it repudiates the idea that the mind is *any* sort of substance – the mind is neither a hidden beetle nor a

[33] If we combine substantialism with privacy, we generate a double boundary, a protective shell surrounding the inner nut. For, if the mind lies concealed 'behind' the body, then the body makes another barrier through which the world cannot penetrate; the mind is cut off from the environment both by its own boundary and by that of the body. A certain conception (or image) of mental privacy thus militates against externalism. But publicly exposing the kernel, by stripping away the shell, still conflicts with externalism if we conceive the mind as like a 'something', i.e. a substance. I think an externalist could reasonably appropriate Wittgenstein's remark that a sensation 'is not a something, but not a nothing either' (304), meaning by it that an intentional state is not substancelike but is not nonexistent either (of course, externalism was not Wittgenstein's point in saying that).

publicly inspectable box. For externalism, moulding the beetle in the shape of the box is exactly wrong: it is an affirmation of substantialism not an abandonment of it. (The body, remember, is 'in the head'.) The mind is not, for the externalist, a beetle in a box – but it is not a beetly box either! Beetles and boxes alike belong to the wrong metaphysical category.

I must now answer a certain objection to the diagnostic suggestion I have been making. I have said that externalism implies that the mind is not a substance, that minds cannot be modelled upon material objects. But, it may be said, this claim is trivialized by the fact that substantialism is patently false on other, quite independent, grounds. For 'mind' is not a sortal predicate picking out a class of *objects* at all, substantial or otherwise. Minds are not, properly speaking, subjects of mental predication: talk of 'the mind' or 'my mind' or 'her mind' is not properly objectual talk – these phrases are in logical reality pseudo singular terms. A listing of all the objects in the world will not include an inventory of all the minds there are. This is not because mental ascriptions are never true, however; it is because talk of minds is best construed as talk of attributes or powers or properties, not of some kind of object of which mental predications are true. The objectual subject of mental predications is the *person* – the person has mental attributes or powers or properties; talk of 'the mind' introduces no further object into our ontology. In this respect, it may be said, minds differ from sets, since sets really are objects.[34] But then, if minds are not even objects, they can hardly qualify as substances – attributes and powers cannot be substances! Admittedly, it will be said, philosophers in the Cartesian tradition have spoken of minds as substances, but their mistake was not internalism but a logico-grammatical howler. And the significance of externalism had better not turn out to be merely that of a shiny new nail in an old and worn coffin. *Of course* the mind isn't a substance: to locate the significance of externalism there would be like saying that relational subjectivism about colour shows that colours are not substances, since they are dependent on what lies beyond them, viz. perceptual receptivities – the point being that colours are properties not objects, so do not even start to qualify for substancehood. Substantialism is therefore a straw man, not worthy to be pitted against externalism.

I am inclined to think that the premise of this objection is basically sound, but that it does not impair the substance (!) of my diagnosis. It is indeed plausible that

---

[34] Somewhat similarly, places might rate as objects under relationalism but not as substantival objects: that is, places may qualify as the denotations of genuine singular terms and as subjects of predication, though they have no being independently of occupying matter. So places are at least candidates for substancehood; they are not simply of the wrong metaphysical category. But, it may be insisted, minds do not reach even the first rung towards substancehood, since mental phenomena are essentially 'attributive'.

minds are not objects (though persons are), that mind talk is attribute talk. The body is an object that stands in a certain relation to the person, but 'the mind' is not analogously related to the person. However, it is not difficult to reformulate my earlier claim in such a way as to respect this logical point. Indeed, I take it that my earlier claim did not *seem* trivial in the way alleged, so it must be susceptible of a formulation which does not invite this triviality objection. The required reformulation is simply this: mental attributes are not substantial attributes. That is to say, if externalism is true of mental attributes, then those attributes are not intrinsic and autonomous: they can be instantiated only in virtue of relations to things in the environment of the subject. Mental attributes are thus quite unlike the intrinsic primary qualities of physical substances – the qualities that determine the extension, shape and boundary of a substance.[35] It is in virtue of possessing such qualities that physical objects count as substances – they determine the ontological category of what instantiates them – and mental attributes are essentially unlike these qualities if externalism is true. Mental attributes are not like the definitive attributes of the beetle in the box (or out of it). Accordingly, if complete externalism were true – no mental attribute is even partially internally constituted – then there would be nothing substance*like* in the correct conception of mind. The defining properties of mind would not be substantial properties, i.e. the kinds of properties that confer substancehood on what instantiates them: autonomy and exclusivity would not be consequences of possessing mental attributes. My earlier objectual-sounding talk of 'the mind' can thus be construed in these attributive terms.

But now this may provoke the following objection. How can I say that externalism implies that mental attributes are not substantial attributes and yet *also* say that it does not imply that persons are not substances? Persons have mental attributes, so how can *they* be substantial while their mental attributes are not? How can externalism permit persons to be autonomous and exclusive and yet not permit their minds to be? Why doesn't the substantiality of persons transmit itself to their minds? The answer to this puzzle is not very hard to find: not every attribute of a substance has to be a substance-conferring attribute. Substances have extrinsic relational properties as well as intrinsic nonrelational ones. There is no pressure to construe *every* attribute of a rock as intrinsic (including its spatial relations to other rocks) just because the rock must have *some* intrinsic attributes in order to qualify as a substance. Similarly, persons could have other

---

[35] We can state the anti-substantival consequences of relationalism about space in terms of attributes too: we can say that spatial attributes do not hold independently of material occupation, so that they cannot confer substancehood on space. Thus spatial attributes are unlike the intrinsic primary qualities of material objects, which are autonomous. So we do not *have* to think of space as an object to make it meaningful to deny its substantival character.

attributes than mental ones in virtue of which they qualify as substances, without detriment to the claim that mental attributes are nonsubstantial.

We are now a short step away from deriving a mildly interesting conclusion about persons (conditionally on the truth of complete externalism). If mental attributes do not confer substancehood on persons, yet persons are substances, then what *does* confer substancehood on them? The only possible answer seems to be that it is bodily characteristics that do. And indeed bodily characteristics are ideally suited to that role, being straightforward physical properties – the kind that confer substancehood on cats and rocks. Persons are substances in virtue of their bodily not their mental characteristics (assuming total externalism).[36] Depending upon how plausible one finds this result, one will be more or less disposed to accept total externalism. If one finds it independently plausible, as I am inclined to, then one will look with some favour on the extreme externalism that leads to it – though there may of course be other decisive objections to total externalism. But if one wishes to link the mind constitutively with the substantiality of persons, then one will see in this result a reason to retreat from full externalism – one will seek some genuinely intrinsic mental attributes to do the substance-conferring job. Later, when I have discussed the plausibility of complete externalism, we will be in a position to return to this issue about persons and decide whether the mind can play any role in determining the substantiality of persons. At present I am only mapping the logical relations between the various doctrines in play.

So far in assessing the significance of externalism for the character of mind I have said nothing about the mind's access to itself. I have not located the primary significance of externalism in its consequences for first-person infallibility or transparency. That there are such consequences I do not doubt (and will treat of them at some length later): distinctions of content, if they are beholden to the external world, will not be necessarily introspectively evident to the subject – mental states may be identical in how they seem in introspection and yet be different mental states. Whether, indeed, one has a certain kind of mental state at all will not be necessarily evident to introspection. World-dependence implies imperfect vision by the introspective eye. The reason I have not focused upon the consequences of externalism for mental epistemology is that I do not think such consequences are *basic*. I do not believe that the undertow towards internalism rests primarily upon a tacit epistemology of mind, namely that introspection is necessarily omniscient within its domain. I think, rather, that it is the metaphysical picture that is fundamentally at stake here – the picture we are apt to have of the kind of being the mind is. In the nature of the case this is not an easy

---

[36] I suppose this result favours bodily conceptions of the nature of persons and personal identity, and disfavours psychological conceptions (such as memory criteria).

claim to establish; we are here in the realm of speculative diagnoses and intuitive pictures, not hard arguments – and what is significant for one person may not be for another. But I can at least indicate my reasons for preferring this order of philosophical priority. In the first place, externalism is not an *overtly* epistemological doctrine: it says how mental states are individuated, what their nature is, not how they are known to their subject – it is, on the face of it, a metaphysical or ontological doctrine. Accordingly, its primary significance should be seen as residing in its metaphysical consequences – what metaphysical assumptions about the mind it calls into question. In general, an overtly metaphysical doctrine has a primarily metaphysical significance: idealism about the external world, or nominalism about abstract entities, say, are metaphysical doctrines whose primary significance consists in their consequences for the *kind of thing* tables and numbers are, respectively. Only secondarily do these doctrines have certain epistemological repercussions. So if we wish to discover what tacit assumptions are disturbed by some proposed metaphysical doctrine, we should look first for distinctively metaphysical assumptions. Secondly, it seems to me that the epistemology of a certain subject matter should be seen as flowing from its correct metaphysics: the facts should be so represented that we can see *why* their epistemology is thus and so. The epistemology of *Fs* always presupposes an underlying metaphysics for *Fs* (consider the different epistemologies of the external world generated by idealism and realism). In the case of the mind, we need to understand what kind of thing the mind is – what it *is* to have a mental state – before we can have any clear idea of the status of our knowledge of the mind. So even if the primary significance of externalism were epistemological, we would still need to ask what underlying metaphysics of mind was generating that epistemology – what the mind is *such that* it has an epistemology of that kind. Thirdly, I doubt that the core surprise-value of externalism could reside in its denial of the transparency of mind to introspection, since this is something that has already come in for a battering on other grounds: we do not generally suppose that all mental phenomena are accessible to perfect introspection. It is true that conscious occurrent thoughts are commonly regarded as prime candidates for transparency, and that externalism denies this, but I doubt that the sense of unease produced by externalism is the same as that produced by such claims as that pains are not always evident to introspection. It is the underlying *reason* for the failure of transparency that causes the basic unease in the case of externalism, not the failure of transparency itself; and this is why a denial of transparency in the pain case, perhaps as a result of some kind of materialism or functionalism, does not occasion precisely the same *kind* of unease.[37] You would need to locate

---

[37] One can imagine (alleged) grounds for denying the transparency of thoughts that parallel the grounds sometimes given for denying the transparency of bodily sensations: for example,

pains outside of the head, make them environment-dependent, in order to tap the
same source of disquiet. And, finally, the epistemological consequences of
externalism have, I think, been noticed and explored more fully than the
metaphysical consequences, and I wanted to remedy that deficiency.[38]

I would, however, now like to connect the metaphysical picture I have been
sketching with the epistemological consequences of externalism, for I think they
mesh in an illuminating way – a way that would not have been apparent if we had
moved straight to the epistemology. The connection involves spatiality and
epistemic access. As I have observed, externalism inserts spatially distant objects
into the content of thoughts. Such thoughts will not be transparent, because the
identity and existence of their constituents will not be evident to introspection. By
contrast, thoughts about one's own sensations (say) will not fail of transparency;
and neither do they incorporate the spatially distant, sensations being right there
with the subject. Opacity of content goes with location of the constituent: if the
constituent comes from the external spatial world, then the content of the thought
will be opaque (or at least not fully transparent). The thought will have the
opacity of perceptual objects, and be prone to the same sorts of illusion. In other
words, the thought's content will not enjoy *immediacy* with respect to the subject:
it will fail of immediacy *both* spatially and epistemically. Indeed, the reason it
fails of epistemic immediacy is that it fails of spatial immediacy. Epistemic
immediacy requires, it seems, the absence of spatial mediation. The epistemic
notion of immediacy is based upon a spatial metaphor; this is why we cannot be
said to have immediate access to what lies outside us. Error obtrudes when the
objects of knowledge lie beyond us – as thought constituents do under
externalism. But now, if I am right that distant constituents are the chief threat to
substantialism, then the failure of epistemic immediacy seems traceable to the
wrongness of substantialism. If substantialism were true, then externalism would
be false – in which case thoughts would have no distant constituents, and so
would not be prone to the opacity entrained by externalism. What is problematic

---

commitment to some form of behaviourism or functionalism that permits mental states to exist
without awareness of them – to be somehow 'masked'. But this would not produce the precise sense of
unease occasioned by externalism. The idea that a mental state may somehow be 'hidden' or 'veiled'
from the subject is not the same as the idea that its very nature makes it extend beyond the reach of
introspection: the *source* of the opacity is different in the two cases. A type of mental state might be in
the head yet possibly cut off from introspection by various kinds of distraction (say), but externalism
implies that what fixes the identity of the mental state inherently escapes the field of the introspective
gaze by extending the state beyond the head. It is the source of this elusiveness that occasions the basic
unease, not what it is a source *of*; not the fact, but the explanation of the fact. So it is wrong to think
that the *distinctive* impact of externalism is to challenge Cartesian conceptions of self-knowledge.

[38] See Davidson, 'Knowing One's Own Mind', Evans, *The Varieties of Reference*, McDowell,
'Singular Thought and the Extent of Inner Space', McGinn, 'The Structure of Content'.

for substantialism is problematic for transparency, and the reason for the former problem is the same as the reason for the latter, viz. spatial separation.

This helps explain the Cartesian combination of the nonspatiality of mind and the epistemic transparency of mind. For, once space is introduced into the mind – in particular, between the introspective faculty and the constituents of mental states – the possibility of error has been provided for: immediacy is then no longer secured. Externalism contradicts nonspatiality, thus leaving room for failures of introspective access; it threatens the latter *by* threatening the former. Conceiving the mind as a nonspatial substance is the metaphysical background to the epistemology of transparency, and this background comes unstuck in the wake of externalism. Thus it is that the metaphysics underlies the epistemology. (I do not pretend that the conceptual links I have just tried to trace are very precise or rigorous. My aim in these remarks has been to hit off some half-submerged assumptions about how the nature of mind and our access to it are connected. We are dealing with a somewhat nebulous constellation of ideas here; I have tried only to give them some intelligible(-seeming) form – make it seem understandable why these ideas have kept each other company. I doubt that strict deductive connections could be established between them.)[39]

I hope I have succeeded in showing that the significance of externalism goes beyond simply challenging certain theories of reference and intentionality. Externalism is more than a mere batch of counterexamples to some optional and rootless philosophical thesis about what fixes the aboutness relation. If I am right, then the opposite internalist view has some fairly deep underpinnings in a way of thinking about the mind that has seemed compulsory to many. This is, I think, why externalism is often reacted to with dismayed incredulity by *beginners* in philosophy. Something, they obscurely feel, is going very wrong here: the mind not in the head but spread out across the world – how can that be! Wittgenstein warns us against the perils of modelling the mind on the material world.[40] My

---

[39] Under externalism the mind is essentially a system of relations between the subject and the worldly objects of his mental states, as with relationalism about space. Accordingly, the subject's introspective knowledge takes these relations as its object, and so there ensues a predictable failure of immediacy. The relata, which comprise mental constituents, are removed in space and time from the subject. So this kind of psychological relationalism is a conception on which immediacy and transparency will intelligibly fail. As the epistemology of space comes essentially to involve that of matter, under relationalism about space, so the (first-person) epistemology of mind comes essentially to involve that of the external world, under externalism about the mind. Full Cartesian transparency requires 'absolutism' about the mind, but externalism conflicts with such absolutism.

[40] In his terminology, assimilating the language-game of using mental words to that of using words for ordinary perceptible objects, and hence interpreting all language on the model of 'name and object'. I might put my point by saying that there is a tendency to construe the meaning of '*x* believes that *p*' on the model of '*x* is square' or '*x* is gold', thus assimilating intentional properties to the properties characteristic of substances. We need, as Wittgenstein would say, to recognize the diversity

suggestion has been that it is the same sort of temptation, or conviction, that causes people to jib at externalism. The proponent of externalism does well, therefore, to go beyond simply brow-beating his internalist opponent with counterexamples and address himself to the underlying conception of mind that causes resistance to these counterexamples. Once this conception is exposed, the opponent might be only too happy to concur with the externalist thesis, not wishing to find himself committed to anything so strange and outrageous as substantialism about the mind. It is not, after all, uncommon to find oneself believing something for reasons which, once they are brought to light, strike one as being quite indefensible – and so dropping the ill-founded belief like a hot brick. Looked at this way, my diagnosis supplies the externalist with the heavy ammunition he needs. On the other hand, as I indicated earlier, substantialism may not be so easy to blast off the intellectual landscape – it has a stubborn tendency to cling resiliently on.[41] At any rate, I think substantialism is one area in which the battle between internalism and externalism may be usefully fought.

4 *The scope and limits of externalism*   I have now given a formulation of externalism, distinguishing weak and strong versions of the thesis, and I have enquired into its significance both for the world and the mind. My question now is whether, and to what extent, the thesis is true. We should by this stage be in a position to know precisely *what* would be true if externalism is, and to appreciate the philosophical repercussions of its being true. I proceed then to get down to cases.

   (i) *Natural kind concepts and indexicals*   Putnam's seminal discussion of whether 'meanings are in the head' focused on the case of natural kind concepts, such as the concept of water. He also remarked that his thesis obviously applies to indexical meaning: for no one could suppose that the extension of an indexical term is fixed by its internally determined intension.[42] What Putnam took to be controversial was the claim that natural kind concepts function like indexical

of the language-games (not that I am very fond of this way of putting it). The externalist in effect takes the dogmatic internalist to be fixated on a misleading paradigm of 'the real'. The danger, then, is that irrealism about the mind will seem inevitable once internalism is seen to be false. (The same kind of danger exists in respect of relationalism about space and time.) But this should be seen as an irrational dread – a kind of agoraphobia about the externality of your mind.

   [41] Wittgenstein, of course, had the idea that there is a persistent and rooted tendency to model the mind on the world of material objects. It is not as if we come to see that this is false and there's an end to the matter. The truth about the mind may run against the grain of how we are prone to think about it. Prolonged therapy may therefore be needed to dislodge wrong philosophical conceptions. We might have an internal fight on our hands.

   [42] See Putnam, 'The Meaning of "Meaning"'.

concepts, that their meaning is not in the head either. The twin earth cases, in which the internal facts are held constant while the surrounding natural kinds are varied, lead, Putnam argued, to the conclusion that the reference of a natural kind term could vary despite invariance in the intrinsic properties of the user of the term. Thus he famously concluded, 'No matter which way you cut the pie, "meanings" just ain't in the head.' In fact this conclusion exaggerates what has been established, since only *some* meanings have been argued to be environmentally determined, not *all*. The appropriate conclusion should have been that a proper subset of meanings are not in the head – a somewhat less resounding announcement. Later authors then pointed out that what went for meanings also went for concepts, i.e. for the contents of propositional attitudes: this is, indeed, but a simple consequence of the principle that the concept expressed by a term is given by what it means.[43] There thus arose the new slogan, 'Mental states are not in the head', where again the implicit universal quantification was not strictly warranted – for only *some* mental states had been shown to be externally individuated.

Now I myself completely accept the lesson of twin earth cases so far as natural kind concepts are concerned: which such concept you have is not determined solely by intrinsic facts, either about the individual or his community; the environment makes a decisive contribution to the content of natural kind thoughts. I also completely accept that the same is true of indexical concepts, at least in this sense: the truth conditions of an indexical thought are context-dependent and hence can vary without variation in noncontextual intrinsic properties of the individual or his community. I accept, in other words, strong externalism about these kinds of content. But I am anxious that we understand what is going on in these examples and assess their purport correctly; in particular, we must not rashly generalize from these cases to other kinds of content – each kind of content must be considered on its own merits.

The essential point about the natural kind examples is this: The appearance (to us) of a natural kind, whether mineral or animal or vegetable, does not uniquely fix its identity. Therefore, if we hold the appearance constant, we do not necessarily hold the reality constant. But our words and thoughts are addressed to the natural kind itself – to its reality – and so they could vary in their reference despite constancy of appearance. So, even assuming appearances to be in the head, the content of natural kind thoughts can come apart from internal facts. In the classic twin earth cases it is assumed that the two natural kinds are experienced

---

[43] I made this point in 'Charity, Interpretation and Belief'. I believe, in fact, that I was the first to make it (at least in print). It is actually pretty obvious when you think about it. Burge makes a number of refinements of the point in 'Other Bodies', which improve on my original formulation of it (the point occurred to him independently).

in the same way – as colourless and tasteless, etc. – while *what* is experienced is different. The operative principle here is simply that the identity of a perceptual object is not determined by how it seems to perceivers. So it is being assumed in effect that seemings belong on the side of the head (so to speak): they are among the internal facts that fail to fix the reference of the term or thought. Viewed in this way, the Putnamian conclusion rests upon a highly compelling and intuitive thesis, namely that perceptual seemings are not necessarily as fine-grained as the reality that causes them.[44] For, once this principle is absorbed and slotted into the right place, it is a very short step to the conclusion that contents need not be in the head: we simply need the assumption that our words and thoughts can succeed in being about reality and not merely about how reality seems to us. In essence, the original twin earth cases showed that (some) contents are not fixed by how things seem to the subject.[45] Of course this is consistent with supposing that seemings are not themselves in the head, but the persuasive power of the examples comes from the fact that *even if we allow that internalism is correct for seemings* we can prove that not all content is in the head. The externalist about natural kind concepts does not therefore *need* to take a stand on whether seemings are in the head in order to derive his conclusion; he can rely on the virtually incontrovertible principle that appearance does not determine reality. Such a principle cannot be appealed to, of course, if we are trying to show that concepts of appearance themselves, or perceptual contents, are not in the head; for such contents the externalist argument is going to have to be far more theoretical and controversial. Indeed, as I shall argue later, externalism about the representational content of perceptual seemings, and about observational concepts, is *not* defensible. The point I am making now is that the form of argument I have discerned in the classic twin earth cases relies heavily upon the appearance–reality gap – and derives its intuitive force from this reliance.

But the intuitive force of the argument seems to be rivalled by another intuition that appears to count against it. Concentrate on the existence-dependence aspect of externalism – the claim that if the object of thought fails to exist so too does the thought. For example, consider a twin earth on which the people are

[44] Saul Kripke makes essentially the same point in terms of 'qualitative counterparts': see *Naming and Necessity*. Different things can be qualitatively similar and yet reference be made to one or the other of them: reference is not supervenient on qualitative appearances.

[45] There is a precedent for this in Wittgenstein's rejection of the idea that meanings (and intentional contents generally) are fixed by 'states of consciousness', i.e. conscious episodes in which some item 'comes before the mind'. He certainly held that the same items could swim before two subjects' minds and yet they mean something different by their words: understanding, he said, is not a 'mental state'. But in his case the emphasis was on behaviour and ability as what makes the distinction, not causal relations to the environment. Still, he rejected the idea that intentional contents are determined by 'qualitative' states of consciousness.

hallucinating a water-like liquid all the time, or on which their demonstrative thoughts lack a reference. The externalist says that such contents are necessarily dependent for their existence upon the obtaining of some suitable environmental relation – hence, no object, no thought. The existence of a thought of a certain type depends upon the existence of thought constituents of the right type; so if these comprise worldly entities, then without those entities no thought of that type can exist to be thought.[46] Now the intuition that seems to tell against this modal claim is just that it seems merely contingent that my thoughts have worldly reference: it seems that I *could* have had these very thoughts in the absence of their actual referents. This 'intuition of contingency' appears to conflict with the externalist's claim of necessity. How can it be that, necessarily, this (say) demonstrative thought – that that cup is chipped – can exist only if that cup exists, while it seems evident that I *might* have been thinking that very thing and yet no such cup exist (I was hallucinating it)? The necessity claim seems belied by an evident contingency. Externalist essentialism thus runs up against an internalist intuition of contingency with respect to the link between thought and its objects.

What I want to suggest is that this anti-externalist argument relies upon a conflation of two sorts of modality: epistemic and metaphysical – as indeed my presentation of the argument was intended to suggest. The externalist can therefore adopt the Kripkean strategy of explaining away the intuition of contingency in a way that renders it quite consistent with his essentialist thesis.[47] The objector is accused of trying to deduce a claim of metaphysical contingency from premises involving a merely epistemic possibility. Call my demonstrative thought D and the demonstrated cup c. The externalist thesis is that D necessarily involves c. The objector invites us to accept that it might turn out that D exists and c does not. The externalist replies that this last possibility is really of the form, 'There might have been a mental state qualitatively just like D which did not involve c but involved some other cup c' or no cup at all', and this does not imply that D (*that* thought) could exist without c. The objector then either concedes that this is what he really meant and gives up the argument, or he splutters that he really did intend to make a metaphysical modal claim about D and c – in which case the externalist will simply disown the intuition so stated. In this way the externalist allows what seems hard to deny without retracting his

---

[46] This is the version of externalism most heavily stressed by Evans, *The Varieties of Reference*. Twin earth cases bear more on the question of identity.

[47] See Kripke, *Naming and Necessity*. Kripke could use this apparatus to handle modal doubts about his own Millian theory of names. Since his view is that the sense of a name is given by its bearer, it will follow that where there is no bearer there is no sense; yet it may seem that I could mean the same thing by 'Venus' even if Venus did not exist. Kripke could diagnose this intuition in terms of a qualitative counterpart of the sense of 'Venus' which fails to be identical to that sense. But, in fact, he makes no such suggestion.

essentialist claim in the slightest. In the presence of strong arguments for externalism this strategy leaves the internalist in a weak debating position.

The strategy just exploited is, of course, exactly parallel to Kripke's strategy when rebutting anti-essentialist intuitions about natural kinds themselves. Kripke explains the intuition that water is only contingently H_2O in terms of some *other* possible substance failing to be H_2O, this other substance being qualitatively just like water. I have just explained the intuition that water-*thoughts* might have been about something other than water (perhaps nothing) as the intuition that some *other* kind of mental state (perhaps not fully a thought at all) might have existed in the absence of water. Illusions of possibility surround both kinds of essentialist thesis. And it is not surprising that the two cases should be thus parallel, since the essentialist thesis is precisely that water – that very stuff, viz. H_2O – enters into the content of thought: the illusion that these thoughts could exist without that constituent is (in part at least) the illusion that that constituent could itself exist without any H_2O existing. At any rate, the latter illusion of possibility fuels the former illusion. The thought is individuation-dependent on the entity, so *its* individuation conditions get transmitted to the thought – hence no water-thought can exist in a world without H_2O. Similarly, a demonstrative thought about a particular organism cannot exist in a world in which no organism has the *origin* that organism actually has – assuming that origin is essential to organisms.[48] This may seem vulnerable to contingency intuitions, but such intuitions can be explained away as mere epistemic possibilities – in this case the real possibility of *an* organism just like the given one, but with a different origin, being the object of a demonstrative thought. Again, what individuates the object individuates the thoughts that are individuation-dependent on the object – the existence conditions of the one get included in the existence conditions of the other. And the apparatus needed to see one's way clear to accepting these individuation conditions is the same in both cases.

Strictly speaking, the twin earth cases show only that some natural kind concepts are world-dependent; they do not show that all are, still less that necessarily all are. The question I now want to take up is whether these stronger claims are warranted. In particular, would it be *possible* for a subject to have natural kind concepts and for these concepts not be open to twin earth cases? Let us be clear to start with that this is not the question whether a subject could have concepts *of* natural kinds such that those concepts are not externally fixed by the relevant natural kinds. This is plainly possible, since someone might think of water solely as 'the liquid I least like to drink': this concept can certainly be possessed in the absence of water, and it will remain the same concept no matter

---

[48] See Kripke, *Naming and Necessity*; also my 'On the Necessity of Origin'.

THE LOCATION OF CONTENT

how we vary the environmental liquids. The question is rather whether natural kind concepts – concepts like *water* and *cat* – are necessarily environment-dependent. I do not intend to propose a rigorous criterion for being a natural kind concept in the intended sense; I shall assume a sufficient grasp on the kind of concept in question – the kind that functions as Kripke and Putnam suggest.[49] But just to fix ideas, let us summarize this as the notion that a natural kind concept is one that is made up of a stereotype plus an extension. Then I think it is clear that externalism (weak or strong) is *not* true of all such concepts. For consider the concept H_2O: this is a natural kind concept in the intended sense, but it is surely possible for someone to grasp it in the absence of water, i.e. H_2O; all that is necessary is a grasp of the concepts that *make up* this concept. Or again, suppose 'coal' means 'wood compressed in a certain way over millions of years' then someone could grasp the concept *coal* by grasping this definition, yet there not be any coal in his world. These are genuine natural kind concepts because they contain a blank space for a hidden essence – the stereotype does not reveal the essential nature of the extension – but they do not require the existence of their extensions in order to be possessed. The reason is clear: they are *complex* natural kind concepts grasped derivatively upon grasp of their constituent parts. Grasp of these conceptual parts may yet require the presence of instances of *their* extensions, but it does not follow that the complex concept can be grasped only in the presence of instances of *its* extension. I take it this point is pretty obvious.

What is not so obvious are the consequences of this for the question whether a subject could possess *all* his natural kind concepts in this world-independent way. I shall argue that he could not. To possess all one's natural kind concepts world-independently would be for all those concepts to be conceptually complex. For if the concept is primitive, then it cannot be possessed derivatively upon possession of its constituent concepts, and will therefore be subject to twin earth cases: this is the situation with *water*, *cat*, and the like. But it does not seem that any natural kind is such that *it* must be represented primitively. Suppose some kind K is conceptualized complexly. Now there are two possibilities: either the complex concept is a natural kind concept or it is not, i.e. either it contains a primitive natural kind concept (e.g. *oxygen* or *wood*) or it does not (e.g. *what I least like to drink*). In the latter case, the complex concept is not a natural kind concept in the intended sense and so falls outside the scope of the modalized externalism we are presently considering. In the former case, it is such a concept but it requires *some* constituent natural kind concept to be subject to twin earth cases. This constituent concept may be in turn complex, in which case we have the same alternatives again. So it seems that in order for someone to possess *any* natural kind concepts

[49] See Kripke, *Naming and Necessity*, Putnam, 'The Meaning of "Meaning"'.

some at least must be primitive and hence open to externalism. At the limit, I suppose, there could be only *one* such concept, the rest deriving their status as natural kind concepts from this one. In consequence, someone could have concepts for all the natural kinds we have concepts for, and these concepts could qualify as natural kind concepts in virtue of containing at least one primitive natural kind concept, and yet that person have only one concept like our concepts *water* or *cat*. It is only if one's natural kind concepts are primitive that externalism will apply to them, and there is no necessity that all or most will be primitive. This is, in fact, an instance of a more general point (to which I shall return), namely that externalism is not directly applicable to constructed concepts.[50] Essentially the same reasoning applies to indexical concepts. Descriptive concepts embedding an indexical component, e.g. *the saucer under that cup*, are not existence-dependent with respect to their actual reference, but they will not qualify *as* indexical unless they contain *some* conceptual constituent which is so dependent. So if there are to be any indexically tainted concepts, then some will have to be subject to externalism – just because some such concepts will have to be primitively indexical. It is consistent with this that someone could possess indexical ways of thinking about all the objects we represent indexically and yet make primitive indexical identifications of only one thing – the rest being achieved by embedding that indexical in complex descriptive-cum-indexical concepts. Increasing conceptual complexity is thus a way of restricting the applicability of externalism.[51] This is why it is too simple to say that all natural kind concepts are susceptible to twin earth cases.

(ii) *Why weak externalism is obviously true* Strong externalism is not obviously true; indeed, as I shall contend, it is false for certain kinds of content. But I think that weak externalism, properly understood, while not exactly being trivially true – for it has important repercussions for the nature of mind – is at least clearly and uncontroversially true of all (primitive) contents. In particular, the truth of weak externalism for singular thoughts follows from fairly elementary semantic and metaphysical principles (unlike strong essentialism for such thoughts – though this thesis too seems to me virtually undeniable). In this

[50] Of course, it may apply to constructed concepts in virtue of their conceptual constituents; but the fact remains that the extension of the constructed concept *itself* plays no essential role in the conditions for possessing the concept. To have the concept *water* you need to be environmentally related to water, but you do not need to stand in this relation to water to have the concept H_2O. It follows that these are not the same concept – something we knew already from the informativeness of 'water = H_2O'.

[51] We might venture the generalization: the more coarse-grained a conception the more the environment contributes to it, the less coarse-grained the less the environment contributes. Ignorance invites an infusion of externalism. Animal conceptions of natural kinds are always coarse and so are inevitably environment-dependent; animal minds lack the conceptual sophistication to prise their thoughts off the environment.

section I shall explain why I say this, and address myself to a pair of objections that seek to deprive weak externalism of any philosophical bite whatever.

The best way to see why weak externalism just has to be correct is to consider the truth conditions of ascriptions of contentful states, and how those truth conditions are determined by the words that go to make up such ascriptions. There seems to be no restriction on the kinds of words that can occur in a content-clause: if a word can occur outside such a clause, in a self-standing sentence, then it can also occur within it. Any sentence can, in principle, be used to say what someone believes. This is simply because any sentence expresses a potential thought. Now one naturally and naively expects that words retain their usual semantic value inside such contexts – or at least that they will not leave their usual semantic value completely behind.[52] One expects, that is, that a principle of semantic uniformity or constancy will operate. We therefore go by the linguistic appearances unless strong theoretical reason can be found not to. Certainly this principle seems eminently reasonable for other sorts of context in which 'that'-clauses can be embedded. Semantic constancy is the rule, the norm. Thus consider negated contexts: 'It is not the case that'. Inserting a demonstrative, say, within such a context does not deprive it of the function of referring to a certain entity: the truth conditions of the whole turn upon whether that entity is thus and so – existential implications are not magically cancelled. We might put this in logical atomist style as the claim that negative facts can contain individuals as constituents. It is the same with modal contexts: placing 'that F' after 'It is necessary that' does not rob it of existential import. Modal facts can also have individual constituents. Vacuous demonstratives do not miraculously acquire a semantic value by being placed inside such contexts: the result of this embedding operation lacks a truth-value just as surely as the simple demonstrative sentence would. Semantic delinquency cannot be ameliorated by confinement within these kinds of context. (Vacuous demonstratives can run but they can't hide.) Thus we have modal sentences that express existence-dependent necessities, e.g. 'Necessarily that dog is an organism.' The same holds for sentences reporting factive attitudes – 'A knows/remembers/perceives that that dog is a poodle', and the like. The term 'that dog' does its usual semantic business here, and so has need of a demonstrated dog if the sentence is to succeed in stating a fact. To put it differently, we can legitimately existentially generalize on the embedded

---

[52] See Davidson, 'On Saying That', where he urges us to preserve our 'pre-Fregean semantic innocence' in the presence of indirect discourse. We should, he says, find it 'plainly incredible that the words "The earth moves", uttered after the words "Galileo said that", mean anything different, or refer to anything else, than is their wont when they come in other environments' (p. 108). His own paratactic theory involves regarding words in content clauses as having their usual reference. (Of course, this general advice applies only to used expressions, not to quotation.)

demonstrative. And these linguistic appearances do not abruptly alter when we come to consider belief contexts. In using a demonstrative to report someone's belief we take it to refer (or else we would not use it), and the report can be *true* only if it *does* refer. If someone says to me, 'Jack believes that that dog is a poodle', and then goes on to add 'but there is no such dog', then I take him to have contradicted himself, to have gone back on an implication. This is just as true here as it is for the other kinds of sentence mentioned above. Untutored semantic intuition tells us that such belief reports have these existential entailments; and this is but a formal mode way of saying that the beliefs reported are themselves existence-dependent. Psychological facts can contain individuals as constituents too. We are dealing here with a semantic *datum* – something any reasonable theory should try to respect, not flout. If anything is counterintuitive, it is the denial of this datum and its (weak) externalist consequences.[53]

Residual resistance to this argument can be further diminished by considering the role of predicates inside belief contexts. Assuming that second-order quantification over properties is legitimate for predicates in simple sentences, it also seems valid enough within complex contexts – negation, modality, factives, belief. For example, for Jack to believe that that dog is a poodle there has to be something (some property) that Jack believes that dog to possess. If there were no such property, then the belief report could not be straightforwardly true. But then, if beliefs can be existence-dependent upon properties, why should they not, for analogous reasons, be existence-dependent upon individuals? Whence this asymmetry between the two sorts of entity? Both belong to nonmental reality; neither is in the head. Surely the same semantic principles are at work for both sorts of contribution to 'that'-clauses. Indeed, much the same holds for other parts of speech: you cannot sensibly use an expression for a nonexistent logical operator within a belief context, any more than you can elsewhere. Proper names are no different. The only way out of this argument that I can see would be to claim, with vast implausibility, that our usual ways of ascribing beliefs are systematically defective, that we should never use anything but pure definite descriptions in belief ascription. But even accepting this revisionary warping of our linguistic practices in the service of a theory would not free belief ascription from existence-dependence altogether, since (as I say) the *predicates* in these ascriptions are also open to existential generalization. And presumably the determined internalist does not want to find himself depending essentially on a prior commitment to mentalism about properties or on rejection of (objectual) second-order quantification. Unless strong reason can be found for repudiating

---

[53] Cf. Kaplan on 'exportation' in 'Quantifying In'. I say nothing here about the difficult question of true negative existential statements involving names and demonstratives. See Evans, *The Varieties of Reference*, for an intricate discussion.

the linguistic appearances – and I know of no such reason – weak externalism goes through cleanly and smoothly.[54]

Some may find the foregoing considerations suspiciously 'linguistic', an attempt to extract substantive metaphysics out of 'ordinary language'. I myself see no force in this complaint, but I offer the following reformulation of the essential point in purely material mode terms for those who do. Beliefs are representations of possible states of affairs. These states of affairs are precisely the states of affairs that may obtain in the world. States of affairs contain as constituents the objects and properties and so on that exist in the world. Since beliefs are relations to these possible states of affairs, they contain whatever the state of affairs they represent contains. So, if a possible state of affairs contains x, then a belief in the obtaining of that state of affairs will also contain x, the belief itself being a state of affairs of which x is a constituent. To identify a belief one has to identify the state of affairs it represents, and to do this one has to identify the objects and properties and so on that make up that state of affairs. The existence conditions of a belief content are thus those of the possible state of affairs the content represents, for to have the belief is to stand in the appropriate psychological relation *to* that possible state of affairs. It is essentially the same with modality: a possible state of affairs can only be necessary (say) if there *is* such a possible state of affairs, and this can be so only if there are appropriate constituents of that state of affairs. And just as modal facts can contain individual constituents as well as universal constituents (properties), so too belief facts can – as with the fact of my presently believing that that cup is chipped. Belief really is a (complex) relation between a subject and certain items in the world, so it can hold between its relata only if they exist.[55] If x does not exist, then there is no such possibility as the possibility that x is F; but if so, then there can be no belief in the obtaining of that state of affairs, there being no such possibility to believe in. Asked *which* possibility is believed to be actual, we cannot answer by identifying it as the possibility that x is F, since that would be to identify *nothing*. Nonexistent possibilities simply cannot be believed to obtain. (A nonexistent possibility is not, of course, the same thing as an *im*possibility.) This is really just another way of coming at the semantic point I made previously, except for the unbuttoned talk of possible states of affairs and their constituents.

It needs to be observed that the foregoing considerations sustain nothing stronger than weak externalism: they show merely that there is an existential

[54] Here, I know, I am slicing cavalierly through controversial thickets. I simply want to insist, in the midst of much clogged semantic theory, on a straightforward intuitive point about the linguistic appearances that should not be lost sight of. Weak externalism has the appearances firmly on its side, and I know of no sound reason to reject these appearances; it is not a piece of arcane theory that we are asked to believe in the face of the appearances – as it is often represented as being.

[55] This conception of belief is already present in Russell's 'The Philosophy of Logical Atomism', IV.

dependence between mental states and what in the world they are about; they do not serve to demonstrate the strong externalist thesis that some sort of causal or environmental relation is built into content ascription. For all that has been said, the constituent objects and properties could be causally quite isolated from the subject of the beliefs in question; he could, indeed, be a brain in a vat, forever prevented from interacting with what he thinks about. This is not surprising, since the considerations advanced were of a purely logical or semantic nature. To derive strong externalism one needs additional substantive arguments, such as twin earth cases, which are in no way already contained in the reasons offered above for weak externalism. Hence there is no legitimate move from weak to strong externalism; in fact, as I shall shortly argue, there are contentful states for which weak externalism is true but strong externalism is false.

It may be felt that weak externalism, so called, is *too* weak to deserve the label 'externalist'. Presumably this charge has little prima facie force in respect of thoughts about particulars, these being bona fide occupants of space–time; but for properties the charge might seem a reasonable one. Let C be a concept and P the property it 'denotes', e.g. the concept *square* and the property of being square. Weak externalism says that no one can have C (in a possible world) unless P exists (in that world).[56] But, it might be said, this existential requirement is nothing other than the requirement that C be coherent, that the corresponding predicate be meaningful; for it is necessary and sufficient for the denoted property to exist that its concept be coherent, that *it* exist. Put it Frege's way: for the reference of a predicate to exist it is required, and its suffices, that the predicate have a sense – there is no more to property existence than that. (I am not here following Frege's own view of the reference of a predicate, i.e. an extensionally individuated function; I am speaking of properties in the ordinary sense.) It will therefore follow trivially from the mere coherence of a thought that weak externalism with respect to properties is true of it. Nor will it lift the weak externalist thesis above the level of triviality to insist that senses themselves are not in the head. That may be true, but it does not generate an interesting species of externalism, since senses do not belong to the world of reference – they live in another sphere altogether.

[56] The question of the existence conditions of properties is, of course, vexed. If we adopt the Aristotelian view that properties need to be instantiated in order to exist, then we get a dependence of general concepts upon the existence of certain particulars: that is, the concept cannot exist in a mind unless some particular instantiating the property exists in the world. So there could not be purely general thoughts in a world in which no particulars instantiate the properties conceptualized. Believing that something is F would imply that at least one thing *is* F. (Description theorists should ask themselves what they think of this result.) Clearly this view makes general concepts more world-dependent than the Platonic view, which does not require actual instantiation for property existence. I will not commit myself on this question, since both views acknowledge the mind-independence of properties (universals), and so both deliver a genuine kind of externalism if concepts are made to depend upon properties.

Besides, the triviality objection can be formulated without reliance on such a view of sense: it depends simply on a point about conceptual coherence.

Now I do not want to embark here upon a thorough examination of the claim about property existence contained in this objection, though I will make two quick remarks. First, I doubt that the coherence of a concept is quite generally sufficient (or indeed necessary) for the existence of a corresponding property: scientifically postulated properties do not seem to have their existence conditions determined in this way, e.g. being phlogistic. Second, in some cases at least, I would say that the existence-dependence goes the other way: a concept will be admitted as coherent only if it succeeds in picking out a real objective property of things – shape concepts seem to me to be like that. What I do want to argue now is that even accepting the suggested existence condition weak externalism is not thereby trivialized, though it does seem to me pretty uncontroversial considered by itself. The reason it is not a trivial thesis is simply that properties are precisely the kinds of item that *things in the world instantiate*. The item that has to exist for me to *think* (say) 'something is square' is the very *same* item that has to exist in order for the material object in front of me to *be* square, viz. the property of being square. This property exists independently of minds (I assert) and it enters into nonmental interactions between material things. It thus has causal powers (when instantiated) that operate out there in the extramental world. It should strike us as more surprising (more significant) than it does that this very objective property also enters into the individuation of mental states: that what is objective and nonmental should enter into the very identity conditions of something subjective, a state of mind. It should, that is, impress us that properties have this dual role: they are instantiated by objects, and they (those very things) are used to identify our states of mind. The nontriviality comes from the reflection that this is (philosophically) surprising, remarkable. It is not similarly surprising that mental states should be dependent upon senses, since senses are not the kind of item that objects *instantiate*: senses are introduced to account for cognitive phenomena, not to explain what happens in the material world. I therefore insist that weak externalism with respect to properties is aptly so called.[57]

---

[57] Put it this way: we simply have no other conception of the concept *square* than as something that denotes the property of being square, so that possessing this concept cannot consist in anything other than standing in some relation (the intentional relation) *to* that property. There is no other way of coming at the concept than as the concept of the property of being square; no other putative specification of the concept would be identifiable as a specification of the concept *square*. It is no orthographic accident that we refer to the concept by italicizing the very word that stands for the property. The concept is essentially property-involving; it is like a cage from which the property can never escape. Concepts are vices designed to trap external properties and hold them rigidly in their grip. The sense of a predicate is a device for imprisoning a property in a thought – but a device that is itself chained for ever to the property.

A new triviality complaint may now replace the one just addressed. This is that the significance of weak externalism depends, not so much on the ontological status of properties themselves, as on the precise way we characterize their relation to the mental states they serve to identify; and the same may be said of objects. Moreover, on the correct way of characterizing that relation, the externalist thesis starts to look dispiritingly anodyne. I have spoken freely of objects and properties as 'constituents' of thought, following an established tradition: and this way of speaking certainly confers interest-value on the thesis it is invoked to characterize. But, the protest runs, the sober truth behind this colourful locution is just that mental states are individuation-dependent on external things – and this does not by itself warrant such excitingly purple language. We do not, after all, say that persons are *constituents* of sensations when we acknowledge that sensations are individuation-dependent on persons – or if we do the trope is readily confessed. So why say that objects and properties are constituents of thoughts in any literal and serious sense? All talk of the mind 'incorporating' worldly items, of its being 'penetrated' by the world, should be regarded as so much misleading hyperbole, even by the committed externalist. We should stick to the literally true talk of individuation-dependence, thus taking the metaphysical sting out of externalism. If the mind has any genuine constituents, the objector concludes, they will be internal not external – though the individuation of mental states still proceeds externally.

My reply to this is that the formulation in terms of constituents *is* warranted and should be taken seriously, and that it is only a lingering attraction to internalism that could underpin the half-hearted externalism just stated.[58] There is, I believe, no respectable motivation for resisting talk of worldly constituents once externalism has been accepted. The key point here is that the objection is not to talk of thought constituents as such; it is not being claimed that contents do not have conceptual constituents, no matter what those constituents turn out to be. Thoughts have conceptual constituents in the same sort of way sentence meanings have semantic constituents (whatever exactly that way is). The dispute between internalism and externalism is not over whether thoughts *have* constituents but

---

[58] Notice that relationalism about space goes naturally with the thought that objects are constituents of space and not merely occupants of it. It is not that space is fundamentally made up of places and their relations, but that objects coincide with these constitutive elements; rather, the objects are what *give* space its form and reality. Only a weak-kneed relationalist would shudder at the idea that objects are the real constituents of space – a relationalist, that is, with absolutist leanings. A full-blooded relationalist claims more than just that we identify places by reference to material objects; he claims that places are constituted by the system of relations between objects. I think a candid externalist should follow the example of the unrepentant relationalist: concepts are nothing other than locations for properties, as places are just what objects take up (for a relationalist). Constituency is the best way of getting at the intimacy of these relations.

over *what* individuates these constituents. According to the objection I am considering, the harm comes only when the externalist, who is right as against the internalist, inflates his thesis by *identifying* these constituents with external worldly items. Now the question to ask this weak-kneed externalist is whether he takes the same view of internalism: does he also believe that the internalist is not entitled to formulate his thesis by saying that his favoured internal items are constituents of thought? Suppose the internalist favours (world-independent) images or behavioural dispositions or bits of cerebral syntax: may he not say that his theory is that these items are the constituents of thought? I suggest that permission would be readily granted for such a formulation of internalism – certainly you may say that your chosen internal items constitute the constituents of thought. Perhaps a claim of literal identity goes a bit too far, since really thought constituents are Fregean senses, i.e. abstract items, but still there is no harm in the picture encouraged by describing the internal items *as* thought constituents. In fact, internalism so formulated has not attracted criticism analogous to that heaped upon the corresponding externalist formulation: it has not been regarded as wildly misleading and hyperbolic. In other words, an asymmetry between the two formulations has been commonly assumed.

But now my question is what could justify this assumed asymmetry except implicit attachment to internalism. According to internalism, content is fixed by a relation to some internal item; according to externalism, content is fixed by a relation to some external item: why should one theorist have the right to describe his preferred items as constituents of content while the other is denied this right? Surely there is a theoretical *symmetry* between the two doctrines in this respect. It will seem otherwise only if you assume that internalism about constituents *has* to be true in *some* way. Then you will take it that externalism is the claim that these internal constituents have to be identified by reference to external things. But this position seems to me both pusillanimous and dubiously coherent: pusillanimous because of the theoretical symmetry, and dubiously coherent because it is hard to see how such alleged internal constituents could *necessarily* be individuation-dependent upon external conditions. I therefore think that full-blooded externalism can and should be formulated in terms of the notion of external constituents. Only a general hostility to the idea that thoughts have constituents of any kind could stand in the way of this style of formulation. And this means that externalism cannot be made to sound nugatory by weakening the relation between content and what individuates it: the world genuinely *enters* content.

Putting this together with my earlier reply to the first triviality charge, we can say the following: content really does *contain* items that are genuinely *objective*. So weak externalism does represent the mind as essentially configured by the nonmental world. Moreover, it is generally true.

(iii) *The limits of strong externalism*   Total strong externalism is the thesis that all mental phenomena are bound to the nature of the environment of the subject: no wedge can be driven between any facet of mind and what obtains (or has obtained) in the surrounding world: the environmental contingencies constrain every aspect of mind: no fissure opens up between them at any point. This is a very interesting thesis, with profound consequences for the general nature of mind and for epistemology. It establishes the strongest possible link (short of identity) between mental states and the environment. I want to know whether this general thesis is true. I have already accepted that it is true for some kinds of content; now I want to chart the limitations of the thesis. When this has been done we shall be in a position to determine the significance of whatever remains of total strong externalism. I shall begin with mental states for which strong externalism looks least promising, working up to more difficult cases.

(1) *Bodily sensations; character traits; the self*   Bodily sensations – such as pains and tickles and orgasms – do not represent the external world. Unlike perceptual experiences, they do not *present* the surrounding world to the subject in a certain way (or purport to). Of course they have their environmental causes – pins and feathers and other fascinating things – but they do not semantically represent those causes. Offhand, then, it looks highly unlikely that we shall be able to construct plausible twin earth cases for bodily sensations: we won't be able to vary their content by varying their environmental relations, because they do not *have* content. Nor will their qualitative character be susceptible to such variation. Let us quickly verify this expectation. Consider an instance of pain caused in me by a pin, and suppose all pains phenomenologically like this one are also caused in me by pins. Now imagine a twin earth on which I have a double equipped with all the same internal properties – brain states, behavioural dispositions, receptor deformations – but whose internal states are caused by feathers not pins: that is, feathers cause in him the same internal effects as are caused in me by pins. Now what does my double feel? Pain, of course! There he is, shrieking, writhing, his C-fibres spiking rapidly – all the signs of a man in pain. He is nothing *like* a man enjoying a bit of a tickle. What matters is what is going on in him, not the external causes of what is going on in him in the surrounding world.[59] It is just that on twin earth feathers trigger my double's pain-subserving apparatus and hence his pain behaviour, instead of pins. Pains are thus in the head, as are tickles and orgasms. There are no Russellian pains or object-involving tickles or environment-dependent orgasms. A subject could enjoy these sensations and they

[59] Our concept of pain is the concept of a state that points towards its behavioural expression; it is 'output-directed'. The external stimuli that cause pain are not in this way part of the conceptual shadow pain casts. The concept of seeing something points in the opposite direction, however, since aetiology is here part of the concept.

be produced quite otherwise than they actually are, so long as the underlying state of the body and brain was preserved. Presumably this is not going to be very controversial. What might be more controversial is a kind of modified externalism about sensations: let the body itself be the environment and ask whether *it* fixes the identity of the sensation. So suppose we consider phenomenologically similar token pains in the muscles of my forearm. Now imagine a twin earth on which my double is internally just like me save for the fact that he has no forearm muscles (on twin earth evolution has not equipped them with arms). What should we say of this case – does it show that a version of strong externalism is true of bodily sensations? I think the answer is clearly No. First, allowing that the imagined world is really conceivable, it is quite unobvious that my double and I will feel different sensations, since the states of our nervous system are being assumed to be just the same – his C-fibres are spiking exactly as mine are. Secondly, such plausibility as the case has depends precisely upon a bodily difference between him and me: but this supports an internalist about bodily sensations, not an externalist, since the body is rated internal in these discussions. To take this case as supporting externalism about sensations would be like defending externalism about natural kind concepts by arguing that these vary when behavioural dispositions vary but not when the environment varies! Behaviourism is just not a kind of externalism; behavioural constraints on mental attributions are internalist constraints, in the sense under consideration here. So the modified position on sensations does not lead to a genuine form of externalism.

Character traits seem much like sensations in the present respect. Whether I am brave or mean or moody does not seem constitutively dependent on my actual environment (except, of course, in so far as my environment affects my internal states). These mental states or propensities are also not intrinsically representational, and it is very hard to see how a plausible twin earth case could be constructed for them. Keep my internal properties the same, including my behavioural dispositions, and you will keep my virtues and vices the same. If I am moody on earth, then my double will be moody on twin earth, no matter how much you gerrymander his environment in an effort to cheer him up. We cannot turn a person from good to bad simply by varying his extrinsic environment; we have to change his internal properties too – centrally his dispositions to behaviour. Emotions are the same, at least in so far as they can be detached from their representational content. My double may be furious that he has been given retaw to drink, which I am furious that I have been given water: but the fury is the same – we are both experiencing the same emotion.[60]

---

[60] Each of these cases has the expressive character of pain. Our ascriptions of these mental phenomena are dominated by what they lead to, not what has led to them. Externalism will not be true

I think much the same is true of the person or self. Personal identity is not environment-dependent. To establish this we need to imagine a twin earth world for which it is an open question whether a given person exists there, and then ask who if anyone we think that person is. Suppose, then, that a person with my body and brain were born and bred in an environment quite different from the environment I was actually nurtured in – different individuals, different natural kinds, etc. This person is also internally indistinguishable from me. His prenatal history, internally considered, is identical too, his parents having the same bodies and brains as my actual parents. Granted strong externalism about at least some of this person's mental states, his mental states will differ from mine; we can even suppose, for the sake of argument, that *all* his mental states differ in their content. We are supposing, then, that this person's external causal history is quite different from mine but that his body and brain are identical with mine (numerically) and that they are in the same intrinsic states. This is to give the externalist about personal identity as much environmentally induced mental variation as possible, so that he has maximum purchase upon the identity of the person. The question, then, is whether that person is me or some numerically distinct person. My firm intuition is that the person in question *would* be me. All that has happened is that I have been transposed to a different environment and spent my life there instead of here. Suppose my parents had been kidnapped before I was conceived and transported by twin-earthians to their alien environment. The sperm and egg from which I actually came then meet in the fullness of time and develop in that environment, so producing a human being with my actual body (externalism about bodily identity is hardly to be entertained). Now consider this human being aged 37 behaving just as I am now, internally just like me. Surely that person *is* me. The self is in the head. Extrinsic relations do not determine personal identity. Perhaps I would not have the same *mind* under these suppositions – identity of mind being arguably tied to identity or similarity of mental states – but it would be the same *person* with a different mind. We need not assume that the person *is* the body or the brain in order to accept this intuition (though such views certainly entail the intuition); it is enough that we recognize that identity of person cannot be pulled apart from identity of body and brain in the way recommended by strong externalism about personal identity. The person is the subject of mental states which are themselves environment-dependent, but it does not follow – and is not true – that the person himself is so dependent. Of course there is no real surprise in any of this, since to identify a person linguistically we do not need to specify some represented state of

of mental phenomena whose individuation is thus behaviourally governed (dispositionally, of course). (To say this is not to be any kind of analytic behaviourist: conceptual liaisons are not conceptual identities.)

affairs – a simple proper name or personal pronoun will do perfectly well. To be a particular person is not to be in any specific representational state; the identity of a person is not the identity of a mental representation. But perhaps this is all too obvious to bear repetition? No one, to my knowledge, has ever in fact advocated strong externalism about persons, and the view has little or no prima facie appeal. The chief significance of its falsity for me is to gain a sense of the limits of strong externalism as a general theory of mental phenomena.[61]

(2) *Complex concepts and some others*   The committed strong externalist may concede what has just been said with a shrug. 'Sure', he may say, 'strong externalism does not apply to nonrepresentational mental phenomena – whoever said it did? What I claim is that it applies to all representational states, specifically to all *concepts*. So let's see you refute me on that!' I shall begin to oblige our total strong externalist about concepts by considering complex or constructed concepts. But first let us note just how strong total strong externalism is. It says that to possess any concept it is necessary to have been in some sort of causal-epistemic contact with instances of the relevant property. This imposes very demanding conditions on concept acquisition and possession; equivalently, it makes it very easy for a thinker to lose his concepts in imagined counterfactual situations – we just remove the instances. The thesis assigns a very large role to the mind-independent world in fixing which concepts a mind may possess: the world does all the generative work, as it were, with the mind itself standing idly by as a helpless and passive mirror of the given environment (here we should be reminded of extreme empiricist doctrines about concept possession).[62] Representational content cannot transcend the actual properties encountered by the subject in their environmental instances. An extreme thesis indeed.

The most obvious problem for this thesis has already surfaced in connection with natural kind concepts: the phenomenon of conceptual construction. In constructing a complex concept from simpler concepts the mind exercises a degree of creativity: it does some of the work of concept acquisition itself, so to say. This constructive operation has the result that concepts come to be possessed

---

[61] This negative result confirms the substantial view of the self endorsed earlier (section 3). The self is not to be conceived as a system of relations involving outer things, as the mind is. The self is as substantial as the body, autonomous and impenetrable. You can model the self on material things and not go far wrong.

[62] The assumption here is that the mind has not the inner resources to generate from within itself concepts that apply to things in the world: it cannot bring to the world what the world has not already conferred upon it. This need not be taken as an anti-nativist doctrine, however, since externalism can admit cross-generational environment-dependence (you need never have been connected to *F*s in order to have the concept *F* but your mother had to be). The claim is rather that real ground-up conceptual creativity is not possible. Minds cannot manufacture concepts without appropriate input from the environment (and not merely as a trigger either).

which need not be instantiated in the thinker's environment or indeed anywhere else.[63] Composing complex concepts out of simple ones by means of Boolean operations is the most obvious way to do this: conjunction, negation, etc. As we can form complex predicates in language, the members of whose extensions we have never encountered, so we can form complex concepts with the same property. This is, indeed, a fundamental feature of what it *is* to possess both language and concepts – creativity is of the essence. To deny this, as total strong externalism does, is to deny something constitutive of concept possession; it is to forget that concepts have an affinity for each other as well as for the world (if I may put it so), so that they may join together and proliferate. The strong externalist is therefore forced to restrict his thesis to simple or primitive concepts, those in the acquisition of which the mind does not exercise conceptual creativity. Of course it is by no means easy to say what conceptual simplicity is or to recognize it when one sees it, and hence to know whether strong externalism has a chance of being true of some given concept. We can expect difficult cases like Hume's missing shade of blue or a shape concept that can be generated from other shape concepts in some analogous way (the missing ellipse). It is, I think, tacitly assumed in discussions of externalism that the concept under consideration is not a constructed concept, as with the original twin earth cases for natural kind concepts, or else it could be readily constructed from its conceptual constituents in an alien environment – people on twin earth could have the concept H_2O provided they are in contact with hydrogen and oxygen. My point is that this simplicity assumption is crucial to the success of the strong externalist argument. Fortunately for the strong externalist, we know that there must *be* a base of primitive concepts (though it need not be the same base for every thinker) for any complex concepts to exist – so he is not going to be deprived of his natural constituency. But we also know that there must be a conceptual superstructure for which his thesis is false. Moreover, there are bound to be more concepts in the superstructure than in the base.

Formal concepts, such as those of logic and mathematics, also seem insusceptible to twin earth cases, despite the correctness of weak externalism for them. The obvious difficulty comes in varying the logical and mathematical environment on twin earth: what could it mean to say that negation or the number 2 do not exist *on* twin earth? For such items the notion of existence and the notion of environmental existence coalesce. We can imagine that on twin earth they mean something different by 'prime number', say, but what is hard is to suppose

---

[63] Yet they must be concepts of some (complex) property; weak externalism must hold true of them. Creativity can transcend the environment, but it cannot outstrip the contents of the world of universals: a concept is always a concept of some (existent) property (so long, at least, as it is a possible property).

them also to be internally indistinguishable from us – applying 'prime number' to the same appearances and the like.[64] What sense can be made of the idea that 'not' denotes distinct truth functions on earth and twin earth and yet those truth functions *seem* the same to both sets of people? The question is barely intelligible. Accordingly, it is difficult to see how the strong externalist might try to show that formal concepts can come apart from internal properties under the impact of a varying environment. On the contrary, it seems evident to me that if two people (or two communities) agree in their internal states and behavioural dispositions in respect of their logical and mathematical vocabularies, then they agree in the logical and mathematical concepts they possess, as well as in the meanings of those words. But the case here is somewhat different from the case of constructed concepts: there we could make *sense* of a twin earth case but our verdict went against the strong externalist; here we cannot so much as set the strong externalist argument in motion. We have here a sort of limit case in which the external and the internal cannot be independently varied. The result is that the strong externalist is unable to claim that formal concepts are individuated by environmental contingencies as distinct from internal features. Strong externalism in effect collapses into weak externalism.

I observed earlier (section 3 (a)) that strong externalism presupposes realism. In consequence, if projectivism or subjectivism about a range of properties of objects is true, then strong externalism cannot also be true of concepts of those properties. The reason is that such properties are individuated by reference to mental reactions in subjects and not vice versa, these reactions being taken as antecedently individuated in some way. A ready illustration of this is provided by Wittgenstein's example of pain patches.[65] Suppose we introduce a predicate 'painy' which applies to all and only those surfaces that cause pain in us; and suppose it is only contingent that certain sorts of surface produce this reaction. Then it is clear that the concept we express with 'painy' is not fixed by any antecedent and mind-independent property of surfaces: a surface is painy in virtue of producing sensations of pain in us; it is not that a sensation counts as pain in virtue of being produced by surfaces of that kind, say having a certain sort of texture. Accordingly, if we try to imagine a twin earth on which different sorts of surface, with a different texture (smooth not rough), produce sensations of pain in people, then we do not thereby succeed in changing the meaning of 'painy': for it applies, by stipulation, to *any* kind of surface that produces pain in

---

[64] Remember that the division of linguistic labour is not at issue here; I am not concerned with the contribution made to an individual's meanings and beliefs by other members of her community. My concern is the relation between the cognitive life of a community of subjects and their (nonconceptual) environment.

[65] *Philosophical Investigations*, 312.

subjects. 'Painy' does not mean *rough* on earth and *smooth* on twin earth; it means *patch productive of pain* in both places. And since pain is 'in the head', so too is the individuation of the concept *painy*.

Now, in so far as this model is applicable to other concepts, the same lesson will be derivable. It is not my aim here to decide which concepts do fit this model; I shall simply mention some concepts which have been construed in this way, establishing only a conditional rejection of strong externalism for such concepts. Thus we have the traditional secondary quality concepts: concepts of colour, taste, smell, sound, and so on. If these are understood to apply to any object which is disposed to produce certain sensations in us, where these sensations are themselves reckoned 'in the head' (or are only weakly external), then we shall preserve these concepts on any twin earth for which these sensations themselves are held constant.[66] Similarly, if we view aesthetic and ethical concepts in this dispositional style, we will obtain the same result (I do not say I agree with this kind of view). Modal and causal concepts construed subjectively will also fail to be environmentally determined. Suppose that on twin earth the people have the same impressions of necessity as we do when observing a causal nexus: then, according to the Humean subjectivist, necessity will be spread on the world in much the same way colour is spread for a projectivist about colour. But then it is a matter of indifference, from the point of view of possessing the concept of causal necessity, what might be true of the mind-independent environment: the conditions for possessing the concept are already supplied by the internal state of felt compulsion or whatever. And so it will be for any concept thus tied to subjective reactions: if they are in the head, then it will be too. Concepts like this function exactly oppositely to natural kinds concepts, the paradigms of environmental determination.

Artefact concepts also elude strong externalism. By an artefact I mean something that is produced by human beings (or some other semi-intelligent life form) in order to discharge a particular function: to be that kind of artefact is then to have that function, that use. Thus being a certain kind of artefact is a relational property; it is to have a particular function *for its maker*. To be a table, for example, is to be used to put things on (roughly) – to have that function for some creature or creatures. Accordingly, something counts as a table if and only if it is used to discharge that function. But now it is easy to see why twin earth cases will not be constructable for artefacts: for keeping the internal facts the same will keep the use of the surrounding objects the same, and this is what determines both the identity of the artefact and the identity of the artefact concept. If people

---

[66] The fact that this isn't so for natural kind concepts shows precisely that they are not secondary quality concepts; so twin earth cases supply a test of whether a concept is dispositional in this way. To be water is not to be disposed to produce sensations of a certain kind in perceivers.

on twin earth treat the flat things around them in the way we treat tables, then these things will be tables on twin earth (not necessarily very good tables) and their 'table' talk will be talk precisely of tables. Altering the chemical composition of what they call 'tables' will certainly not alter the meaning of the word for them. Artefact concepts are tied to ways of treating things, not to what the thing is independently of its being so treated; so if we keep these ways fixed in imagining our twin earth, then we will kept the concepts fixed too. Here we see the difference from natural kinds: for water is water no matter how you treat it. We could, of course, choose to mean by 'water', *what we use to quench our thirst, bathe in, etc.*, thus making 'water' express an artefact concept; but then twin earth cases for that meaning and that concept would not be constructable either – XYZ will be 'water' in *that* sense. Again, the semantic contrast with natural kind words is what defeats the strong externalist's strategy.[67] Weak externalism, however, applies indifferently to both sorts of word (and concept).

(3) *Psychological concepts*   An interesting class of concepts to consider is the class of concepts *of* mental states: is strong externalism true of the possession of these concepts? Here the environment consists of psychological subjects themselves – the mental states of the people around one. The question is then whether the mental states of others fix the content of my mental concepts. What happens to my mental concepts if we vary my psychological environment while keeping my internal states the same? Are the constituents of my psychological thoughts strongly dependent upon the contingencies of my mental environment, i.e. upon what mental states people around me actually happen to have? We can divide this question into two parts: (a) are my *singular* thoughts about mental states, my own and others', dependent for their existence and identity upon the actual mental states they are about? and (b) are my *general* psychological concepts strongly dependent upon the mental kinds with which I am in fact surrounded? I shall answer Yes to (a) and No to (b).

Suppose I see that your arm is burnt and I say, pointing at the burn, 'That pain must be dreadful'. Then I have, it would seem, made a demonstrative judgement about a token sensation of yours. I have made the same sort of judgement about your pain as I might make about my own when I say of myself 'This pain is dreadful.' And there seems nothing to prevent me making such demonstrative judgements about other mental states of yours – your emotions, visual experiences, beliefs, and so on. Now if these appearances are not misleading, we can apply our general theory of demonstrative concepts of these judgements. And if we do, we can derive two results. First, weak externalism is true of such

---

[67] Fundamentally, it is the epistemic distance between the essence of a kind and the way we represent it that determines whether strong externalism will be true of it (for us). Projected essences will lie at no distance from our conceptions of them.

judgements: they contain other people's mental states as constituents and are therefore existence-dependent with respect to those mental states. If you had not been feeling any pain, then I could not have judged that *that* pain was dreadful: we can existentially generalize on the embedded occurrence of 'that pain', given that the ascription to me of that judgement is in fact true. The argument from semantic uniformity is as sound here as it was for demonstratives about physical events or objects. Second, we can derive strong externalism too: if we keep my internal properties the same and change the sensation you felt for another with the same visible symptoms, then my judgement will differ in its content, being a demonstrative judgement about another sensation. The case is just like substituting one material object for another in respect of a demonstrative judgement about such an object. So my singular thoughts about other minds are not in my head; they have constituents drawn from within those other minds. Your mind penetrates mine; mine embraces yours (a comforting conclusion). I have mental states with *contain* your mental states, which could not indeed exist without them. Our mental states are, on reflection, *inter*dependent, since you can (of course) make like judgements about me. (This is more than can be said for my material-object thoughts – here the dependence is all one way.) In fact, there can be nested hierarchies of dependence in the case of thoughts about other minds. Suppose that in response to my original judgement about your pain you say, 'That's a compassionate thought.' Then you have thought something that contains my thought as a constituent, which in turn contains your pain as a constituent. Assuming transitivity of the constituency relation, your thought now contains your own pain as a (deferred) constituent, as refracted through my thought. I may then go on to remark, 'I don't deserve that charitable thought', thus incorporating your thought into mine which contains an earlier thought of mine which contains a pain of yours. And so it goes, one mental state nesting snugly within another, existence-dependence being transmitted upwards between the thinking subjects. (One can imagine frames of mind in which one might rather enjoy stacking up the mental dependencies with another person – so long as it was the right person.) At any rate, it seems clear enough that singular thoughts about other minds are strongly external. They work like singular thoughts about other *persons*: when I judge of someone 'She seems very intelligent' I express a thought that contains another person as a constituent. And what I can do for other people I can also do for their psychological states.

Turning to question (b), let us first note that weak externalism is as true here as it is for other kinds of general concept, since mental predicates, used to specify the content of psychological judgements, denote mental properties in the same way physical predicates denote physical properties – properties that other people may instantiate. The claim that seems to me to be wrong is rather the stronger claim that which mental property a mental predicate denotes in my language is fixed by the mental properties people around me actually instantiate. Let us test this claim by constructing a putative twin earth case. Suppose, then, that we vary the mental lives of the people around me (while keeping mine fixed) in the following way: what they see as red people on earth see as green and vice versa. I apply my psychological predicates to others and to myself just as I do on earth. So the experiences of others that prompt me, on the strength of their behaviour, to ascribe 'experience of red' and 'experience of green' are inverted on earth and twin earth: on earth what I call 'experience of red' are experiences of red, while on twin earth I apply this phrase to experiences of green (and similarly for 'experience of green'). The environmental causes of these utterances are permuted in the two situations.[68] But note: *my* experiences stay the same from earth to twin earth. There is nothing question-begging in this, of course, since the claim under examination is not the (ludicrous) claim that my *experiences* are fixed by my psychological environment; what we are considering is the claim that my *concepts* of experience are fixed by the actual experiences in my environment. Now the strong externalist thesis is that 'experience of red' on twin earth has experiences of green as its extension; it denotes the property of having an experience of green. At the level of concepts, I express the concept *experience of green* on twin earth with that predicate. The phenomenological kinds with which I am surrounded are thus said to fix the sense of my experiential vocabulary in the same sort of way that the natural kinds around me fix the sense of predicates like 'water'. We can think of (some of) the experiences around me as an 'initial sample' which I use to confer meaning on my mental terms – their extensions are fixed by a relation to phenomenal similarity with this original sample. Now is this suggestion plausible?

If there are problems with it, they will not recapitulate the problems we found with strong externalist accounts of concepts of projected or subjective properties. For the properties denoted by my mental concepts are not spread by me onto the world: they are, in the relevant sense, objective properties – properties that would be possessed by other people even if I did not recognize their possession. Nor is the problem one of conceptual complexity all the way down, as it were: for plenty of our mental concepts are primitive in the sense that we do not come to

---

[68] We need not assume full-strength spectrum inversion to make this case, i.e. total behavioural identity accompanied by inversions of colour experience. It will suffice that I and my double apply our mental words to people around us in the same way. These two surrounding groups may differ behaviourally in ways that make no impact on him and me. Experts could tell the difference, but we cannot. What matters is that these groups put us in the same internal states, despite the differences in the experiences that cause us to be in these states. It is the same with the usual twin earth cases for natural kinds: experts could tell the difference between water and retaw, but they affect us amateurs in the same way. Here too we do not need to assume total indistinguishability by all conceivable tests.

have them by construction from simpler concepts. Nor are mental kinds artefacts. The problem comes, rather, from the dual role of mental concepts in first- and third-person ascriptions. The strong externalist thesis looks viable when we are considering third-person ascriptions; indeed it looks to have the (supposedly) desirable property of guaranteeing the general truth of our judgements about other minds, since *whatever* mental states others around me have my concepts will necessarily include them in their extension. But when we shift our gaze to first-person ascriptions the strong externalist thesis can be seen to have intolerable consequences. For consider: on twin earth my words 'experience of red' are said to express the concept *experience of green*, this being the kind of experience people around me have when I apply those words to them (by hypothesis). But now I also apply those words to myself on twin earth in the way I do on earth: I have the same dispositions towards self-ascriptions of mental predicates and I apply these predicates to *the same mental states*. It follows that I say and judge of my experiences of red that they are experiences of *green*! The problem is simple: they have different experiences from me on twin earth, so if their experiences fix my experiential concepts then my own self-ascriptions of those concepts will turn out to be uniformly *false*. It is the exact converse of the epistemological position that results from letting *my* experiences fix my experiential concepts: for then I get them uniformly wrong and myself right. Since a logical gap can open up between my experiences and other people's, binding my *concepts* of experience to one or the other set of experiences can have one of two epistemological consequences: either the concept fails to fit their experiences (if it is bound to mine), or it fails to fit mine (if it is bound to theirs). The strong externalist thesis yields the latter result; an internalist thesis yields the former result. The price of strong externalism about mental concepts is thus hyperfallibility in one's self-ascriptions of those concepts.

It does not seem to me that this is a price we can reasonably be expected to pay. The epistemological cost here is too steep. Things may not look so dire when we are contemplating me on twin earth – so what if I can't describe my mental states correctly there! – but in fact the hyperfallibility seeps back to life on earth. For the question must inevitably arise: what if the people around me *on earth* have radically different experiences from me? Suppose they have spectrum inversion with respect to me: that is, unknown to me, the situation on earth is really the same as we stipulated the situation on twin earth to be. Then, granted strong externalism, my mental predicates *now* express the concepts they *would* express on twin earth, so that right now my self-ascriptions are just as riddled with falsehood as they would be on twin earth. The logical possibility that others here and now have different mental states from me thus generates, in conjunction with strong externalism, the logical possibility that I am here and now systematically wrong

THE LOCATION OF CONTENT

in my self-ascriptions. For all I know, whenever I think (the sentence) 'I have an experience of red' I am wrong because, despite the fact that I have an experience of red, I am *really* judging that I have an experience of green. Not only is this terribly hard to swallow – it is also not at all easy to get one's mind around. One wants to know what on earth could be going *on* psychologically in the situation envisaged.[69] We are here confronted by a mind-bending species of radical scepticism about self-knowledge: the problem, not of other minds, but of one's mind. Namely, how can we now be sure that our mental concepts are not so constituted that they are systematically false of our mental states? This problem is unique to strong externalism about mental concepts; nothing like it afflicts concepts of material things, including concepts of human bodies. It suggests that there is an inherent limitation in strong externalism to concepts relating to the nonpsychological world.

How might the strong externalist try to wriggle out of this problem? I can think of three possible escape strategies, none of which works. First, it might be suggested that the psychological environment be taken to include one's own mental states, so that these are given some role in fixing the identity of one's mental concepts. But then my mental concepts will be (possibly) pulled in two directions, with a consequent threat of ambiguity and conceptual fault-lines. And if the experiences of others do succeed in forming a univocal concept out of this individuative tug-of-war, we will still have an unacceptable hyperfallibility. On the other hand, if we let my experiences dominate, so eliminating the problem of one's own mind, we are in effect simply giving up strong externalism about mental concepts – those concepts will then be uniquely fixed by what is going on in *me*. Indeed, allowing my own experiences any role is already conceding the essential victory to the opponent of strong externalism. It is no form of strong externalism to insist that my pains fix the meaning of 'pain' in my language! Second, someone might try claiming (with evident desperation) that the mental states of others necessarily fix the identity of my mental states themselves – that, for example, whether I am capable of feeling pain or seeing red is somehow constituted by the capacity of others to enjoy these mental states. The claim would then be that we simply cannot imagine a possible situation in which others have radically different experiences from me, which is what generates the problem I have urged. This would, of course, equally deprive the strong externalist of his strategy for refuting his opponent, since he would not have produced a case in which the internal and the external come apart and yet our intuitions go with the

---

[69] What conceivable source of cognitive error could ever induce me to believe of my (vivid) experiences of red that they are experiences of green? Surely I could not be so cognitively deficient, so entirely inept at forming true beliefs. What kind of cognitive slip-up is being envisaged here? Where, pray, did my best belief-forming efforts go wrong?

external facts. But it is also both unmotivated and deeply implausible. Unmotivated, because it does not have the authority of an established theory of content determination to back it up – how could it since it is not an externalist claim about *content* at all but about that which mental contents *represent*? Implausible, because we really do not want to make mental states like pain or colour experience socially determined (as distinct from *concepts* of such states). That would (a) deprive a lifelong Robinson Crusoe of such mental states, (b) make interpersonal divergences of kinds of mental state (colour blindness, etc.) logically impossible, and (c) cut mental states off completely from the internal physical facts about a person's body – a physical double of me in pain could not be declared to be in pain until we had verified that others around him also felt pain. I take it, then, that this second possible avenue of escape is solidly blocked. Third, the strong externalist might try restricting his thesis to third-person uses of mental terms, conceding that first-person uses are fixed by internal facts about the speaker. This may seem to get the best of both epistemological worlds: third-person ascriptions will turn out to be true no matter how much other minds differ from mine, and first-person ascriptions will carry on enjoying their old familiar infallibility. The difficulty with this rather optimistic line is obvious: it introduces the possibility of a fundamental ambiguity in our mental vocabulary; it splits our mental concepts right down the middle. Suppose other minds are different from my own in the way described above. Then 'experience of red' means one thing when ascribed to others and another thing when self-ascribed. Similarly, the concept I employ in ascribing experiences to them will not be the concept I employ in ascribing them to myself, though it will seem to me that it is. Indeed, in the situation envisaged I *cannot* employ the same concept in both sorts of judgement; there is a logical bar to my carrying a mental concept from a first-person context into a third-person context and vice versa. If it were allowed that I could accomplish this routine-seeming transposition, then surely that is what I would endeavour to do – for I want my mental words to mean the same in both sorts of linguistic context – but then again we have the unwelcome result that my self-ascriptions are going to turn out to be hyperfallible. So the strong externalist had better claim that I *cannot* succeed in my linguistic intention in the case in which others have different mental states from me – or else he has not avoided the original problem. Matters might look slightly more hopeful for the strong externalist if it could be supposed that the possible semantic divergence was in principle recognizable by the subject – if he could *tell* when his mental words mean one thing in first-person utterances and another in third-person utterances. But of course it is precisely this that is being denied: the sense of my mental words is precisely as opaque to me as are the experiences of others – my access to the former is no better than my access to the latter. Thus it is that scepticism about other minds, when conjoined with strong externalism, leads to opacity in what my mental words mean and in what mental concepts I am employing. But even if the subject could recognize the semantic and conceptual divergence when it occurs, that would not be of any great help to him, since he is still constrained to operate as he would had he not recognized the ambiguity. So the ambiguity strategy looks doomed as well. What we want is a theory that permits univocity of concept even in the possible case of a divergence of mental states. In effect, this is to permit the possibility that our third-person ascriptions might be systematically mistaken. (I shall return to externalism and scepticism later.)

And there is a further point to be made. If the strong externalist's conditions are regarded as supplying anything approaching sufficiency, then they are in a certain respect much too weak. The thesis, to repeat, is that environmental relations to mental kinds necessarily confer the corresponding concepts on a thinking subject. This allows me to acquire concepts for kinds of mental state which I do not myself enjoy, and which may be quite unlike any that I enjoy. To take an extreme example: I could come to have concepts of a bat's sonar-related experiences by having such experiences occur in my psychological environment and by going through the right extension-fixing rituals. The bat's experiences would be the typical causes of my application of some introduced predicate to them, and of my judgements as so expressed. I might, that is, come to be related to the bat's experiences in much the same way that I am now related to natural kinds whose hidden essence I do not know. As a result, according to strong externalism, I come to have concepts for these alien types of experience. But this seems implausible: for it is a compelling principle that I cannot come to have the concept of an F without knowing what it is to be F; and in the case of experiences I cannot know what they *are* unless I know what they are *like*.[70] In other words, I would not (could not) come to know what it is like to have a bat's sonar experiences just by standing in such causal relations as the strong externalist deems sufficient; but then I do not really have the *concepts* of such experiences. Call these experiences B-experiences: then it will not be true to say that I have mastery of the concept of B-experiences – at best I have introduced a predicate 'B' whose extension is the set of B-experiences. But I do not really *understand* this predicate. The case is quite otherwise with 'water': I do come to have the concept *water* by standing in the right environmental relations to water. The asymmetry traces to a special feature of experiential concepts, namely that there is an ineliminable dependence upon one's own case in coming to grasp them. I do not grasp the concept *B-experience* because I do not have B-experiences or anything like them. I cannot know from my own case what it is to have such an experience.

[70] See Thomas Nagel, 'What is it Like to be a Bat?'.

Strong externalism flouts this requirement: it makes instantiation in the environment pivotal to concept possession, not instantiation in *me*. In this way it makes the acquisition of mental concepts too easy. Clearly this is a feature of mental concepts that has no parallel for material concepts: there is no need for *me* to instantiate the material properties for which I have concepts. So there is here a basic obstacle in the way of generalizing strong externalism from material concepts to mental ones. Given the essential role of one's own case for mental concepts, it looks as if internalism is going to find a secure niche in our account of them; weak externalism is the only kind of externalism we are going to get here. Again we see that not all concepts behave like natural kind concepts, those paradigms of the strongly external.

(4) *Perceptual content*   In having perceptual experience the world seems to us to be a certain way; it presents itself to our experience as containing various objects and properties. Experience, we may say, *represents* the states of affairs so presented (or apparently presented): perceptual representation is the converse of perceptual presentation. The way in which experience represents the world constitutes its *content*, the way it makes things seem. The content of an experience determines what it is *as of* – how the world *would* actually be presented *if* the experience were veridical. The content of experience is thus objective in the sense that it represents (or purports to represent) how things stand in the external world. Perceptual experiences are therefore potential candidates for strong externalist theorizing. The strong externalist says that the content of experience is environmentally determined: how things can seem to you is fixed by how things objectively are around you. Only if a feature of the world has been actually presented to you can it be *re*presented by you.[71] The content of experience is strongly individuation-dependent upon the character of the perceiver's environment. My question is whether this application of strong externalism is defensible. This is not, of course, the same as the question whether in order actually to perceive a certain feature that feature has to be present in the perceiver's environment and be causally responsible for the experience. The answer to that question is certainly Yes, since *perception* is a causal concept that requires the presence of what is perceived. But that question concerns the conditions of *success* of a perceptual experience. My question is rather whether its *seeming* to you that the world is thus and so depends upon its being environmentally thus and so, and upon your being in some suitable contextual

---

[71] Presumably the strong externalist about perceptual content will want to qualify this formulation to allow for generativity in the perceptual system: he will want to accept that representational primitives can be combined to yield perceptual contents that apply to nothing in the perceiver's environment. In other words, he will want to allow for the perceptual analogue of conceptual creativity and complexity – a concession which limits the scope of strong externalism.

relation (presumably some species of causation) to instances of its being thus and so. Suppose a perceiver has an experience as of a square thing (of such and such size and shape, etc.): the question is whether it follows from this fact that his environment contains (or has contained) square things with which he has interacted in some fashion. (Of course this follows if the fact is that he is *seeing* a square thing; but that is not the present question.) More generally, is the content of experience necessarily a function of the actual environmental contingencies? Is the causal link between world and experience *individuative* of experience?[72]

I shall begin my treatment of this important question by addressing a preliminary question about externalism and observational concepts. This question is of interest in its own right, and answering it should serve to sharpen the question about perceptual content. The question is this: can we construct a twin earth case for observational concepts under the assumption that we keep the content of experience fixed? As I stressed when discussing natural kind concepts, it is standard to keep the perceptual appearances constant in setting up the twin earth world, and then it is argued that natural kind concepts can still vary. I want to enquire whether the same can be done for observational concepts: that is, can we give a *classical* twin earth argument for their environmental determination? So for the moment I want to just assume that perceptual content can be held constant through environmental changes and focus on the concepts applied in response to the registration of such content. After this I shall relax the assumption and enquire into perceptual content itself.

What do I mean by an observational concept? I do not wish to get embroiled here in the difficult question of how precisely one's intuitions about observationality can be given a rigorous formulation. Crudely, I intend concepts that can be applied simply on the basis of experience without collateral information. For example, one can tell just by looking that a suitably presented object is square (assuming veridicality), because its being square is *given* in experience. By contrast, one cannot tell just by looking that something is water, since the identity of the substance is not immediately given to experience — it is a matter of underlying chemical structure.[73] But it doesn't much matter for my purposes how we draw the line, i.e. on which side particular concepts fall; my interest is in any concept that is tied in this direct way to the perceptual appearances. For convenience let us consider the concept *square*. Then my question is whether

---

[72] Burge advocates a view of this kind in 'Individualism and Psychology'. However, my own discussion of the view was composed before reading Burge's paper, so I should not be taken to be offering a reply specifically to Burge's position. I mean to be discussing a broad family of causal theories of perceptual content (perhaps more extreme than anything Burge himself would wish to endorse).

[73] See Jerry Fodor, *The Modularity of Mind*, on observationality: also Christopher Peacocke, *Sense and Content*.

possession of this concept is environment-sensitive in a case in which the perceptual appearances are held constant.

To hold the perceptual appearances constant is to suppose that on twin earth things seem the same way to people as they do on earth: in particular, things seem square to them. So suppose that the environmental variation consists in substituting round things for square things, so that the internal states produced on earth by square things are produced by round things on twin earth (and vice versa if you like). In short, round things produce (by some trick of the atmosphere let us suppose) experiences as of square things on twin earth. People there then apply, just as we do, the predicate 'square' to the world on the basis of these experiences. Now what does 'square' mean on twin earth: *square* or *round*? This is tantamount to the question whether the identity of the concept is fixed by its typical environmental cause or by the subjective seeming that prompts its employment. Under our temporary assumption that the content of these seemings is not itself strongly external, this is the question whether strong externalism is true of observational concepts. Well, is it?

That the answer is intuitively obvious (isn't it?) should not deter us from enquiring into its rationale. On twin earth, I take it, they exercise the *same* observational concepts as we do. The identity of the concept goes with the identity of the prompting experiential content, not with the distal cause of experiences with that content. There are two main reasons for this. First, to deny it would be to sever the observational concept from its definitive inferential role: to have the concept *square* just is to apply it on the basis of experiences as of square things. Observational concepts are applied simply on the basis of experience without collateral information: how then could someone (rationally) apply the concept *round* simply on the basis of an experience as of something square, i.e. without the benefit of collateral information (such as that round things look square on twin earth and that *here* is twin earth)? Since there have to be *some* concepts of this kind if *any* concepts are to be applied, we know that the twin-earthians must have some concepts for which the current version of strong externalism is false. And note that we could not suppose, compatibly with strong externalism, that the twin-earthians had the bridging belief needed to convert their square-experiences into a reason for judging something to be round – viz. the belief that square-looking things are really round – since that would be to credit them with the concept *square*, and they will not have this concept if there are no square things up there – as we may suppose there are not. The basic point here is that the twin-earthians could have no possible *reason* for applying their observational concepts as the strong externalist supposes, given the nature of such concepts (this is assuming, of course, that there is no cross-modal corroboration going on). Observational concepts *must* go by how things appear.

Second, what would the strong externalist say about the locution 'I have an experience as of a square thing', as uttered on twin earth? He cannot plausibly deny that 'square' means the same when embedded in this locution as it does in simple predications of objects. But if it means the same, then we have another hyperfallibility result: the subject is having an experience as of a square thing but he is *judging* (according to strong externalism) that his experience is as of a *round* thing, since 'square' means *round* on twin earth. First-person authority evidently counts for nothing on twin earth. Leaving aside the political repercussions of adopting this kind of strong externalism, this result must surely strike us as philosophically quite unacceptable. We may not be completely infallible about our experiences, but surely we could not be quite *so* fallible – never getting it right at all! Better to let the twin-earthians' beliefs about the world be systematically wrong than their beliefs about how the world *seems* to them. My strong externalist combines illusory experience with true world-directed beliefs and false experience-directed beliefs; but the correct combination here is surely that of illusory experience with false world-directed beliefs and true experience-directed beliefs. Error has been shifted inward by the strong externalist, instead of staying out there where it belongs – between belief and the external world.

The case of observational concepts is essentially different from that of natural kind concepts because in the latter case there is no conflict or rivalry between how things seem and how they are. The experiences enjoyed on earth and twin earth are both compatible with a range of different natural kinds, so we are not forced to *choose* between world and experience in fixing the concept. If we were to suppose that people on twin earth have experiences as of *water* and yet are surrounded by retaw, then we would be faced with a comparable choice between the content of experience and the environmental contingencies – and then it would not be so clear that 'water' does not mean *water* on twin earth. It is precisely the assumption that their seemings are not to be so characterized that makes strong externalism go through so smoothly for natural kind concepts. But with observational concepts the connection with experience is much more intimate and constitutive.

Have I cheated by simply presupposing that perceivers on twin earth have the concept *square*? Wasn't this just built into the stipulation that they have experiences as of square things? It is true, I agree, that on certain views of what it takes to have a perceptual experience the assumption of concept possession follows trivially. Thus it is with analyses of experience in terms of dispositions to make judgements, these being concept-deploying exercises: its seeming to you that there's a square thing consists in your judging, or being disposed to judge, that something falls under the concept *square*. But I would reject such analyses for familiar reasons, and I think that the correct view of perceptual content does not render my conclusion nugatory.[74] We can first note that even if perceptual content were inherently conceptual, it would not follow immediately that perceptual judgements share that content; for it might be that the concepts featuring in such judgements are fixed by something other than the conceptual contents of experience – by the environment, say. So the question of the conceptual content of observational judgements is not prejudged by a prior determination of the conceptual content of perceptual experiences. And the gap between these two kinds of content will widen into a gape once we begin to appreciate the important differences between experiences and beliefs: experiences are phenomenological states, beliefs are not; experiences belong to sensory modules, beliefs live in the central cognitive system; and so forth.[75] But secondly, I do not myself believe that there is any significant sense in which perceptual content is conceptual. Like other writers, I would argue (though I will not do it here) that perceptual content is pre- or nonconceptual: it feeds information into the conceptual system without itself being conceptual.[76] (We need this level of content if we are to attribute perceptual content to creatures without beliefs, I would say.) Granted this kind of conception of perceptual content, it is very much an open question whether what determines it also determines observational concepts proper; there is at least *room* for a version of strong externalism that limits itself to genuine concepts. Put in these terms, my own conclusion above was that observational concepts are necessarily tied to preconceptual perceptual contents. And finally, even if we insisted on characterizing the experiences of twin-earthians in some supposed non-representational (but still phenomenological) vocabulary, I think my conclusion would still hold. That is, if we stipulated that their sense-data, construed nonrepresentationally, are to be the same as ours, then I still think we should suppose that they share our observational concepts, since even such sense-data would constrain the identity of concepts applied on the basis of their reception. However, this last point is difficult to evaluate in view of the obscurity

[74] Basically, the problem with such theories is that they mistake a contingent link between perception and belief for a necessary or constitutive link. Perceptual experiences may or may not lead to corresponding judgements; they are more neutral with respect to belief than the dispositional analysis recognizes. Certainly there are kinds of perceptual experience I could have that I would *never* give credence to. In addition, such analyses cannot capture the phenomenological aspect of perceptual experience.

[75] See Fodor, *The Modularity of Mind*, on the different roles of experiences and beliefs within our cognitive economy – in particular, with respect to 'encapsulation'.

[76] See Evans, *The Varieties of Reference*, on nonconceptual content and perception. The general point here is that the concept of information is not essentially the concept of conceptual information. Concepts are just *one* way of carrying information about the world – and a very sophisticated way at that.

(incoherence!) of the notion of sense-datum in play; I mention it only for those (unlike me) who think they can make decent sense of the notion.

My interim conclusion, then, is that observational concepts are not strongly external (though of course they are weakly external). Moreover, this is not a trivial claim, even when we suspend the question of the strong externality of perceptual content – to which I now turn.

Let us be clear that we are considering a phenomenological notion here: conscious seemings, states there is something it is like to have.[77] And we are asking whether these subjective states owe their identity and existence to the objective environmental contingencies. Looking square is subjectively distinct from looking round – is that distinction a matter of a difference in how these experiences relate to instantiations of squareness and roundness? Is this what the distinction *consists in*? I want to argue that this strong externalist thesis is false, for a number of intricately related reasons. I begin, as usual, by trying to set up a crucial thought experiment involving our favourite planet. We are to keep the internal facts the same on twin earth, but now we must drop the assumption that these include perceptual seemings, since it is now their externality that is at issue. The internal facts we now freeze are: intrinsic states of the body and brain, behavioural dispositions nonenvironmentally specified and proximal stimulations identified without reference to their distal sources. What we keep fluid are the relations between these facts and the properties of the environment. And our question is whether we can drag perceptual content along with these environmental variations, thus detaching it from all that is internal. This is the same as the question whether any of the three kinds of internal facts mentioned exercise a constitutive hold over attributions of perceptual content.

Following the pattern already laid down, let us suppose that our perceiver (call

[77] So we are considering properties of organisms that determine the form of their subjectivity, and hence the accessibility or otherwise of this subjectivity to other organisms. In so far as experiential content determines subjectivity, the strong externalist is in effect trying to explain subjectivity in terms of objective relations to an objective environment. For example, he wants to explain the subjective experience of seeming to see a round object in terms of a causal relation between the organism and round things. Or again, he is out to explain the representational content of a bat's sonar experiences in terms of the characteristic environmental causes (high-pitched sounds) of those experiences. So there seems to be a clear sense in which subjective features are being explained in terms of objective facts. This raises the whole question of whether such a project can possibly succeed: strong externalism would seem to come under Nagelian strictures against reducing the subjective to the objective. And this in turn raises the forbidding question of how the subjectivity of consciousness is related to its content: What constraints on a theory of content are imposed by the fact that contents are part of what makes a conscious experience the subjective state it is? How does subjectivity relate to the determinants of content? How should our theory of what an experience is *like* connect with our theory of what it is *of*? These are hard questions, and questions that would take me away from the main line of my discussion. I shall not pursue them in this book, though I suppose they will have to be faced some time. The whole question of consciousness and content needs thorough examination.

him Percy) has the distal causes of his internal states inverted on twin earth: if S1 is the state caused on earth by square things, then on twin earth S1 is caused by round things; and if S2 has round things as its earthly cause, S2 has square things as its twin-earthly cause. Let us take it that these state descriptions include each of the three sorts of internal fact that we are keeping constant – behavioural dispositions and proximal stimuli as well as bodily states. Clearly we are assuming that the laws relating distal causes and S-conditions are different on twin earth from what they are on earth: for example, the light rays are warped in some way from object to retina. Nevertheless, the causal relations are as reliable and uniform on twin earth as they are on earth (presumably there is nothing sacrosanct about the optical laws prevailing on the surface of our planet). For simplicity, let us assume that no other sense is involved in transactions with these visually perceived objects. Now, assuming all this, the strong externalist is in a position to make his argument: he will say that the case is one in which the internal facts are identical but the perceptual content differs, thus establishing that it is not internal facts that fix perceptual content but external relations. If this is right, then internalism is refuted and externalism vindicated. On earth S1 is correlated with experiences as of square things, while on twin earth S1 is correlated with experiences as of round things; and similarly, mutatis mutandis, for S2 with respect to experiences of round and square.[78] Is this plausible?

Included in these internal state descriptions are descriptions of Percy's behavioural dispositions, as well as his actual behaviour. His body moves through space, and so do his limbs, in the same way on earth and twin earth. He traces a path through space as he walks about, and his hands and fingers trace their smaller paths too. Suppose that on earth S1 includes moving in a certain sort of rectilinear path – as it might be, around a square building. Or it might include tracing a square shape in the air with an extended index finger. By hypothesis, S1 includes the same behaviour on twin earth: Percy carves out the same path as he moves his legs (or hand). On earth, we would say, he moves in this way *because* the world seems to him to contain a big square object (or he has been asked to trace the shape of a TV screen in the air). For S1 is correlated with such experiences, and agents behave as their experience indicates (given appropriate beliefs and desires). But on twin earth, according to strong externalism, S1 is correlated with the world seeming to contain a round object; so Percy is *not* there behaving as his experience indicates. Similarly, if S2 includes moving in a curvilinear path, then on earth Percy's behaviour fits his experience while on twin earth it does not – for on twin earth, according to strong

[78] Burge constructs a thought experiment of this form in 'Individualism and Psychology', though he considers a different sort of content from the sort I consider. (I did not know of his when I concocted mine.)

externalism, it seems to him, when he is in S2, that he is seeing a square object. As we might (somewhat tendentiously) put it, he behaves on twin earth *as if* it seemed to him that objects of certain shapes were there, but in fact (says the strong externalist) it does not seem to him that way at all. In other words, the strong externalist is committed to envisaging a radical breakdown of the usual connections between spatial behaviour and perceptual content. Percy's spatial propensities are seriously out of synchrony with how things spatially seem to him.[79] To judge from his S1 spatial behaviour alone one might be forgiven for supposing that it looks to him as if there is a square thing there; but the strong externalist claims that such behaviour is not the true arbiter of content – we have to look outwards to the distal cause to decide how things seem to Percy. In the event of a mismatch between behaviour and environmental cause, we are advised to plump for the environmental cause. Instead of being guided by the behavioural effects of an experience we should go by the external cause of the experience. Look at causal history, the strong externalist advises, and ignore causal powers – the range of behavioural effects brought about *by* the experience. Aetiology trumps aftermath.

This recommendation seems to me to be both contrary to intuition and theoretically unsupportable. We have three elements to coordinate here – environment, experience, behaviour – and the strong externalist thesis gets their alignments exactly wrong. In making experience necessarily fit the world, while allowing behaviour to be environmentally inappropriate, strong externalism introduces a fracture at the joint between experience and behaviour. It becomes quite incomprehensible why a perceiving agent should ever function in the way suggested – moving squarewise when it seems to him that there is a round thing there. Matters would become intelligible if the agent had some belief to the effect that square things look round to him, but of course that is out of the question in the present case. A quick way to appreciate the bizarreness of what the strong externalist is claiming is to consider Percy's action-directed propositional attitudes – his intentions and tryings. These too will be said to have their content fixed by the actual environment, so the strong externalist has Percy intending to negotiate a round object and trying to move in a suitably curvilinear path: these volitional attitudes have *round* as part of their content. But Percy puts these into effect by moving squarewise! Normally we would suppose that this could only

---

[79] Strong externalism is committed to claiming that the world as perceptually apprehended diverges from the world as acted in: the subject is not doing what his experience says he should be doing. Percy is functioning like a split-brain subject, the agent Percy operating independently of the perceiver Percy. But his brain is whole! There is no reason for the disconnection – just a mistaken theory. We should restore Percy's unity by rejecting strong externalism, thus plugging action back into perception.

happen if Percy's motor system was completely fractionated, medically pathological, the limbs refusing to do as Percy told them. But Percy on twin earth does not suffer from such physiological problems; indeed, his nervous system is exactly like his normal double on earth. Surely it is far more plausible to suppose that he acts as his experience indicates, thus aligning perceptual content with his behaviour, not his environment. In this way inappropriate action goes with delusory experience, as appropriate action goes with veridical experience. The sensori-motor system is rightly so called: perception and action function together in an integrated pattern of links, actions being sensitive to sensory deliverances. So when it comes to a competition between action and environment, in the fixation of perceptual content, action wins. Aftermath beats aetiology.[80]

And there is another dimension to this. It is very tempting to describe the kind of behaviour Percy gets up to in functional or teleological terms. We naturally want to say that the *purpose* of his moving in a square path is to negotiate square objects successfully, that this is the *function* of his moving like that. Now I shall be discussing teleological accounts of content more fully in chapter 2, but I want

---

[80] Burge's example involves the substitution of cracks and shadows as between the actual and the counterfactual situation. It is supposed, implicitly, that there is no conflict between the verdict suggested by behaviour and the decision to go by the distal cause; the behaviour is not more appropriate to one kind of environmental cause than the other. This assumption enables Burge to avoid a conflict between behaviour and distal cause, so that the way is open to let the environment individuate the content of the experience. In this respect his example resembles classic twin earth cases for natural kinds, since here too there is no conflict between behaviour and distal cause, just underdetermination of the latter by the former. It seems to me, however, that it is precisely this assumption which renders Burge's case unpersuasive. For the crucial question is whether the experiences causally associated with cracks and shadows (of the same shape, darkness, etc.) really do differ in their content: do they present the world differently to the subject? This is the question whether the two environments *seem* the same to the perceivers in them, i.e. whether the cracks and shadows produce phenomenologically identical experiences. And it seems to me that they do, since these cracks and shadows look exactly alike to perceivers. But then we do not have a case in which genuine perceptual content – how the world seems to the perceiver – has been made to vary with environmental variation. And this is precisely because the alleged difference of phenomenological content does not show up in behaviour – which is just what we would expect if we were told the experiences represented the world in the same way. This is not to say that the two sets of experiences might not convey or carry different sorts of 'information' according to the identity of their typical causes; but it does not follow from this that they have different *contents*. Experiences of water carry different information (in some sense) from experiences of retaw, since the two are nomically related to different liquids; but they surely do not differ in their phenomenological content. Burge's cracks and shadows have the same appearance too, so they are phenomenally indiscriminable – which is to say they give rise to the same perceptual contents. The upshot is a dilemma for the strong externalist: either he produces a case in which behaviour and environment conflict (my case), in which case behaviour dominates; or he produces a case in which they do not conflict (Burge's case), in which case it is not plausible to discern a genuine difference of experiential content. I do not think a case could be produced that did not impale the strong externalist on one or the other horn of this dilemma.

now to indicate the relevance of teleological notions to the present issue. Suppose, for the moment, that we are entitled to characterize behaviour of this kind in terms of the (biological) notion of function; and suppose that such characterizations constrain content in some important way.[81] Then, if Percy's functional properties are preserved on twin earth, so too will be the content of the implicated representational states, specifically his perceptual states. That is, if his squarewise movements have the function precisely of negotiating square things, then the perceptual states that lead to these movements will partake of this function and have their content fixed accordingly. They could not have the strong externalist's preferred content (viz. *round*) because to negotiate round things is evidently *not* the function of Percy's squarewise behaviour.[82] A teleological theory of content may thus be invoked to back up the intuitive verdict I have been urging. The delicate question, to which I will recur in chapter 2, is what precisely the relationship is between biological function and environmental contingencies. I have just in effect assumed that behaviour and contentful states can in principle have a function that is specified by reference to a property that is not actually instantiated in the organism's causally impinging environment. Pulling function and environment apart in this way enabled me to cite function as contradicting the strong externalist's causal thesis. And, as I shall argue later, this assumption of a possible dissociation seems to me entirely correct (as a conceptual thesis): it requires simply that a function could in principle exist without that function ever actually being fulfilled. But even *if* this were not possible, and some deep necessary relation had to hold between a function and a certain kind of causally impinging environment, it is important to see that this does not favour the strong externalist. For, first, such a necessary relation would prevent the strong externalist from arguing against his opponent by separating out internal and external factors – on the reasonable assumption that the operative notion of function cannot be radically pulled apart from behavioural dispositions of the sort with which I have been concerned.[83] And, second, given the correctness of the

---

[81] This is not to say that one can *analyse* content in this way, supply a reduction of it to behavioural and/or teleological notions. The claim is rather that such notions govern our ascriptions of content; they supply regulative principles to which we ought to conform in our ascriptions of perceptual contents.

[82] I have not tried to say just what it is that fixes the function of a trait or piece of behaviour, though I have assumed that it is not the typical environmental cause of the events in question. I am relying here on an intuitive sense of function, and trying to remain neutral on substantive issues concerning the analysis of function itself.

[83] Presumably we do not want to countenance just any combination of causal powers and function, so that any old behaviour can count as an attempt to fulfil a given function. There must be constraints linking the function of something and its actual capacities and dispositions. It would be ludicrous to say of a blade of grass, for example, that it has all the functions of a human body. Objects need to have enough structure to make them candidates for having certain functions; their causal powers must be of

functional account of content, it will be functional properties that wear the theoretical trousers in the fixation of content, not the environmental causal relations that are claimed inevitably to go *with* these individuatively fundamental functional properties. However, this is a topic for later, and one that shifts the whole discussion into a different conceptual domain. The point I want to make now is just that teleological considerations *seem* to be operative in guiding our intuitions about Percy's perceptual contents, and these intuitions count powerfully against the strong externalist's theory. Fitting Percy's behavioural dispositions into a teleological framework gives a theoretically motivated rationale for reposing confidence in the intuition I have urged.

It will be observed that the behavioural descriptions I have cited contain predicates that refer to particular shapes: Percy is disposed to move *square*wise, i.e. in a square path. These behavioural descriptions are not, then, entirely intrinsic; they refer to properties of the space around Percy, not to properties of Percy (*he* isn't square). But it would be a confusion to assimilate this use of 'square' with that favoured by the strong externalist. In these behavioural descriptions 'square' is not being predicated of material objects with which the subject is in causal contact: there are no square *things* on twin earth, so nothing square has ever caused Percy's experiences – these are always caused by round things, remember. Indeed, the behavioural descriptions in question could be instantiated by a mobile perceiver stranded in empty space (the agent in a void) – a situation in which the strong externalist will presumably hold that *no* perceptual contents are available to the subject (at least none that are as of external states of affairs).

What the presence of these shape predicates does bring out, however, is the weak externalist strand in the account I favour. The behavioural dispositions that go with a square-representing perceptual content must themselves be specified by using a predicate that refers to the property of being square. The content of the experience must be so specified, and so must the behaviour that constrains that content. But of course this only gives us weak externalism since that predicate does not need to be instantiated by (material) objects in the perceiver's environment.[84] (This is clear also for functional descriptions: a kind of behaviour can have the function of negotiating square objects without it being

a kind such that they could in certain circumstances fulfil the assigned function. It would be difficult to be very precise about these constraints, but I assume they are operative, so that the function of perceptually controlled behaviour harmonizes in some way with a nonfunctional description of the behaviour.

[84] If you are worried that 'square' is instantiated by empty regions of space in Percy's environment, then substitute some other predicate that cannot be instantiated by empty space; or change the case to 'square material object'.

entailed that there are, or were, any such objects around the perceiver.) All that is required is that the perceiver satisfy these weakly external behavioural descriptions. (From this it appears to follow that there could not be a wholly disembodied perceiver whose experience represented the world as containing square objects: this seems to me a desirable result.)

Acknowledging the weak externalism present in my preferred account allows us to resolve two puzzles that might seem to arise once strong externalism about perceptual content has been rejected. The first puzzle is this: how can weak externalism be true of perceptual content if such content is supervenient upon 'internal' facts of the three kinds I have distinguished? That is, if it is sufficient for a certain kind of perceptual content that these internal conditions obtain, then how can it also be *necessary* to include some objective property in the specification of that content? Surely, if perceptual content is so supervenient, then we must be complete internalists about perceptual content, thus denying objective content to perceptual representations. That would, of course, be a disaster, but we are not, fortunately, driven to suffer it. For the whole thrust of my argument has been that we need to appeal to (weak) externalist descriptions *of behaviour*: we need to conceive of behaviour in terms of properties that objects might (I said, *might*) instantiate. [85] We must describe the body as tracing a *square* path through space; we must see behaviour as (potentially) appropriate to *square* objects; we must characterize the function of squarewise action as that of negotiating *square* things. Accordingly, the supervenience base for perceptual content already *includes* relations between intrinsic bodily states and the property of being square. So the weak externalism inherent in attributions of perceptual content is reflected right there in the supervenience base – thus resolving the puzzle. Only a full-blooded internalism about content-constraining behaviour could make the puzzle seem irresoluble. But this is neither mandatory, nor natural, nor the conception I have operated with.

The second puzzle takes us back to the Matching Problem, discussed in section 3. That problem, you will recall, was said to arise when the individuation conditions for a kind of content made no allusion to the individuation conditions for the states of affairs represented by that content, and vice versa. For how, in that case, could there be any match or fit or harmony between them? I therefore

---

[85] I hope it is clear that I am not intending to propose a behaviour*ist* account of perceptual content. I am simply trying to discover which other facts about a perceiver – internal or external – might be supposed to constrain or regulate ascriptions of such content. If you like, I am seeking the 'criteria' for ascribing perceptual contents. And so far I have been saying that the distal cause of a type of experience is just defeasible evidence for its content, evidence which presupposes that other facts about the perceiver support the same ascription; while behavioural-teleological facts provide self-sufficient criterial evidence for an ascription of content – they call the shots when it comes to deciding how things seem to the subject.

made it a condition of adequacy that some individuative dependence be demonstrated between content and represented state of affairs. Now once we reject strong externalism for perceptual content that problem looks set to loom, since such content is no longer fixed by a causal connection with the environmental feature represented. But it should now be clear that the account I have proposed has the resources (in principle) to deal with this problem of matching. For we are, in effect, individuating (teleologically specified) behavioural dispositions *by reference* to objective properties, those that enter the content of the associated experiences. So whatever individuates those properties (as it might be, their causal powers) also individuates those behavioural dispositions, which in turn constrain the ascription of perceptual content. The matching problem would only look pressing (or insoluble) if the relevant behaviour were conceived wholly internally, without allusion to the properties represented in the experience. But this is a conception we have stoutly and steadfastly repudiated. Instead, what makes the disposition the disposition it is cannot come apart from what makes the represented property the property *it* is.

I have not attempted, except in a sketchy way, to offer any real *theory* of perceptual content to pit against the strong externalist theory. I have traded upon the behavioural facts to motivate my rejection of strong externalism, and I have hinted at a teleological conception of how content is fixed. But this is far from giving anything like noncircular necessary and sufficient conditions for an experience to have a certain content. I am, indeed, sceptical that any such reductive conditions *can* be given, though I will edge closer to a positive theory of content in the next chapter.[86] My aim so far has been the more modest one of giving some shape to my intuition about the twin earth case I initially set up. But I do not intend this profession of modesty as any kind of retraction or concession; on the contrary, I think the argument I have given is about as good an argument as could be given in this area, in view of the nature of the area. We should not, here as elsewhere, confuse philosophical cogency with philosophical theory. For, ultimately, it is a matter of mobilizing intuition in the right direction, not replacing intuition with some supposedly independently motivated theoretical structure. Theories come and go; intuitions stay robustly on. So you can agree with my intuition without falling for my theory – though I would prefer it if you did both.

[86] We would need to understand consciousness a lot better to provide such a theory; we would need to know what is necessary and sufficient for a conscious experience to have a particular content. And this presupposes some sort of account of subjectivity, the what-it's-likeness of experience. I am not claiming to have anything of that ambitious kind to offer. But we can still say what sorts of facts we do not want conscious contents to float free of; we can say what sort of background they need to be embedded in. We might even be able to say what sorts of facts would determine an experiential content when slotted into a general theory of consciousness. . .

Strong externalism is often backed up with a kind of theory: a body of principles that provide necessary and sufficient conditions for content. The theory is not always made quite explicit, but it is, I think, commonly taken to provide some independent motivation for the strong externalist thesis. That it is an inherently clear and coherent theory is supposed to confer those virtues on the thesis supported by the theory. I want now to delve a little deeper into the workings of this underlying theory and expose some problems and obscurities with it. This should serve to further wear down any resistance that might still be felt to my rejection of strong externalism: for it is not a thesis that upon inspection keeps the best of theoretical company. The theory I have in mind might be called the causal theory of perceptual content (hereafter CTPC).[87] If I am right in what I have said so far, then this theory has already been refuted, but it is worth tackling the theory head on, if only to get a bit clearer about why strong externalism does not *have* to be true – given that it is not.

CTPC is easily stated, at least in a rough way. It says that the content of a type of experience is conferred by its typical distal cause: whatever property in the environment reliably causes experiences of that type *is* the property the experience represents. So it is both necessary and sufficient for experience-type E to be as of property F that tokens of E be regularly caused by instantiations of F. The theory is naturally construed genetically: experiences come to *acquire* their contents by dint of regular causal interactions with environmentally instantiated properties. If you want to give E the content F, then the thing to do is to subject instances of E to bombardment with instances of F (if this is not too colourful a way to put it). Experience picks up its content by causally locking onto the properties instantiated around the perceiving subject. Instances of E start life empty of content and then acquire it by receiving the causal impact (or im*print*) of external objects.

I think there is a circularity lurking within the heart of CTPC, a circularity which does much to explain the air of platitudinous truth that the theory can seem (in certain lights) to have. The circularity comes into focus when we ask what *sort* of causal relation it is that confers content. It cannot, of course, be any old causal relation – or else any property instantiated along the incoming causal chain would come to be represented by the experience. We need to single out the right kind of distal object, viz. the kind of object that is perceived once the content has been

---

[87] Versions of this kind of theory can be found in Burge, 'Individualism and Psychology', and Fodor, *Psychosemantics*. Fodor restricts himself to a sufficiency claim, saying nothing about the necessary conditions of content. Then what would he say about the same array of contents in a creature which lacked these causal connections? If he wishes to allow for content in the case of the brain in a vat, then he cannot avoid the question what fixes content in this case – and by hypothesis no causal theory will work here. Sufficiency is not sufficient for a general theory of content. His conditions will not serve to naturalize content for possible creatures that fail to satisfy them.

acquired. But now it seems unavoidable that the causal relation we need to isolate be identified as the perception relation itself. The theory then is that experiences come to have their content by virtue of being *perceptions* of the property in question. And I think that intuitively it is just this idea that lies behind CTPC: thinking of the perception relation that holds between our (mature) experiences and their objects, we suppose *that* relation to be what originally confers content on our experiences. And indeed what other sort of causal relation *could* be operative in fixing the right content? But now it should be obvious enough where the circularity lies: an experience can only count as a perception *of* an F if it *already* has the content F.[88] What it is for a token experience to qualify as a perception of some property F already includes that experience's having the content F. For an experience cannot count as a perception of something unless it has some suitable representational content. But then, of course, we cannot use the perception relation to *explain* what it is for an experience to have content. Putting it genetically, perception is coeval with content (or subsequent to it), so we cannot suppose that the perception relation could precede and confer content. Perception presupposes content, both conceptually and genetically. The capacity to perceive requires the capacity to perceptually represent, so the latter capacity cannot be bestowed by the former.

This is an elementary point, but absorbing it plunges CTPC into obscurity and difficulty. For what other conception of the content-conferring causal relation is there available? Before I pursue this question further, however, let me draw a contrast between CTPC and the causal theory of reference that puts the circularity objection into perspective. I suspect that the attraction of CTPC derives in part, and perhaps very largely, from an analogy with causal theories of reference. I want to point out that there is a crucial disanalogy between the two sorts of theory, and it is this that generates the circularity I have alleged. Suppose we set out to explain predicate reference by means of typical causal source (or some such): we say that 'F' in my language refers to the property F in virtue of the fact that my utterances of 'F' are typically produced by instances of F. The predicate acquires its reference by way of the causal impact of F-things on my uses of it. Now we can ask of this theory what kind of causal connection it has in mind; and we know that it cannot be just any kind or else predicates would be multiply ambiguous, referring to every property typically implicated in the causal chains leading up to their use. But in this case we are not compelled to invoke notions that already presuppose that predicate reference has been fixed. For we can appeal to relations such as perception. We can say that my utterances

---

[88] The case is not like explaining perception in terms of causation plus representational content, since content does not presuppose perception (as in hallucination). But perception does presuppose content. There can be seemings without seeings but no seeings without seemings.

of 'F' are typically produced by my perceiving instances of F: such a relation is necessary and sufficient for 'F' to refer to F. This theory is clearly not circular (at least not without very substantial extra argument): it explains one relation, viz. reference, in terms of another, viz. perception – and this latter relation does not (on the face of it) already build in the former. (Even if perception involved an internal language – the Language of Seeing – this would not prevent us explaining semantic reference in a *public* language in terms of perception.) In short, semantic content can be noncircularly explained in terms of perceptual content, if it can be explained in this way at all. But it is perfectly clear that perceptual content cannot *itself* be explained in this way: that would be to try to explain something in terms of itself. I suspect, however, that enthusiasm for CTPC is sustained by implicitly assuming that the two cases are analogous – by assuming that CTPC can help itself to whatever CTR can. The basic point here is that CTR, as I have expounded it, explains one kind of content by reference to another more fundamental kind; but CTPC is trying to explain that more fundamental kind, forgetting that it is fundamental. The tacit assumption is that we have available some noncircular restriction on the kind of causal relation that confers content – as CTR does. But, at the least, it has not yet been shown that we do.

What, then, are the prospects for discovering such a restriction in the case of CTPC? What is needed, clearly, is some way of characterizing the experiential relatum of the perception relation that does not presuppose that it is already endowed with content. Once this is to hand we will be able to define a relation 'perception*' that is exactly like perception except that it does not entail that the experience has content. Then we will be in a position to say that experience comes to have content in virtue of the regular obtaining of perception* between experiences and instantiated properties. Now what will these noncontentful characterizations be like? Presumably they will be fit to feature in psychophysical nomic generalizations relating environmental properties and noncontentful experiential kinds. These kinds must be such as to be apt for differential triggering by external properties: if an experience is of noncontentful kind K, then it will be apt to be triggered by property P. The thought then is that when this selective triggering has happened frequently enough kind K will turn into a contentful kind representing P. So there are two requirements that CTPC needs to meet in characterizing experiences: (a) the characterization must not presuppose content, and (b) the characterization must make experiences apt for elicitation by specific kinds of property. The only way I can see that these requirements might be met would be by recognizing a prerepresentational yet intrinsic level of description of experiences: that is, a level of description that is phenomenal yet noncontentful – something like traditional sense-datum properties of experience, in fact. These properties, as we might say, *dispose* an experience to acquire a particular content under the impact of the triggering external properties.[89] Now what should we say about this whole conception?

I want to make two points about it. The first is just that this is indeed a conception of experience that CTPC seems driven to accept. It must therefore face up to the obligations incurred by adopting this conception; it must convince us that it is legitimate. And I myself have considerable doubts about this idea of a prerepresentational phenomenology latent in perceptual experiences – as if such experiences were really just like bodily sensations except with a kind of representational overlay. However, I shall not here pursue these doubts, being content to have raised them. Certainly CTPC, once this commitment has been teased out of it, begins to lose its initial air of innocent good sense: it now looks to conceal some alarmingly problematic doctrines. The second point is that, by invoking a prerepresentational level of phenomenology, CTPC is in danger of sacrificing its explanatory aims. For it has thereby conceded that it cannot account for *all* the phenomenological features of experience. This may not at first seem like a very large concession – until we ask two questions. One question relates to the 'apt for' relation that holds between prerepresentational features and the contents they anticipate: these features, we said, *suit* the experience to acquire a certain content. But this dispositional property holds in *advance* of content-conferring causal interactions; it cannot then be explained in *terms* of such interactions. It follows that CTPC has no explanation of what it is for an experience to be phenomenologically *fit* to acquire a certain content; and this looks dangerously close to accepting that it cannot, after all, offer us a full theory of content – the explanans sits perilously close to the explanandum. (Besides, the whole explanatory structure is beginning to seem terribly obscure, as if we were just defining properties into existence to keep the theory afloat.) The other question is this: is it being supposed that the transition from prerepresentational phenomenal properties to content proper is really a *phenomenological* transition? Is there to be a difference in what it is *like* to have the relevant experiences after the content-conferring process has done its work? Here a dilemma threatens: either there is, in which case the difficult question must be faced as to what exactly it consists in; or it is not, in which case CTPC is not a theory of phenomenological properties at all – which is what it was advertised as being.[90] Again, it is not that

---

[89] Perhaps Peacocke's 'sensational' properties of experience might be invoked here, assuming them to exist: see his *Sense and Content*.

[90] Here again we observe that the causal theory is apt to degenerate into a theory, not of experiential content itself, but of the 'information' that might be derived from knowledge that an experience of a certain kind occurred; that is, the information consequent merely upon nomic connections, e.g. about the state of the subject's optical apparatus.

I think these questions knock CTPC flat; what they do is bring out the obscurities and problems lying buried in the theory. For my own part, I would prefer to avoid these problems by denying the conception of experience that leads to them: perceptual experience has none but representational properties (at least so far as consciousness is concerned). But denying this conception leaves CTPC with the original circularity problem I raised. Whether it can command any other resources to evade the problem I shall not now enquire. It is clear, at any rate, that the task is by no means trivial. So the theory behind the strong externalist thesis is not in the best of health. It staggers under the weight of a hitherto unresolved circularity.[91]

Let us now shift our attention towards Percy's sensory periphery. I have dwelt upon what Percy does, his motor outputs; I shall now focus upon what he receives, his sensory inputs. Remember that included in Percy's internal properties are the proximal stimuli that assail his sensory receptors: for example, the patterns of light, of certain intensities and wavelengths, that are incident at the retinae. We were invited, in setting up a twin earth case, to keep these constant while varying their distal origins, presumably by warping the passage of light from object to eye. It was then claimed, by the strong externalist, that perceptual content would follow the distal stimulus – the properties of the object – thus inducing a change of content, despite the identity of the proximal stimulus. Subjecting a perceiver to the same barrage of proximal inputs, from birth to death, is no (logical) guarantee of sameness of perceptual content (and not because of any innate determination). We might put this claim as the principle that the distal *dominates* over the proximal – it overrides it. Perceptual content can, as it were, leapfrog over the proximal stimulus (the totality of them) and pick up on the outlying distal cause of the nearer slice of stimulation. Thus it is that on twin earth content can concern roundness, despite the fact that the proximal stimuli are identical to those produced on earth by square objects. Is this view of the relative priorities of the proximal and distal plausible? I shall argue that it is not.

We can begin by noting the connection between downgrading the proximal stimulus and failing to do justice to the perceiver's behavioural dispositions. The connection goes via the brain. Brain states constitute the causal basis of behavioural dispositions. But what puts the brain into these states (inter alia) are the proximal inputs that excite afferent nerve activity, culminating in the brain. You get the same afferent activity, and hence the same central brain states, other things being equal, if you use the same proximal stimuli; nerve endings are sensitive to what reaches them, not to what lies at the distal portion of the causal chain – they cannot leapfrog. This is an application of a general principle about causation, proximity and intrinsic change: viz. the intrinsic changes wrought in a material object by the action of some other material object are sensitive only to what is causally most proximal to that object – billiard balls cannot play leapfrog either. Presumably the application of this principle to the brain and its proximal inputs is not going to be contested: if two brains start off in the same physical condition intrinsically, and you subject them to the same patterns of proximal causation, then you will end up with a pair of brains in the same physical condition intrinsically, the distal origins being as may be. So sameness of behavioural dispositions in Percy is (partly) attributable to sameness of proximal stimulations.[92] But then proximal stimuli play a decisive role in determining what determines content. We could not have those dispositions without those proximal stimuli (other things being equal), and if we have those stimuli we get those dispositions (again equalizing other things). Respect for the proximal stimulus issues from, or goes with, respect for behavioural dispositions. We expect that perceptual content will be sensitive to what behavioural dispositions are sensitive to, neither more nor less: and this is (equalizing initial conditions) the pattern of proximal stimulation.

The thesis to be established, then, is that perceptual content reflects proximal not distal stimulation. I shall argue for this by considering the general nature of the perceptual mechanism. My argument will proceed in two stages: first I argue that a perceptual system *could* conform to the proximal fixation of content; then I argue that actual perceptual systems, such as our own, do conform to this – indeed, that it is very hard to see how a perceptual system could *not* work in that way.

To establish the possibility claim, consider how we might construct a simple pattern recognition device that works in the way I suggest. Suppose we want to make a device that gives a certain output when certain shapes are presented to it; so the purpose of the device is to produce distinctive outputs for particular inputs. Imagine that the presented objects are to be placed behind an opaque wall (perhaps they are too bright for us to look at) and the device is to deliver its outputs to us on the other side of the wall. Let us suppose that the output mechanism consists simply of a pen that draws shapes on paper when suitably triggered by the mechanisms of the device. The device will need a transducer: something that takes the effects of a distal object, say light playing upon it, and converts or codes them into some other form, ultimately into movements of the pen. Make the transducer a photographic plate with suitable contraptions attached to do the energy conversions. We then set the device up in such a way that when it receives a certain pattern of light at its transducer it causes the pen to

---

[92] These dispositions can be specified as above: moving squarewise and the like.

draw a certain shape; the transducer is thus made to incorporate a projective function from proximal inputs to figural outputs. Suppose we arrange it so that the light normally received from a square object (at a certain position and orientation) triggers the transducer to cause the pen to draw a square figure. Once all this has been set up (and there have been bigger engineering problems) we can use the outputs to predict what manner of object lies behind the opaque wall, at least as to its simple shape. We have contrived a kind of law linking object and representation by exploiting the effects on the transducer (proximal stimuli) which are produced by the object. The output thereby contains *information* about the 'environment' of the device. The question now is whether strong externalism is true of this device.

Well, let us construct a twin earth case for it. Suppose we migrate with our precious device to a planet on whose surface light is twisted in some peculiar way: the pattern of light that reaches suitably placed objects from other objects that are round is just like the pattern of light that is reflected from square objects on earth. Our device suffers no internal alteration as a result of the trip. We are, let us suppose, unaware of the unearthly behaviour of light in our new habitat (perhaps we are not seeing creatures). We set up our dear device as before. What will it do when it is presented with a round object? Why, it will automatically sketch out a square for us of course! (Or gouge out a square figure if we are using touch not sight.) It will do this because it has been inflexibly constructed so as to convert a certain incident pattern of light into a certain shape. The proximal stimulus is all the transducer has to go on, and it responds to it mechanically and faithfully. It would not be physically possible for it to give a different output without some alteration in its internal machinery – without, that is, incorporating some other function from proximal input to figural output. Moreover, we would take it, upon receipt of the device's output, that there was indeed a square thing on the other side of the wall – thus falling into understandable error. It is, I think, very tempting to describe the device as subject to a certain sort of illusion (or proto-illusion); certainly we, the users, would be victims of an illusion. The point is that, given the design of the device and our purposes in making it, we would say that it was indicating the presence of square objects behind the wall.[93] And if it

---

[93] That is to say, the representational content of the drawn square is that there is a square thing there. In another sense of 'indicate' we can say that the drawn squares indicate round things, since there is on twin earth a regular causal connection between the two; this is the sense in which clouds indicate or mean rain. It is vital not to confuse these two senses of 'indicate', since the latter is very far from the former. I suspect that causal theories subliminally trade on this confusion, giving them a prima facie plausibility they have yet to earn. The crunch comes when causal theories try to account for error or misrepresentation, a notion that has no application in the case of 'natural meaning'. Cf. Fred Dretske, 'Misrepresentation'.

It may help to equip my device with a motor unit that causes it to behave in certain ways when it

had always operated on twin earth we would still say the same thing. The device need *never* have been actually triggered by a square object for it to output square figures and for it to be taken by us to indicate square objects. It just needs the right proximal inputs to set it in motion. In other words, there could (logically) be a pattern recognition device of this simple sort that systematically misrepresented its 'environment'; and it could only do that if its outputs were not fixed by their typical distal cause – but by how those outputs are hooked up to the proximal stimulus. The device was made under certain assumptions about the laws linking distal and proximal cause. Once these laws are abrogated, as they are on twin earth, the assumptions are falsified, and the poor machine just keeps churning out illusory outputs – it systematically malfunctions. The device, as it were, conjectures the character of its environment – better, mechanically computes a hypothesis about it – on the basis of two things: the proximal input, and some built-in empirical assumptions about the proximal/distal relation; and if the device is placed in an environment where those assumptions are false, it will systematically compute the wrong distal hypothesis. If a pattern recognition device has such fixed assumptions hard-wired into it, then it will take proximal inputs into illusory outputs, *no matter how long it has operated in the environment in question.* All the causal interaction in the world will not change the 'content' of its outputs if these assumptions (and the proximal stimuli) are held fixed. For these assumptions (and those stimuli) are all it has to *go on*. Since it seems to me that there clearly *could* be a device that functioned in this way, I take it then that I have established my first possibility claim.

Think now, if you will, of naturally evolved pattern recognizers: say, frogs. And let us assume that frogs have genuinely mental states when they see things (there is something it is like, though not perhaps very much, to be a frog). A bug heaves into our frog's visual field, a pattern of reflected light hits his retinae and is transduced into nerve impulses, these are centrally processed and the frog's sticky tongue shoots dramatically out. The content of the frog's visual experience, we may suppose, was something like: bug at velocity v and distance d. Somewhere in the frog's visual system assumptions are embodied about the relation between retinally incident light and the likely distal cause of this light. These assumptions are (presumably) contingent and empirical. They amount to a kind of inverse of the function from distal to proximal. Evolution has obliged the frog (one supposes), by coding these assumptions into its genes, to be exploited in the seizing of edible bugs in the course of time. Each time a new bug comes haplessly into view the frog's visual system performs a computation premised on retinal input and the assumptions it embodies, the result of which is a useful

---

draws its figures; this will give us an extra basis for ascribing the content *square* to its drawn square (as it did for organic Percy). I am also assuming this is an *analogue* representation device.

distal representation. This representation then feeds into the frog's motor system to produce the right tongue trajectory. Now: what happens to the frog's distal representations if we transpose it to a counterfactual environment in which the assumptions are false but all of its internal properties are preserved? (We can suppose, if we like, that the frog has been there since conception.)

We know for sure that its tongue will shoot out as if there were bugs there, even if we wickedly arrange it so that there are not. But we also know that proximal inputs will be processed in the same way, according to the same assumptions, and as a result the same distal representations will be generated – just as we would expect from the tongue-shooting behaviour. The frog's visual system, designed as it is, will be fooled by the new environment, imprisoned within the rigid operating principles it embodies. It will behave, in effect, just like my simple device, chained to its design and to what hits its sensory surfaces. The frog can no more leapfrog to the distal source than my device can. The only way to restore veridicality to the frog's experiences would be to rewire its internal design, install a new set of assumptions: but that would be to vary the internal facts. If this is not obvious, then consider that the built-in assumptions must figure in processes that feed into the frog's motor system: if the assumptions are varied, thus leading to distinct perceptual contents on receipt of identical proximal stimuli, then what is fed into the motor system varies too, giving rise to distinct kinds of behaviour. Our attributions of computations and representations to the visual system are constrained by the sensori-motor links – by what the organism *does* with its visual information. Thus fixity of visual operating principles (identity of proximal/distal assumptions) may be inferred (keeping proximal stimuli constant) from sameness of vision-driven motor activity. Behaviour, operating principles and proximal stimuli may each be triangulated with respect to the others; and perceptual content (distal representations) can be extracted from these three elements without recourse to what is actually and typically going on distally in the perceiver's environment. Our frog's twin earth double thus enjoys the same perceptual contents as his earthly prototype.[94]

Once again we see teleological ideas at work here. The visual systems of terrestrial organisms are designed (one assumes by evolution) to project distal representations of their environment on the basis of their (rather exiguous) proximal inputs, with a view to exploiting these representations in the control of

---

[94] Note that we could switch the natural kind of the environmental specks that trigger the frog's experiences: organic bugs on earth, tiny buglike robots on twin earth. But if these look the same the frog's experiences will have the same content. What would Burge say of such a case? Presumably that we have induced a shift of perceptual content. It is hard then to see how he can avoid the result that qualitative doubles (perceptible objects with exactly the same appearance) can give rise to distinctions in how things seem to the subject – a result which comes close to being contradictory, I think.

behaviour, thus enabling the organism to negotiate and survive in its environment. The rules of projection from proximal stimulus to distal representation embody empirical facts about the relation between objects and the way they strike the organism's receptors. So if we abrogate these facts, varying the distal features while keeping proximal stimulation constant, we get no change of perceptual contents, provided we keep the design the same. And we keep the design the same if we preserve the sensori-motor links by holding behavioural dispositions and abilities steady.[95] If it is the function of a visual representation to guide behaviour whose function is to negotiate (say) square objects, then the representation has the content *square* (this is meant only as an approximate formulation). But it is (logically) possible for the visuo-motor system of an organism to have such a function even though it is rarely or never fulfilled: biological purposes are not *necessarily* successful – as indeed other kinds of purpose are not.[96] We infer the function of behaviour by (roughly) determining what *would* make it successful – say, the avoidance of square objects – not by determining what the actual regular environmental cause of the behaviour is. Similarly, perceptual states may have functions that are not fulfilled (they are always illusory), and these functions constrain their content; typical environmental cause is at best a crude and fallible guide to these functions, behaviour being the more reliable arbiter. This, I think, is at least *an* important part of the reason why it seems intuitively correct to say that the frog's double has the same perceptual contents as the frog: we have preserved function on twin earth. On earth function and causation go regularly together – the bug-catching function of the perceptual state is typically accompanied by the actual causal presence of a bug – but on twin earth we keep that function while erasing the causative bugs. Consequently, we keep content. It can *look* as if regular environmental causation is doing the work in the fixation of content because it (contingently) goes with function, but the true picture emerges when we disentangle function and causation – then function dominates. So the functional story explains some of the attractiveness of the causal theory, while dislocating it from a position of theoretical centrality. (Again, I am not intending to advance a full-blown teleological theory of perceptual content here; I am merely locating our intuitions within a more articulated conceptual framework.)

The outcome of these reflections for the role of the proximal stimulus should now be clear. We cannot coherently suppose the visual system to latch onto distal

---

[95] Again, I am not saying it is logically sufficient for a specific experiential content that we observe the same pattern of sensori-motor links; the claim is rather that this is criterial in some weaker sense.

[96] Do not be misled by the contingencies of evolution here: frequent failures to function correctly lead to extinction, but this is not a matter of conceptual necessity. The teleological theory does not, in fact, require the truth of evolutionary theory; creationism allows for function too.

properties if we keep both proximal stimulus and operating principles the same. Nothing more can contribute to perceptual content than what can be recovered from the proximal stimulus in conjunction with the built-in assumptions, these together having the ultimate function of controlling behaviour. We might say that the assumptions, when married to the organism's motor system, are a sort of complex function (in the mathematical sense now) from proximal stimuli to behavioural responses; and the perceptual content of a visual representation caused by a given kind of proximal stimulus is fixed by that function. This makes the environmental presence of the property so represented in principle dispensable.

I said that my argument would have two stages, a possibility claim followed by the assertion that this possibility is actualized in organisms like frogs and human beings. I think it should be apparent that the second stage has already been completed; for in exploring the possibility in question we have uncovered reasons why perceptual systems *have* to work in this way. What we have done, in effect, is to excogitate, more or less a priori, the approach to the study of vision adopted by Marr and his associates (of course I did this with Marr's approach firmly in mind).[97] So what I am saying is that the Marrian conception of the workings of the visual system is, implicitly anyway, opposed to CTPC. In consequence, it is opposed to strong externalism about perceptual content (I do not mean that it is presented by its scientific practitioners in this light). If this is right, then the best empirical theories of vision confirm the philosophical conclusion I have been urging: my possibility claim is taken by these theories to be the way actual visual systems operate. Indeed, given the various constraints on how visual systems could operate, it is hard to see how visual systems anything like ours and frogs' could work otherwise. Marr is vividly aware that vision must mesh with action, and this mesh (as I have argued) cannot be respected if we follow the strong externalist: he purchases necessary veridicality (at least by and large) at the cost of behavioural epiphenomenalism, since the veridical experiences could be generally completely out of synchrony with the organism's behavioural dispositions.[98] The way the world seems to the organism plays no role in shaping

---

[97] See David Marr, *Vision*.

[98] The link between visual representations and the behaviour they control becomes as loose-hinged as that between the environment and behaviour. The psychological causal basis of behaviour becomes as remote as the environment in the explanation of behaviour. The sense in which the environment is epiphenomenal then applies also to visual representations; the causal powers of the representation get radically decoupled from its content (it disposes the subject to move squarewise though it is as of a round object).

The view I take of Marr's theory is exactly opposite to that suggested by Burge in 'Individualism and Psychology'. For an effective criticism of Burge on Marr see Gabriel Segal, 'Seeing What is not There'. Segal and I see seeing similarly, though we came to see it so separately. Where I stress the role

what the organism does. This consequence of strong externalism seems to me radically contrary to the general perspective presupposed by Marr. I therefore enlist Marr's empirical framework in support of my own philosophical position. This, then, completes the second stage of my argument.

I come now to the epistemological consequences of strong externalism about perceptual content. Perceptual content consists in the way things seem to the subject, in phenomenological features of experience. Strong externalism claims that such phenomenological distinctions consist in relational distinctions with respect to the environment. Now environmental distinctions themselves are detectable by means of perception, by the exercise of the senses; whereas experiential distinctions are ordinarily supposed to be detectable, not by means of the senses, but by introspection. The way we tell the difference between objective states of affairs and the way we tell the difference between subjective experiential states of ourselves are not the *same* way – they require the exercise of different 'faculties'. Perception tells us how the environment is; introspection tells us how the environment seems to us: such, at least, is the traditional view.[99] The question is whether this traditional view can be maintained once strong externalism is accepted. For, on the face of it, some modification of that traditional view seems called for by strong externalism, since introspectively detectable distinctions are being made to depend upon the existence of perceptually detectable distinctions. How, if at all, can introspection then maintain its traditional autonomy from perception? How, in particular, can it retain its traditional epistemological privileges? And, if it cannot do so, is that any objection to strong externalism?

The traditional view of the relation between knowledge of experience and knowledge of the world insists upon what we might call the Cartesian Asymmetry: our knowledge of the character of our experiences is not dependent upon our knowledge of their supposed environmental causes, and hence is not afflicted by the same sources of fallibility; whereas our knowledge of the world does depend upon our knowing the character of our experiences. It is this asymmetry, specifically its first component, that strong externalism seems to challenge, since it makes the very identity of experiences dependent upon the actual environment, thus apparently making our knowledge of experience

---

of behaviour in attributions of perceptual content, Segal says that such attributions must always be given a 'top-down motivation', i.e. the representations need to be exploited by the perceiver in getting around the world. He uses this feature of Marr's approach to argue against Burge's view of the philosophical assumptions of that approach.

[99] I am not using 'introspection' in any theory-laden way here; in particular, I am not taking it to be inward-directed perception. I simply mean whatever enables us to have beliefs about our own mental states, however that faculty is to be conceived.

dependent upon our knowledge of the environment. The conflict between strong externalism and the Cartesian Asymmetry can be spelt out as follows. Our perceiver, Percy, has enjoyed a particular course of experience in the actual world, and he has enjoyed it in a particular environment. But two things are logically (or metaphysically) possible for Percy: one, that he might have enjoyed a quite different course of experience; the other, that he might have been placed in a quite different environment. His experiences could have had different contents, and he could have had different states of affairs around him. Since these are both logical possibilities about Percy, he is clearly not in a position to rule them out by arguing that his actual experience and actual environment are logically necessary. Percy must admit that both these things are real metaphysical possibilities. But, the Cartesian tradition claims, there is a vital epistemological asymmetry between Percy and these two possibilities. For suppose they were realized – suppose Percy were in a possible world in which they were actual: then, with respect to the first possibility, it would necessarily *seem* to Percy that his experiences were different; while, with respect to the second, it would *not* necessarily seem to him that his environment were different. Varying experiences necessarily involves varying how things seem to the subject, but varying environments does not necessarily vary how things seem to him – for the relation between seemings and the environment is fundamentally contingent. But now, if experiential distinctions necessarily show up in how things seem to the subject, then Percy is *now* in a position to rule out the logical possibility that his experience is taking a different course from the course it seems to him to be taking; but since environmental distinctions do not *necessarily* show up in how things seem to the subject, Percy is not now in a position to rule out the logical possibility that his environment is different from the way he takes it to be. If our seemings were different, they would necessarily seem different; but if our environment were different, it might seem the same. Seemings cannot seem to the subject to be other than what they are, but realities can. Hence the Cartesian Asymmetry.

It is just this asymmetry that strong externalism appears to dissolve. For it says that a change of the subject's environment (considering Percy in a counterfactual environment) necessarily changes the content of his experience, so that this possibility is equivalent to the first possibility, viz. that his course of experience has been counterfactually varied. Indeed, we can *only* realize that possibility *by* changing his environment. Accordingly, if we can rule out one possibility, we can rule out the other: an epistemological *symmetry* follows upon a mutual entailment between environmental truths and experiential truths.[100] This

---

[100] Of course this entailment need not be point-by-point. Strong externalism affirms a general dependence; it does not say that every experience must be veridical. What it says is that it follows from

equivalence cuts both ways, of course. Either our knowledge of experience inherits the insecurity attaching to our (so-called) knowledge of the world, or our knowledge of the world inherits the infallibility of our knowledge of experience. This second response to the strong externalist's epistemological symmetry offers the hope of a swift and decisive rebuttal of scepticism about the external world. I shall not discuss this response now, reserving it for my later discussion of externalism and scepticism. The first response, which I shall now discuss, finds self-knowledge to be as infected with doubt as our knowledge of the external world has traditionally been taken to be: I am as uncertain whether it seems to me that I have experiences *as of* square things as I am whether I actually do perceive square things – that there are in objective fact square things around me. Introspection thus comes to suffer from the same kind of fallibility as perception is traditionally supposed to. The gap between subject and world opens up between subject and experience.

We need to be careful how we state the fallibility that results from strong externalism. It is customary to distinguish infallibility from self-intimation, and to define these two notions as converses of each other. A subject is infallible with respect to a range of propositions if and only if it follows from the fact that he believes any one of them that it is true. A range of propositions is self-intimating for a subject if and only if it follows from the fact that any one of them is true that he believes it. Neither of these notions quite captures the failure of first-person authority that seems intuitively to result from strong externalism. Consider the judgement-form 'I have an experience as of an F.' This expresses a belief in whose content a contentful experience features; in particular, the content contains the concept F. Now strong externalism says that the identity of F is fixed by the environment. But then F has that identity *both* within the context 'experience as of' *and* the context 'believes he has an experience as of'. It is the same concept that crops up in both places: in giving the content of the experience, and in giving the content of the subject's belief *about* that experience. So whatever it is that the subject experiences, according to strong externalism, will also be what he believes he experiences, since the environment fixes both of these in one fell swoop. But then infallibility and self-intimation, as defined above, *will* be satisfied by strong externalism, in virtue of the constant meaning of the word 'F' in both sorts of context. The subject will have the experiential states he believes himself to have; and he will believe himself to have the experiential states he does in fact have. Strong externalism ensures that the content of introspective beliefs will not come apart from the content of experiences. Clearly we need a slightly different notion

the fact that an experience has a certain content that experiences of that kind are generally caused by things of the kind represented, not that they invariably are. Cf. Burge, 'Individualism and Psychology'.

of introspective access if we are to pinpoint the epistemological intuition in question.

This intuitive notion is most naturally stated in terms of 'telling the difference' between experiential states: that is, in terms of the idea of *discrimination*. Let us say that mental states of a certain type are *transparent* to their subject if and only if he can discriminate them from each other in any possible situation. Intuitively, their identity is completely evident to the subject – he sees right into it. There are mental states that fail of transparency in this sense: knowledge is not transparent, for example, because the subject cannot discriminate knowledge from mere belief just on the basis of introspection. Beliefs about natural kinds are not transparent either: if my beliefs were about retaw not water, this would not be a difference of belief discriminable by me just by introspection. On the other hand, bodily sensations are plausibly regarded as transparent: I can always tell the difference between (intense) pain and (mild) pleasure. A useful criterion of transparency is this: if you replace one type of mental state with another in me, while allowing me to retain my memories of the mental states I have had, then I will judge accurately whether you have given me a new (type of) mental state or just another instance of the old type – I will be able to discriminate between them on the basis of (accurate) memory. Now the Cartesian tradition does, I think, suppose that perceptual experiences are transparent in this sense: differences of perceptual content are always subjectively discriminable – differences of seeming are seeming differences. This property of introspection is not, however, strictly entailed by the notions of infallibility and self-intimation, since they are consistent with its absence: whatever perceptual content you give me I will (per accidens, as it were) get it right, but without knowing *which* content it is I am getting right. This is because the definitions of those notions say nothing of the subject's epistemological relation to the identity and difference of his mental states. With this richer notion of transparency to hand, then, we can say that, according to strong externalism, perceptual content is opaque not transparent. It is no more transparent than the environment is: just as I cannot necessarily be relied upon to discriminate environmental differences, so I cannot necessarily be relied upon to discriminate experiential differences. Since I can fail to tell the difference between an environment of square things and an environment of round things (I behave the same way in both), I can fail to tell whether my experiences are as of square things or as of round things. I can introspect conscientiously from dawn till dusk and still not discover which type of experience I enjoy. Since I cannot necessarily distinguish the actual environmental situation from a number of other possible ones, I cannot necessarily distinguish my experiential contents from the possible ones that *would* result from the realization of those other environmental possibilities. If one of these environmental possibilities is my being a brain in a vat surrounded by empty space, then I cannot tell whether my experience is now as of being such an envatted brain – seeming to see empty black space or the electrodes that stimulate my afferent nerves or simply nothing whatever. The general principle underlying this result is that if discriminating Fs depends upon discriminating Gs, and I cannot discriminate Gs, then I cannot discriminate Fs. Thus it is that the undiscriminating character of perception stains the discriminative power of introspection – according, that is, to the strong externalist who takes the first fallibilist way with the anti-Cartesian symmetry.

I have already, in this chapter, held it against various strong externalist theses that they conflict with first-person authority; so it will come as no surprise now if I say that I do not find this consequence credible in the present case either. It seems to me that the faculty of introspection has greater discriminative powers than strong externalism is equipped to recognize. This is not a conviction I can hope to prove to someone who is prepared to swallow the opacity of experience as something forced on us by an independently correct theory, but I can, I think, at least ply your intuitions in the right direction. But first let me just assert that it really *does* seem to me that I can, in all circumstances, tell the difference between an experience as of a square thing and an experience as of a round thing (or between different types of colour experience): presented with both simultaneously I could always tell that they were different; and presented with them at different times (or in different worlds) they would always make a differential impact upon my introspective faculty. In this respect perceptual experiences are, I assert, like bodily sensations: distinctness is always apparent distinctness. I could not have distinct (types of) perceptual experience and be disposed to react to them in exactly the same way, as if they were (phenomenologically) identical. Phenomenological distinctions *must* always be introspectively registered. So, at least, I am prepared confidently to assert.[101] Only a philosophical theory could induce us to deny this, and in the present case a theory that has not stood up to scrutiny on other grounds.

To spur intuition, then, consider a more extreme form of strong externalism than any considered hitherto: namely, that perceptual content necessarily varies the moment the environment changes. Suppose, that is, that if we place Percy in successive environments, varying the external causes of his (constant) internal

---

[101] Here I feel a bit like G. E. Moore confidently asserting the existence of his hands as part of what it is common sense to claim that one knows; only *his* confidence had not the solid backing of a faculty like introspection. I really *am* quite positive that it does not now seem to me that I am a brain in a vat; it never crosses my mind to doubt that what I appear to be seeing are books, skyscrapers and snow. Honestly. But I can be made to wonder whether I am really seeing these things (I am no dogmatist).

states, then we get instantaneous variation of content; to fix ideas, let him spend every other day on twin earth, where round things supplant square things as causes of internal state S, so that the experiences correlated with S jump from one kind of content to the other daily. Assuming that the environmental differences are not themselves discriminable by Percy, this extreme form of strong externalism has the consequence that Percy cannot tell the difference between how things seem to him on successive days – so far as he is concerned, it is all one with him perceptually. Nothing in Percy's behavioural dispositions will bear witness to these differences of seeming; he goes on just as if things seemed the same to him, though they in fact seem different (says this extreme strong externalist). Now let me ask the following question: what if we allow Percy to retain accurate memories of how things seemed the day before? Would these equip him to make a judgement of distinctness as between his seemings on successive days? Percy remembers on Wednesday that things seemed F to him on Tuesday, while they in fact seem G on Wednesday. Presumably our externalist will say that this will not improve Percy's discriminative powers, since his present introspective belief and his introspective memory belief will themselves be infected with the same opacity as the experiences themselves. If Percy is rational, and convinced by strong externalism, then he will answer our request for a judgement of experiential identity by saying, 'How should I know? – it depends whether I've had my environment changed since yesterday.' But this strikes me as deeply counterintuitive: surely if a person remembers how things seemed to him in the past, and he knows how things now seem to him, then he has all he needs (and could possibly want) to decide whether things seem the same now as they did then. It really will seem to Percy that his seemings have changed, if they have changed in fact; his memory will tell him so. Our extreme strong externalist is flying in the face of what has the look of something undeniable. And the absurdity of his view seems yet more blatant when we consider that Percy's behavioural dispositions are the same, according to the strong externalist, whether his perceptual contents are varying daily or not. Percy comports himself on twin earth every other day just as he would had he stayed on earth for that day, but we are told that his perceptual contents and introspective beliefs are radically different during these daily sojourns to twin earth. On Tuesday he believes that he has experiences as of square things and moves squarewise; on Wednesday, duly beamed up to twin earth, he believes (truly) that he has experiences as of round things and yet he *still* moves squarewise. Not only do differences of experiential content not show up in behavioural dispositions, neither do differences in what is *believed* about one's experiential content – and this makes it even more difficult to make sense of the subject's deeds. We need to keep experiential transparency if we are to avoid this kind of result. Differences of seeming should always give rise to corresponding behavioural differences.[102] But now, if this is the right thing to say about Percy's perceptual contents in this temporal case, then it is also the right thing to say about comparable counterfactual cases too, since there is no relevant difference between the two sorts of environmental variation: differences of counterfactual seemings with respect to the actual world should be just as transparent as differences of later seemings with respect to earlier ones. It therefore seems to me that the traditional transparency of perceptual seemings is not up for strong externalist denial: the givenness of the given is something given; the reality of seemings is a seeming reality.

If I cannot strictly *prove* that experience must be such that introspection is necessarily sensitive to changes in it, then perhaps I can offer some sort of explanation for why this should be so. Explanation can sometimes boost credence where argument gives out. A plausible naturalistic account of *why* introspection is so sensitive to perceptual content may thus ease acceptance of the claim that it is. Naturalized Cartesianism may be more palatable to some than Naked Cartesianism. Anyhow the question of explanation is of independent interest. Let me enquire, then, how it might have come about that introspection got to be as reliable about perceptual content as I have urged that it is. What does reliable introspection *do* for its possessor? What purpose might such high reliability, amounting to virtual infallibility, serve? If we could identify such a purpose, preferably one with a solid biological rationale, and if we could show how reliable introspection fulfils it, then we would have explained *why* introspection has the Cartesian property. We would have explained this feature of the mind (certain minds) in the same sort of way biologists explain why organisms have various physical or behavioural traits – for example, why giraffes have such long necks or bees are so good at colour discriminations.[103] Why, to get right down to

---

[102] This connection is apt to seem contingent, thus generating the possibility of an inverted spectrum and so forth, because of the general mind–body problem: the links between mental and physical facts seem breakable, tenuous. Any theory of content that invokes physical facts will then be susceptible to such intuitions of contingency. I think we should try to separate this source of doubt from sources closer to the theory of content as such. Strong externalism is not implausible just because it uses physical relations to the environment to explain content; it would be on the wrong track even if there were no general mind–body problem. By contrast, the way in which behaviour can seem to float free of conscious contents is a reflection of the general mind–body problem, not a defect in this way of coming at content. We might be tempted to think that only a theory of content that eschewed all reference to physical facts could avoid the apparent contingency of the link between mental and physical – a theory that regarded content as answerable to nothing save the autonomous configuration of consciousness itself. But this, I would say, is a delusion spawned by the impression of contingency that the mind–body relation can seem to present. However, to sustain this position would take me too far afield.

It is worth noting explicitly that strong externalism itself implies the possibility of inversions of perceptual content without any behavioural sign.

[103] We are trying to explain the pay-off in having a certain sort of biological excellence. Fireflies

basics, do the genes prefer introspective infallibility – what is in it for *them*? Where is the benefit to the biological subject? (I am here assuming that human introspection is universal and fixed and hard-wired enough to admit of an explanation in terms of evolutionary biology – its super-reliability is not a matter of 'culture'. However, my explanation does not actually depend on this assumption.)

What is needed is some function for transparency that confers a serious point on it – something that makes it *worth* possessing from a biological point of view. We must not think of it merely as some kind of otiose and decadent luxury, a device for self-absorbed wallowing, encouraging an immobile dreamy posture and sublime indifference to what is going on around you – the contemplative Cartesian locked up in his own thoughts. No, we need to see it as contributing to the organism's active life in the world, as a valuable aid to survival, a vital piece of psychological machinery. We need, that is, to understand how it helps the organism negotiate his environment – how the inward gaze can serve an outer-directed purpose. At any rate, that is the explanatory question I here set myself: what world-directed purpose did natural selection have in mind when it installed the capacity for infallible discrimination of perceptual contents in our brains?

Let us first identify the function of perceptual states themselves. This is plainly to provide the organism with reliable information about the condition of the environment around it, so that food can be found, predators eluded, mates procured. Clearly the more reliable perception is the better for the organism, provided high reliability does not have counterbalancing disadvantages (such as an unwieldy visual system that slows the organism down). Too much perceptual illusion spells trouble for the genes, so natural selection will favour the veridical perceivers (other things being equal). Still, we know that naturally evolved visual systems are by no means illusion-free. They function well enough in their natural environments most of the time, but they can be tricked if we contrive a kind of environmental stimulus they are not equipped to interpret correctly – in an extreme case by producing total hallucinations by means of direct cortical stimulation. Perception, like most other evolved capacities, is a kind of compromise with the environment, a product of optimization within certain parameters and trade-offs with other functional demands.[104] Visual perception,

are, I understand, extraordinarily good at discriminating the noises made by members of their own species. We get some explanation of this excellence when we learn that they are surrounded by predators that are very good at trapping them by imitating the noise fireflies of different species make. There needs to be a good reason for such excellence, because mediocrity takes less out of you. Why are we not merely mediocre at discriminating our own mental states? It might take less energy, and there don't seem to be any predatory mimics of our mental states to contend with!

[104] Cues to depth, for example, are reliably present in the environment, but they can be removed, so producing distance illusions of various kinds. Presumably if such cues were often removed by

say, isn't entirely perfect, even for visual experts like us, and the imperfection comes with the territory. Nevertheless, in an ideal world, where the engineering problems were less severe, and the environment more hospitable, the senses of organisms *would* asymptote to the unimprovable – natural selection would see to that. It is just that the environmental constraints as they actually are place limits on the reliability of perceptual systems.

Now what I want to explain is why introspection is so much more reliable than perception – why it is less vulnerable to error and illusion. To discover this, we must first ask why introspection exists at all – then we can ask why, given this explanation of its existence, it should exhibit such high reliability. Well, why might it be useful to be able to register, in the form of beliefs, that one is having a particular kind of perceptual experience? I think the answer must be that this enables one to control one's behaviour more effectively than if one did not have such beliefs. Suppose, then, that the introspective beliefs did *not* exist though the perceptual experiences did: what benefit would be thereby sacrificed? Presumably the experiences would then have to shape and control world-directed beliefs directly. But this type of cognitive system would, it seems, lack the kind of *flexibility* characteristic of cognitive systems that feature knowledge of the experiences received. For the introspective belief buffer, acting as an intermediary between perception and world-directed beliefs, can, as it were, put an experience in neutral – it can decline to be guided by it in the formation of beliefs about the world. The subject can judge, *of* a perceptual experience, that it is not to be trusted, and hence not to be acted upon. But this is possible only if introspective beliefs are available to the subject. Judgements of veridicality or its opposite require the capacity to form beliefs *about* one's experiences. Higher-order mental representations, such as introspective beliefs are, permit the cognitive system to query and edit what it receives at the lower level. This is very clear in the process of (what might be called) *perceptual collation*: the juxtaposition and comparative evaluation of perceptual experiences received at different times or through different sense modalities. This process, which involves the weighing of disparate sources of sensory evidence, assists in weeding out misleading sensory impressions, and results in a more sophisticated procedure for making decisions than a system that lacks this facility. In other words, the advantage of having beliefs about one's experiences is that each experience does not have to be taken at face value: one can, so to speak, sort through one's experiences in order

nature, as it were, visual systems would have to compute depth in some other way. As it is, they depend on reliable contingencies. But there is no biological point in building in such failsafe devices if they are very seldom needed, given the extra burden the visual system would then have to bear. The cyclop's single eye may serve its owner's purposes well enough, and it is harder to build and service a binocular system that a monocular one.

to arrive at the most considered and globally informed decision possible. If a cognitive system has the capacity for introspective knowledge, then it is less at the mercy of momentary impressions than a system without this capacity. Being able to think 'it seems to me that such and such' is what permits one to append the qualification 'but things may not really be such and such.' Introspective beliefs permit one to make the distinction between appearance and reality, and hence maintain a critical attitude towards sensory intake. (It does not particularly matter to this explanation that there could conceivably be other ways of achieving the same kind and degree of cognitive flexibility. What matters is that this is *one* way, and it is the way natural selection seems to have hit upon.)

We have, then, a world-directed naturalistic explanation of why the introspective faculty for perceptual experiences exists: it enables us to know the world better. But we have not yet explained what I undertook to explain, namely the super-reliability of the deliverances of this faculty. How come we are so good at telling how things seem to us? To answer this we need to remember the biological ideal of infallibility and what might stand in the way of fulfilling that ideal. Cognitive systems (or subsystems) aim at absolute reliability because (other things equal) truth is more conducive to survival than falsehood. Now the system that is responsible for gaining knowledge of the external world consists of two subsystems, on the view just sketched: there is the subsystem that generates perceptual experiences, and there is the subsystem that generates beliefs about these experiences. Both work in tandem to produce maximally reliable beliefs about the world. The process of producing these latter beliefs is thus a two-stage process in which both stages have to be reliable if the final output is to be: the experiences should match the world, be accurate representations of it; and the beliefs about these experiences should match the experiences, be accurate representations of them. The perceptual subsystem should be maximally discriminative about the world, and the introspective subsystem should be maximally discriminative about experiences of the world. If *either* subsystem fails in its duty, then the whole system will be liable to form false beliefs about the world. We can think of this two-stage process in terms of sensory modules and a central cognitive system.[105] The goal of the total system is to arrive at true beliefs about the world. To do this the sensory modules must first process the proximal input and deliver up a distal representation. Once this has been done, that representation (the output of the module) must become input to the central system and be suitably processed by it. On my suggestion, this works by first producing a belief (within the central system) to the effect that the sensory module has just delivered up an experience with a certain content; then the central system weighs

---

[105] See Fodor, *The Modularity of Mind.*

this sensory evidence up, collates it, and finally prepares it for impact on the motor system. The key point for us is that this second stage is itself a process of forming a representation of something else, just as the first stage is. Now why is it that the second stage of representation formation is so much more reliable than the first? Why is the central system so good at registering the output of a sensory module? Well, if it were less good than it is, then the total system would be less effective, because less reliable with respect to the world; so there is a premium on introspective perfection. An organism will therefore have perfect introspective discrimination *if it can*. The same is true for perceptual discrimination, as I said earlier. And now the central point is this: introspection can approximate more closely to the ideal than perception because there are simply more *opportunities* to go wrong in the latter case than in the former. The perceptual system is more prey to the vagaries of the environment than the introspective system is prey to slip-ups in the delivery of modular outputs to the central system. Given the conditions under which the two subsystems operate, it is simply *harder* to design a system that always gets it experientially right about the world than a system that always gets it introspectively right about its own psychological states. Vision, say, has to perform the incredibly difficult task of recovering an accurate distal representation from fragmentary proximal inputs – and all *sorts* of things might happen between the distal and the proximal stimulus to prevent the visual system from making the right 'inference'. It can seem, indeed, like a miracle that the visual system ever manages to do what is required of it; the gap between 'data' and 'hypothesis' is perilously wide and strewn with the corpses of mistaken 'inferences'. And this is, as it were, an inherent engineering problem: given the way the world is (e.g. how light behaves – or sometimes misbehaves), and given how visual systems must operate, absolute perfection must remain a distant ideal not achievable in the hard world (just think of the visual problems you have on a dark night). But – and this is the central point – the introspective faculty does not have to cope with these engineering problems: its task is just *much easier*. The whole process goes on inside the head, for one thing: there is no need to infer boldly to hypotheses about the remote environment from the exiguous and fleeting traces it leaves on your sensory surfaces.[106] All that is necessary is that the sensory module should be properly hooked up to the introspective faculty – a simple matter (looking at the mechanics) of wiring in the right neural connections. There is thus no yawning de facto gap that needs to be riskily bridged by a set of 'assumptions' about what in the world might have produced the current retinal image. It is as if the only task for introspection were to report on the character of the retinal image itself. The introspective faculty does not

---

[106] Scare-quote 'infer' here if you prefer.

have to span a perilous proximal/distal chasm; it gets the visual module's output on a plate.[107] Thus it is that the biological ideal of representational infallibility can be achieved for introspection but not for perception. Knowing what the genes favour, and knowing the constraints they face, we would predict precisely the epistemological asymmetry that we in fact find. If we were introduced to other naturally evolved creatures from Mars, equipped with perception and introspection, and we were told that the environmental constraints on Mars were like ours on earth, then we would expect to find the same sort of asymmetry – imperfect perceptual systems but high-fidelity introspective systems. For what would *prevent* natural selection from fulfilling its ideal in the case of introspection? Once you have got introspection set up in the workshop, it is not a terribly difficult engineering assignment to tune it up to perfection; but not so for perception. Experience is transparent to introspection because nothing really stands in the way of its being so; but there is plenty to prevent the transparency of the world to perception.

Seen in this light, we would not *expect* strong externalism to be true of the perceptual experience of any creature endowed with an introspective faculty. Given the function and nature of introspection, we would expect the very transparency strong externalism denies. So if my theory of introspection is anywhere along the right lines, then we have an extra reason for doubting strong externalism about perceptual content. In order for introspection to be as discriminating as it (predictably) is, it needs to classify experiences without reference to their causal history; so transparency requires that experiences be otherwise individuated than aetiologically. Experiences individuated as strong externalism says would not serve the purpose for which introspection of them exists.

This implies that if a creature had a rather fallible introspective capacity the pressure against strong externalism about its experiences would not be as powerful. And it would be even less powerful for a creature wholly without introspection. For we would not need to save transparency by denying strong externalism where such creatures are concerned. If it were not for the other objections to strong externalism, then we would have no particular reason for rejecting it in their case. But once we equip a creature with infallible

---

[107] You can therefore trick the visual system by sending in the right proximal inputs and watch it compute a false distal hypothesis; but there seems no way to trigger the introspective system save by sending in experiences themselves – and so failing to fool it. The only way for me to cause in you the belief that you have an experience of red is to lay on an experience of red; not so for the belief that there is a red thing in the environment – here I need not lay on a red thing, just an experience of red. In the case of introspection, activation conditions for belief coincide with truth conditions; but perceptual beliefs can be activated in ways that do not presuppose the fulfilment of their truth conditions.

introspection, perceptual content is (so to say) driven inwards – or at least prevented from being dragged outwards all the way to the environment. And indeed I think that reflection on such creatures does suggest that strong externalism is somewhat more plausible-seeming in their case: we are more inclined to allow that perceptual content is a matter of something like causal links to the world when there is no introspective infallibility to draw it inwards. This seems to be so for machines with (quasi-)representational states, as well as for very simple organisms that have perception without self-consciousness.[108] Putting it naturalistically: once evolution found a use for introspective infallibility it had to ensure that perceptual states were individuated independently of the environment; up till then it didn't really matter all that much.[109] Cartesianism thus became a biological necessity.

That concludes my case against strong externalism about perceptual content. I want now to remark some consequences and corollaries of the position I have reached.

Any position on the content of perceptual experience will have immediate implications for the content of mental *images*. Images are modality-specific, commonly derived from perceptual experience, and subject to the same sorts of processing principles as perceptual experiences.[110] They also have the phenomenological character of perceptual experiences, and represent by means of this phenomenology (what the mental state is like determines what kind of thing it represents). We may expect, therefore, that images will have their content fixed in the same sort of way perceptual experiences do: my image of a red sphere, for example, will have its content fixed as my perception of a red sphere does. That is, strong externalism will not be true of mental images either – and for the same sorts of reasons. For: that thesis will lead to a dissociation of image content and behavioural dispositions; it will not do justice to the proximal stimulus; and it will yield an implausible fallibility in our introspective knowledge of our mental images. I shall not restate my earlier arguments for these claims as they apply to perceptual experience so as to make them applicable to the case of images, since that would be unbearably tedious and (I take it) unnecessary; I assume it is obvious enough how the restatement would go.

[108] For such cases, however, the notion of representational content is apt to degenerate into that of mere informational content, i.e. natural indication.

[109] Imagine that the input to the introspective faculty had its content individuated by the actual distal cause of the token experience in question: then introspection would be precisely as reliable (or unreliable) as perception. If you want an introspective faculty that is more reliable than this, then you had better not individuate its inputs in this radically external way. But making the environmental individuation global rather than point-by-point only improves introspective reliability by degree; experiences are still not cut out to be transparent to introspection. Compare sensations of pain: they would not serve their biological purpose if there was always a real doubt about whether you had one.

[110] For various papers on images, see Ned Block, *Imagery*.

Apart from the intrinsic interest of the question, the fixation of image content can serve to add extra weight to the position I have taken on perceptual experience: for I suspect that strong externalism and a causal theory of content will seem even less attractive for images than for perceptions, at least prima facie.[111] There is not, I suspect, the same impulse to insist that content comes causally from the environment – probably because images are not given to us *as* caused by the environment. Images thus *seem* more autonomous with respect to the environment; we feel we could easily have these very images however the external environment was disposed – while our having these very experiences strikes us as more dependent on things outside us.[112] This feeling is, of course, not correct for perceptual experience (if I am right) – not, that is, as a claim about the very conditions of having a certain experiential content – but one can at least understand how it might *look* as if there were an asymmetry here between images and perceptions. But now if image content is acknowledged to be environment-independent, then this acknowledgement will act back on the case of perception, since it is hard to see how strong externalism *could* be true of perception but *not* true of imaging, given the intimate connections and similarities between these two types of mental state. How could it be that a subject could have an *image* of a square thing while living in an environment devoid of square things and yet could not have an *experience* as of a square thing? Wouldn't the cognitive machinery necessary and sufficient for the former achievement work also for the latter (when plugged into the general machinery proper to perception)? If you cannot run a twin earth case for images, then you cannot run one for perceptions – that seems an eminently reasonable conditional.

It may be of interest, however, to consider how one might *try* to construct a twin earth case for images, because there are empirical psychological results that provide a quite sharp refutation of the strong externalist's claim about images.[113] So, suppose I am a subject in an experiment on image-related tasks. I am asked to form an image of something and then to answer some question on the basis of the properties of this image: say, I am asked to imagine a certain building and to report on the shape of some portion of it. It takes me a certain amount of time to

---

[111] It is notable that image theories of intentionality are often opposed to causal theories; this opposition would not come naturally if images themselves positively invited a causal theory.

[112] The occurrence of images seems more subject to the will than the occurrence of perceptual experiences, which cannot simply be summoned to the mind. This may encourage the idea that the content of experiences must be fixed by something outside the subject. That would be a non-sequitur, but one can see how it might operate to favour a causal theory. No comparable temptation arises for images. Certainly I know of no theorist of content who has advanced environmentalism about the representational powers of images.

[113] I am thinking of experiments on tasks involving image rotation, e.g. R. Shepard and J. Metzler, 'Mental Rotation of Three-Dimensional Objects'.

reply (my 'response latency' as the psychologists say). Now imagine that on twin earth my internal double is also the subject of just such an experiment, but on twin earth the shape I am asked about on earth does not there exist. Suppose, instead, that some other shape entirely features in the causal history that leads up to my double's forming his image. He then gives his answer to the experimenter's question, and (by hypothesis) his response latency is the same as mine. My image of a certain shape and his image of another shape have led to identical response latencies, these being one kind of behavioural fact. But now suppose that it is a psychological *law* that the two imaged shapes in question have different response latencies associated with them – his should take twice as long to process as mine, say. Then the strong externalist claim conflicts with a psychological law that characterizes image-processing mechanisms in human beings. We have established that response latency is some function of the figural properties of images, and now we are told that for the twin-earthian this law breaks down – even though he is a normal human subject falling within the intended scope of the law. But this is absurd, since the processing mechanisms functioned identically in the two cases. To preserve the law we must reject strong externalism about image content. This is just a special case of the general point that strong externalism (about certain sorts of content) cannot properly respect behavioural dispositions. (Weak externalism about image content, however, does not have any of these troubles.) End of point about images.

Some mental contents are strongly external, and some are not. Natural kind concepts, for example, are, while observational concepts are not. But is there any system in this dichotomy? Is there any independently motivated division of concepts with which this one correlates? Well, there do seem to be two other (connected) distinctions which map pretty neatly onto the present distinction: the modular/central distinction, and the observational/theoretical distinction. To take the latter distinction first: if a concept belongs to the appearance of things, then it turns out to be only weakly external; while if it is a concept that goes beyond the appearances – as natural kind concepts do – then it gets to be strongly external as well. If we call concepts that in this way transcend appearance 'theoretical', then we can say that theoretical concepts are strongly external while untheoretical concepts are not. Thus the strong/weak distinction correlates with the 'inferentiality' or otherwise of concepts, i.e. whether they go beyond the appearances. The modular/central distinction is connected, since sensory modules are limited to observational contents, theoretical concepts being the business of the centre. So the representations handled by the modules, with their distinctive processing principles and functional architecture, are characteristically only weakly external; while the representations uniquely manipulated by the central system are characteristically strongly external. The mapping here may not be perfect, but it is close enough to be suggestive. Modular representations are more confined to the head than central representations. Perhaps the kind of processing that goes on in sensory modules requires that the implicated representations not be strongly external: the whole content of the representation needs to be fully *accessible* to the processes operating on it. However, I will not pursue this question further here, leaving it as a topic for (as they say) future research. The point I wanted to make is just that the strong/weak dichotomy is not arbitrary; it hangs together with other principled distinctions among concepts.

The difference between natural kind concepts and observational concepts, with respect to externality, seems to me not surprising when one examines the phenomenology associated with the two sorts of concept – the relation between phenomenal similarity and similarity of content. In the case of perceptual content and concepts tied to it, how the world seems fixes which properties are represented as true of it: when you have an experience as of a square thing it precisely seems to you that something is *square*. The represented property enters into the very phenomenology of the perceptual seeming. To specify what it is like to have the experience it is necessary to advert to the represented property.[114] Thus phenomenal similarity coincides with similarity of content. But it is not so with natural kind representations: distinct natural kind concepts can be applied to the world in a surrounding of phenomenal identity. The world could seem exactly the same to two subjects yet they apply distinct natural kind concepts to it. Natural kinds do not themselves enter into seemings, as shapes and colours do. There is no phenomenological kind such that to specify *it* one must advert to some natural kind. One does not, strictly, have experiences as of water (say), but only as of a colourless, tasteless liquid (which is why people on twin earth have the same experiences as us when they direct their minds towards their distinct liquid). This is what it *means* for some concepts to be observational and for others not to be. Now in view of this intuitive difference we can say the following: in the fixation of observational concepts phenomenology suffices, while in the case of natural kind concepts there is slack between phenomenology and content. This slack needs to be taken up by something, and environmental relations are what

---

[114] I would resist the idea that the features of experience that determine their subjective phenomenology are somehow nonrepresentational. This is true of bodily sensations such as pain, but it is a mistake to assimilate the phenomenology of perceptual experiences to this kind of 'raw feel': their phenomenology essentially involves (is constituted by) how they represent the external world. So their subjectivity is essentially world-involving. The objective property of being square is (partly) what confers a certain subjective character on experiences as of something square (along with the specific sense-modality in question, of course). Weak externalism is built into the very phenomenology of perceptual experience; the objective is a constituent of the subjective. Here is one respect in which the gulf between subjective and objective is not as impassable as might be supposed: some subjective facts cannot obtain without the existence of certain objective entities – indeed, they are individuated by reference to such entities.

take it up. But where there is no such slack there is no such need, and so environmental relations are not called for. Strong externalism steps in to top up phenomenology, as it were. If only phenomenological facts were relevant to fixing content, then we would have no natural kind concepts; but we could still have our full quota of observational concepts. Weak externalism is necessary if we are to characterize representational perceptual seemings, and hence attribute observational contents; but that is all the externalism we need in fixing these contents. But in the case of natural kind concepts weak externalism about seemings is not enough, since the seemings do not include or fix natural kinds. It is the existence of this representational slack that motivates strong externalism for natural kind concepts. Where the slack does not exist, notably for perceptual contents, neither does this motivation for strong externalism; it needs, therefore, to be motivated in some other way – and I have in effect argued that there *is* no other way. So the asymmetry between the two sorts of concept, with respect to externality, traces to a different relation to phenomenological seeming.[115]

Finally, the relativity of observationality should be noted. A property that enters the content of one creature's experience may not enter the content of another's. Observationality is not a feature of properties as such, but of properties in relation to a particular creature's sensory and cognitive apparatus. So we cannot take a particular property, say squareness, and say of *it* that any mental representation of it must be only weakly external; just as we cannot take a natural kind and say that any concept of *it* must be strongly external. It all depends how a given creature mentally represents these items. There could be a creature for whom squareness is a theoretical property, inferred (say) from (successive) perceptions of angles – this creature .never actually *sees* a full square shape. Similarly, there could be a creature for whom being water is an observable property: that is, in giving the content of the creature's perceptual experiences we have to specify water itself – what it is to be water. Thus if the creature had microscope eyes, then it might have experiences as of H_2O; and so we would have to advert to that very substance in order to specify the content of the experience. For this visually acute creature it is a matter of straightfoward observation that the glass contains water – no inference beyond the appearances is necessary. By contrast, the visually obtuse creature would need to bring a bit of theory to bear in order to tell that it was confronted with a square.

[115] Phenomenological content is fixed by the very structure of consciousness, so to speak; but this structure does not uniquely determine a natural kind content. In the former case, then, consciousness does not need to be boosted with environmental relations – as it does in the latter case. Natural kind contents do not come within the 'phenomenal field' of perceptual consciousness, but observational contents do (almost by definition). Perceptual consciousness can only present appearances, not the realities underlying appearances; these realities need then to be made into intentional objects in some other way, e.g. by means of causal relations to the environment.

How does this relativity bear on the question of strong externalism? In this way: its truth-value will be reversed for the two types of creature just mentioned. It will be true for the obtuse creature's concept of squareness, and it will be false for the acute creature's concept of water. To verify this, quickly run through a couple of twin earth cases for these creatures' concepts. In the case of the obtuse creature, vary the environmental shape while keeping the internal facts constant, including its perceptual seemings. I think it will be apparent that the concept shifts (assuming that behavioural dispositions are not fine-grained enough to pin the represented property down uniquely – just stipulate this). In the case of the acute creature, try doing the same with the substance perceived. This will require envisaging a visual illusion: XYZ molecules will have to look like H_2O molecules to the creature's double. In this case I think the plausible view is that the concept does not change: 'water' still refers to H_2O on twin earth. For it *seems* to the acute creature on twin earth there that it is surrounded by H_2O molecules, and this supplies all that is necessary for locking the reference of 'water' onto water. If the real essence of a natural kind enters into a creature's perceptual experience, then there is enough richness in the experience to single out a unique natural kind – so varying the environment will not override the dictates of the experience. (Of course there may be some vagueness as to whether a certain property enters a creature's experience directly, so that observationality is not a sharp concept. If so, there will be cases in which it is a vague or indeterminate matter whether strong externalism is true for the concept in question. But this vagueness does not – it should go without saying – undermine the distinction.) In sum, the creature-relativity of observability implies a like relativity in the thesis of strong externalism: it must always concern the environmental determination of a concept *with respect to* a kind of creature. Normally this relativity is implicit in the specification of the concept, but I think it is conducive to clarity to acknowledge it explicitly.

That concludes my discussion of strong externalism about perceptual content. I have discussed it at some length because of the theoretical centrality of perceptual content, as well as because of its intrinsic interest. Perceptual representation is arguably the most basic way in which the mind represents the world; it underlies all the other ways. So if I am right that strong externalism is not true of perceptual content, then the most basic of the mind's representative capacities is not subject to environmental individuation. This puts in proper perspective the cases for which strong externalism *is* true.

I proceed now to assessing the upshot of our results so far for a number of issues to which externalism has been supposed relevant.

5 *The philosophical bearing of externalism*   I argued for three main claims in the previous section: that strong externalism is true of only a proper subset of mental contents, and these not the most basic; that weak externalism is true of all representational contents, no matter what their subject matter; and that there are some mental phenomena – the nonrepresentational kinds – for which not even weak externalism is true. We can already see, then, that the mind is not individuatively monolithic, that mental kinds are of fundamentally different kinds. We cannot generalize from one sort of mental state to all the others; there is no common essence here. What I want to do now is bring this mixed picture to bear on four issues: substantialism, physicalism, scepticism and psychological explanation.

(i) *Externalism and substantialism*   Earlier (in section 3) I suggested that if total externalism were true of the mind then it could not be a substance; alternatively, mental attributes could not be substance-conferring attributes. This is because externalism conflicts with the idea that the mind is autonomous (or self-subsistent) and exclusive (has impermeable boundaries). I shall not repeat the arguments I gave for this conditional contention. My task now is to determine the bearing upon substantialism of what has emerged as the *correct* version of externalism – its scope and limits. We can then finally declare whether or not the mind *is* a substance.

I think that the results of section 4 do establish that the mind is not a substance: the final composite conception of the mind is still a conception on which substantialism is false; its externalist component is enough to give this result. I anticipate two grounds of resistance to this conclusion; they both stem from regarding total strong externalism as the *only* truly anti-substantialist thesis from among the range of theses we have considered. The thought here would be this: only if *every* mental feature – including things like pains and character traits, as well as items such as perceptual experiences – were individuated by relations to the actual environment could it follow that the mind lacks the intrinsic properties needed to confer substancehood on it, since to qualify for that status the mind requires merely that *some* of its properties be instantiable independently of other substances, and only *total* strong externalism excludes that weak existential claim. Not *all* of a substance's properties need to be intrinsic, so the mind might qualify as a substance in virtue of a proper subset of its properties, viz. those that are not strongly external – which, by my own showing, are numerous and basic.[116]

---

[116] This would be the analogue of a 'semi-relational' view of space (or time): I mean, a view which regarded some of the structure of space as constituted by material objects but some as not so constituted – say, its three-dimensionality as nonrelational and its Euclidean geometry as relational. (I am not saying this would be a plausible or even a coherent view.) Such a mixed view would hold that space is partially autonomous with respect to objects, so that subtracting the objects would destroy

Now, as I said, this line of argument has two prongs: that weak externalism is not itself anti-substantialist, and that anyway there are other mental states that are not even weakly external. Let us consider these two prongs one at a time. Suppose, for a moment, that strong externalism were universally false; or consider a type of mind to which it had no application. Take it, that is, that only weak externalism is true of minds. Then it would certainly be correct to say that the mind is not *environment*-dependent, that the existence of its mental states does not depend upon causal or other relations with things around the subject. But it would not follow – and it would not be true – that the mind is not *existence*-dependent with respect to items in the world. Whether these worldly items are particulars or universals, weak externalism still makes the mind dependent upon what exists beyond the subject: particulars at some spatial distance, or objective properties that particulars (may) instantiate.[117] (Note that this latter

some of its properties while preserving others. Would this intermediate conception still imply that space is not substantival? It depends how crucial to the essence of space we take the autonomous properties to be: if the autonomous properties are few and incidental, then the essential nature of space will not be absolute and substantival; if they are many and central, then the essential nature of space can be pulled apart from what it materially contains. Presumably if the three-dimensionality of space were object-dependent, this would be enough to undermine a substantival interpretation of space – even if other spatial properties could obtain independently of objects. I am suggesting that something like this is true of the mind: the essential structure of the mind is determined by the intentionality of its states, so that if this structure is externally fixed the mind is relational to its core. Taking away the extrinsic content of mental states is thus like taking away the three-dimensionality of space (or the direction and ordering of time). So I think that a double aspect account of content, of the kind defended in my 'The Structure of Content', is still an account on which the externalist aspect undermines the substantialist conception of the mind – despite the presence of a further intrinsic aspect. A mind is something that has representational states, and there *are* no such states if *only* the intrinsic aspect is present – only 'place-holders' for such states.

[117] Putting the point in Plato's way may help to underline it, put it into BOLD. There is the world of minds and their states, and there is the abstract nonmental world of universals which exists independently of minds. Objects participate in this latter world by instantiating properties, and minds hook up to it by having thoughts in which these properties occur. So minds are shot through with these objective entities, structured by their relations to the Platonic world. But then minds instantiate their characteristic properties by standing in certain relations to properties that they do not themselves instantiate (representing is not the same as instantiating), and they cannot have these characteristic properties unless those other properties exist. No substance has this dual relation with the world of universals, this double dependence. Combining Plato with Brentano: the essence of mind (what distinguishes the mind from other things) is its 'directedness' onto the world of universals (as well as particulars). The mental is thus made to depend upon the nonmental. And if the existence conditions of properties are made to require their instantiation (the Aristotelian view), then thoughts aimed at the world of universals may fail to reach their target, thus producing abortive thoughts – thought-attempts that fail to concern any possible state of affairs. Concepts without properties are empty – not real concepts – and so the Aristotelian view puts concepts under the same risk of nonexistence as properties must suffer. If solipsism were true, along with Aristotelianism and externalism, then no would-be thought would manage to be a real thought and there would only be a would-be mind not a real mind (minds being things that are capable of having thoughts of a certain range and richness). If

dependence is not a dependence upon properties that the mind *itself* can instantiate. The mind does not – generally – instantiate the properties it represents. Perhaps the temptation to suppose that it does, so that an impression of red (say) is said to be a red impression, helps explain why substantialism has seemed so plausible to many philosophers: for if the mind *has* the properties it represents, then of course it will be metaphysically *just* like a material substance. So let us be very clear in our own minds that this temptation is a big mistake.) Therefore weak externalism conflicts with autonomy and exclusiveness. Perhaps the clearest case of this conflict is in respect of thoughts about the mental states of others; for in this case we have items of the *same kind* as the thought itself entering the content of the thought as its propositional constituents. Weak externalism welcomes worldly items as constituents of thoughts and perceptions just as much as strong externalism; *how* they come to be constituents is of secondary importance, so far as the issue of substantialism is concerned. Internalism is what is required for substantialism, but weak externalism directly contradicts internalism. I therefore think that the first prong of the objection is ineffectual.

How incisive is the second prong? The claim will be that, just as a material substance has both intrinsic and relational properties, the former qualifying it as a substance, so the properties of mind bifurcate in this way – and the intrinsic properties of mind qualify it as a substance equally. This suggestion needs delicate handling. The intrinsic properties in question are bodily sensations, traits of character, the nonrepresentational aspect of emotions and any wholly intrinsic features there may be to representational states. The question, in effect, is whether *these* can play the substance-conferring role played by intrinsic primary qualities in the case of material substances. I do not know of any absolutely knock-down reply to the claim that they can, but I think there are a number of considerations which tell strongly against the idea. The fundamental point to insist on is that representational states really are the characteristic and definitive properties of what we call 'mind'. This is essentially Brentano's thesis that the essence of mind is intentionality; or again, Descartes' doctrine that thought is the essential attribute of mind. We do speak of other sorts of state as 'mental', but there is an element of courtesy or secondariness about this. A

no particulars, then no properties; but if no properties, then no concepts; but if no concepts, then no minds with thoughts. The idea that there could be nothing but a mind is thus mistaken if we combine externalism with the Aristotelian view. The only thoughts available to such a being would be ones that contained properties that being itself instantiated – all the rest would be sham. In particular, there would not even be perfectly general thoughts containing concepts potentially applicable to material particulars. In this way we get the anti-solipsist consequences of strong causal externalism without going beyond weak externalism. (Of course, we need the Aristotelian view to get this result – and it is not an uncontroversial view. I am not saying I agree with it: but disputing it is what is necessary in order to rebut the above argument – an interesting result.)

creature with only bodily sensations, say, would not be naturally described as having a mind; while a creature with only thoughts seems the paradigm of a minded being. Presumably this is why we tend to speak of pains (say), not as states of the mind, but as states of the body. Similarly, it sounds odd to describe traits of character as properly 'states of mind'. And any purely internal aspects of representational states that there might be would hardly count as conferring mindedness on a creature in the *absence* of the associated representational contents. These kinds of intrinsic state thus seem too accidental to the notion of mind, and are too exiguous in themselves, to perform the role played by primary qualities in the case of material substances. We feel that intrinsic primary qualities really do form the *core* of our idea of a material object, but those nonrepresentational features of mind do not analogously form the core of our idea of a mind. The definitive features of mind are representational, whether they are perceptual states or propositional attitudes, and these are inherently incapable of acting like primary qualities of material substances. So the core of mind is not substantial. The intrinsicness of *some* (so-called) mental states is not going to overturn the ontological classification imposed by these central and definitive mental features. I therefore conclude that anti-substantialism about the mind is not seriously threatened by the second prong either, despite superficial appearances. We may thus finally declare that the mind is not a substance, and this because of externalism. All we need to do now is live with this result.[118]

(ii) *Externalism and physicalism* Any conception of the physical basis of mental states must be informed by a correct analysis of the individuation conditions of those states. Unless we know what it *is* to have a certain mental state, we cannot determine the form of its physical substrate. The contours of the physical bases of mental states must be moulded according to the shape of the mental states so based. My question, then, is how the physical basis must be sculpted in order to provide for externalism.

What seems immediately clear is that the physical basis cannot be located wholly within the head. We cannot site the mind at the place of the brain, and we cannot make intrinsic brain states the (full) basis of representational mental states. Suppose we tried simply to identify the mind with the brain: that is, suppose we count 'x's mind' as a singular term like 'x's brain', and then assert 'x's mind = x's brain'. Then we should run up against the following problem: x's mind is essentially not a substance, whereas x's brain essentially is a substance; but then, by Leibniz's law, they cannot be identical. Mind and brain differ in their

---

[118] A word of advice on how to live with it: do not use your imagination to try to get a grip on the correct view, because your imagination is too dominated by the world of perceptible substances. Think of relationalism about space and tell yourself it's a bit like that. On no account model your conception of mind on the brain. And don't think it is going to be easy to live with it.

metaphysical category, so there can be no identifying them. Nor, I think, is this objection met by weakening the identity thesis to a claim of exhaustive constitution – saying that the brain constitutes the mind in rather the way a piece of bronze constitutes a statue. For, though Leibniz's law then becomes inapplicable, we will still have the transmission of *some* properties through the constitution relation, and one of them is precisely what we do not want, namely substancehood. Surely if X is wholly constituted by Y and Y is a substance, then X is a substance – as with the statue and the piece of bronze. But the brain is a substance and the mind is not, so the one cannot wholly constitute the other. The relation between minds and brains is going to have to be a lot less intimate than the relations of identity and constitution can allow. Intuitively, the problem is that the characteristic and definitive features of the brain are different in kind (in category) from those of the mind – the former being intrinsic, the latter extrinsic. This is also what prevents us identifying representational mental states with intrinsic brain states: these mental states are not, as brain states literally are, situated within the head. A modal argument quickly puts paid to any hopes of identification here: you could have the same brain states in a world in which the objects of the corresponding mental states did not exist, but you could not have those mental states in such a world – Leibniz's law again delivers the nonidentity result. Nor will retreating to a constitution thesis help: for if brain states wholly constitute mental states, then it looks as if mental states will have to exist in any world in which their constitutive brain states exist – but this will be false of the worlds in which the objects of the mental states do not exist. What has been omitted are the extrinsic relations definitive of the mental states. Intrinsic (in the head) physicalism cannot then do justice to externalism about the mind.[119]

However, there is no reason that I can see why physicalism *has* to assume this intrinsicalist form; it can happily go extrinsic. Physicalism does not have to be brain-centred; there are plenty of other physical facts in the world. Consider

[119] Strictly, there are a number of qualifications and caveats that need to be made to these remarks, but I think they are fairly obvious and routine. See Burge, 'Individualism and the Mental' for a more extended discussion; also my 'Philosophical Materialism'.

Awareness of the need to accommodate external determinants of thought within physicalism is present in the following remarks from Thomas Nagel's (early) 'Physicalism': 'Many intensional predicates do not just ascribe a condition to the person himself but have implications about the rest of the world and his relation to it. Physicalism will of course not require that these be identical simply with states of the person's body, narrowly conceived. An obvious case is that of knowledge, which implies not only the truth of what is known but also a special relation between this and the knower. Intentions, thoughts, and desires may also imply a context, a relation with things outside the person. The thesis that all states of a person are states of his body therefore requires a liberal conception of what constitutes a state – one which will admit relational attributes' (p. 111). In retrospect, at least, this passage contains the key idea of what later became externalism about content. (I am grateful to Anita Avramides for drawing this passage to my attention.)

physicalism about the perception relation. What it is, physically, to (for example) see an object cannot consist simply in intrinsic physical states of the perceiver, since seeing requires the holding of a (causal) relation to the seen object. But this relation can be described physically: it consists in the transmission of light from the object to the eyes. Combining this physical relation with the underlying neural processes gives a physical basis with the right sort of structure: *it* goes where seeing goes – right out to the object. And a similar story could presumably be told about knowledge and remembering, which also reach out into the world. There is clearly nothing anti-physicalist about invoking physical relations between the organism and the physical world – of course there isn't. But then the physicalistic externalist can make the same sort of move, taking perception as his model. The only interesting question is how precisely the physical relations in question are to be characterized. No consideration of principle frustrates the externalist physicalist. Relationality is not in itself a problem.

How does the distinction between strongly and weakly external mental states bear upon the character of the underlying physical relations? As we have just seen, the strong kind of externality poses no new problem. Basically, this is a matter of causal relations to the environment, relations of the same general kind as underlie the perception relation: a given natural kind, say, makes a physical impact on our sense organs and so forth, and we end up with thoughts concerning that natural kind.[120] The physical relations to the environment will be different on earth and twin earth, so we can readily explain the difference of content by reference to these physical differences. But weak externalism does, I believe, introduce a new puzzle for the physicalist to deal with. Consider a representational state, say a perceptual experience, whose content is specified by reference to a property with which the perceiver has never been in causal contact. It is of the essence of that state that it should involve a relation to a certain (external) property – let it be our old friend squareness again. But what, physically, might that relation consist in? It cannot consist in the kinds of physical relations involved when a perceiver actually *sees* a square object – the instantiated property interacting with light in a certain way and a reflected pattern of light striking the retinae as a result. For this perceiver has never stood in such causal-physical relations to instances of squareness. So physicalism about merely weakly external mental states cannot follow the model of perception; it cannot exploit physically describable causal relations to the property represented. The brain in a vat provides an extreme and vivid set-up in which such a theory would be manifestly inapplicable. If the envatted brain can have all the weakly external mental states we have, then *none* of these can be explained in terms of extrinsic causal-physical

---

[120] This is not intended as any kind of physicalist analysis of having such a concept. I am merely sketching the shape of the realizing physical basis of environmental determination.

interactions with the represented properties. It looks as if we are going to need a radical rethink about the kinds of physical relations we can rely on invoking.

I suggest that we turn to behavioural facts about the subject. What we need are behavioural descriptions that make reference to the property represented by the mental state: that is, we need weakly external behavioural descriptions. Then we can say that behaviour so described provides the physical basis of the mental state in question. We have more than one option here. Either we can describe the behaviour in terms of its spatial properties, or we can introduce more functionally loaded descriptions. On the first option, we hold that the physical basis of an experience as of a square thing consists in being disposed to move in some sort of squarewise path (given other mental states, of course). This proposal might take the form of a standard functionalist definition in which the definiens contains behavioural descriptions embedding predicates of external objects.[121] Alternatively, we might wish to boost the behavioural descriptions with teleological or functional (not in the sense of 'functional' just used) concepts: behaviour whose biological function it is to promote survival in the face of square things – or some such. Assuming that the notion of biological function is physicalistically acceptable, this would give us (if it were correct) a suitable physical relation to the property of squareness – the relation, in brief, of *adaptiveness to*.[122] This gives us a richer kind of physicalism than the kinds we usually get: teleological physicalism (as we might call it) takes biology seriously, regarding it as the proper home of the kinds of physical facts that underlie mentality. And I myself would urge that this is the right approach to adopt quite independently of coping physically with weakly external content. At any rate, it seems that the flexible physicalist has the resources to accommodate relations to properties that do not essentially involve the physical *impingement* of the property on the organism. The property comes in, rather, as what the organism's behaviour is designed to adapt *to*.

From a formal or structural point of view, we might compare weakly external content with measurement (a comparison that will bulk large in chapter 2 and 3).[123] In attributions of mental content we assign some (propositionally

[121] So the basis of an experience of square is specified as 'some state of the perceiver's nervous system that disposes her to move in ways geared to square things'. More technically, we take the Ramsey sentence of a theory that relates the organism's internal states to the property of being square. Such a definition might equally be fulfilled by a brain in a vat: we just make the dispositions conditional on having a body (of a certain sort). Basically, the idea is to relate the contentful state to a discriminatory ability on the part of the perceiver, where the ability is essentially specified in terms of the properties it discriminates. Again, this is not a reductive analysis; it simply says what physical facts are 'correlated' with certain kinds of content.

[122] Or what Ruth Millikan calls 'relational proper function': see her *Language, Thought and Other Biological Categories*. I shall be discussing this notion more fully in chapter 2.

[123] For a discussion of propositions as indices see Brian Loar, *Mind and Meaning*. My idea is slightly different, though, since I am concerned to let the constituents of propositions be the base

embedded) object or property to the subject as a way of mapping out his psychology, thus modelling his mind in a space of nonmental items. In attributions of size or distance or temperature we assign some number to the measured object as a way of mapping the relations between objects (or between properties of a single object), thus modelling them in a space of nonphysical (because abstract) items. Now we can ask what the physical basis of both sorts of assignment consists in; and in neither case can we appeal to causal impingement, since neither numbers nor properties (in the merely weakly external case) impinge upon the objects to which they are assigned. We cannot, for example, say what it is physically for a glass of water to be 62 degrees centigrade (to be in that measurement relation to the number 62) in terms of the number's causal impact on the glass of water. Nor would we dream of trying to say this. Rather, we appeal to physical facts about the water and the way these facts are conventionally coded in a numerical structure. We do not, then, worry unduly about whether it is possible to be a physicalist about the property of being 62 degrees centigrade.[124] Somewhat similarly, we need to explain the assignment of (propositionally embedded) external items to mental states in noncausal terms, appealing instead to the physical facts about the subject that make a given assignment the right one. And, as I have suggested, these will be behavioural facts, plausibly teleological in character, which incorporate relations to the assigned property. In both cases we see that there are more ways to be a relational physicalist than by relying upon straightforward causal relations between the relata involved in the fact to be physically explained. It seems to me, then, that we can find physical facts moulded into the right shape to accommodate externalism. There need be nothing physically mysterious about externality *as such*.

(iii) *Externalism and scepticism* One form of scepticism, perhaps the most basic, starts from the assumption that how things seem and how they really are are logically independent questions. There is no deductive bridge from one to the other, either in the particular case or generally. The sceptic then goes on to claim that we cannot rationally rule out, on the basis of how things seem, a range of distinct logical possibilities concerning how they really are, all of which are incompatible with what we take ourselves to know about reality − and that accordingly we do not know what we take ourselves to know. The standard ways of trying to defeat this simple-seeming sceptical argument are either to deny that we cannot rationally rule out the rival possibilities or to allow this but deny that it

indices, these being objects and properties and the like. Worldly items make up the coordinate system we apply to states of mind (though they need a propositional context in order to do so). The 'parameters' of mind are objective things. We get a fix on a contentful state by relating it to its worldly parameters − rather as we fix a position in space by means of mathematical coordinates.

[124] See Hartry Field, 'Mental Representation', the appendix.

follows that we do not know what we take ourselves to know. The externalist strategy, however, is to question what the argument – and these replies to it – assume, namely that seemings and realities can logically come apart in the way envisaged.[125] The sceptic's assumption is that one could enjoy precisely the seemings one does in fact enjoy even if one had never been in environmental contact with realities of the kind one's seemings purport to represent. Thus one could have just *these* experiences and beliefs and yet be floating damply and isolatedly in a vat, so long as something put one's brain into the same internal states it is now in (implanted electrodes or some such). But the strong externalist denies precisely that; he ties one's representational contents down to one's actual environment, so that there is no *possibility* of experiencing all *this* unless reality is like *that*. Strong externalism makes it a strictly necessary condition of having a certain range of seemings that one's environment be a certain way, the way those seemings generally represent it; so, conversely, it is strictly sufficient for one's environment being a certain way that one has a certain range of seemings. Moreover, this strict sufficiency has been established by a priori philosophical argument, on the basis of the principles of individuation of representational contents, and so it is licit to move inferentially from truths about the content of one's mental states to truths about the external world – the move is, indeed, deductive. The link between truths about appearances and truths about realities is conceptual and necessary, despite the agreed distinctness of the two realms. Strong individuation dependence thus blocks the crucial starting assumption of the sceptic – that more than one kind of environment is logically compatible with how things seem with respect to the environment. It is not, of course, that only one kind of environment *is* logically possible; it is rather that, *given* a fixation of contents, a unique environment is thereby determined. So *whatever* environment a subject found himself in, and however internally like a subject placed in another environment he was, he would necessarily have representational contents that (generally) reflected how things are around him. According to the strong externalist, we can all now say, 'No matter which logically possible environment I am in – even the brain in a vat environment – I know that my experiences do not systematically mislead me, for they have a content that is fixed by the facts of that environment, *whichever* one it may be. How things are cannot then be other than how they seem.' This style of argument is commonly directed against scepticism regarding the external world, but its form can be deployed also against the sceptic about other minds. Suppose that strong externalism about mental concepts is true. Then my mental concepts are logically (individuatively) tied to

---

[125] See Putnam's discussion of externalism and the brain in a vat in *Reason, Truth and History*. Davidson takes a similar line in 'A Coherence Theory of Truth and Knowledge', though he differs from Putnam in important respects.

the actual experiences of those around me: whatever they are, so my concepts must represent them. There is indeed a whole range of distinct logical possibilities concerning these experiences – among them the possibility that I am surrounded by insentient and unsapient robots – but whichever of these is in fact realized my concepts are necessarily fixed by it. Thus my beliefs about (or perceptions of) other minds are guaranteed to match whatever is in fact true of them, at least by and large. Again, it is the starting assumption of logical independence (between my third-person beliefs and your mental states) that this anti-sceptical strong externalist challenges.

This is a bold and exciting line of argument against the sceptic. It suggests that epistemology has fretted at the cruel feet of the sceptic for so long because it has never enquired into the conditions of mental representation. Epistemology needed the philosophy of mind (and language) in order to rid itself of its sceptical problems. Tacitly assuming an internalist theory of content-determination, it was powerless to counter the sceptic's impregnable-seeming argument. But adopting the correct externalist theory, on grounds quite independent of scepticism, yields the bonus of a refutation of that persistent epistemological irritation. At last we have a *principled* reason for banishing the sceptic! However, delightful as such banishment would undoubtedly be, I do not believe that externalism can make it proper and legal. Scepticism survives the externalist threat. I shall now make four criticisms of it, sprinkling enough cold water to dampen the externalist's excitement.

Let me first agree that the argument, as I have presented it, is valid: it does follow from strong externalism about seemings that truths about reality may be inferred deductively and a priori from truths about the content of experience. If I have an experience as of a square thing, then it *follows* (if strong externalism is true) that there are square things in my environment and that I have had experience of them. However, as a refutation of scepticism, the mere validity of this inference is obviously not enough. First, and most obviously, the argument needs to be sound – the premises have also to be true. But I have spent the better part of this chapter arguing that strong externalism is *false* of perceptual content, so the key premise in the argument fails.[126] And the truth of weak externalism does not sustain the argument, since it does not entail the necessary causal

---

[126] Someone might accept that strong externalism is false for perceptual content but deny that perceptual experiences play any epistemic role in justifying our beliefs about the external world, holding that strong externalism is true of all beliefs that do play such an epistemic role – so what we believe must be largely true though our experiences can be as illusory as you like. Something like this seems to be Davidson's position in 'A Coherence Theory of Truth and Knowledge'. I have criticized this position in 'Radical Interpretation and Epistemology'. Briefly, I think it is impossible to sunder what is believed about the world from how it is experienced; the relation between them is normative and justificatory.

condition on perceptual content exploited by the strong externalist argument. The truth of an attribution of perceptual content may indeed have implications for the subject's behavioural dispositions, and so entail something that goes beyond the experiences themselves, but these implications peter out before we get to any truths about the environment beyond the subject – they tell us nothing about the *veridicality* of the experiences in question. And the same goes for mental concepts and scepticism about other minds: we rejected the strong externalist thesis for these concepts too, and so opened up the logical gap upon which the sceptical possibilities trade.

Second, the concepts for which strong externalism is true do not afford even a local vindication of the externalist's anti-sceptical argument. Go back for a moment to individual and natural kind concepts: does it follow from strong externalism that beliefs involving such concepts must be generally true? When I believe that there is water in the oceans or that this cup is white am I guaranteed to be correct in what I believe? Clearly not, since strong externalism applies to the possession of particular concepts not to the propositions in which these concepts occur. Even if every concept makng up a particular belief were strongly external, it still would not follow that the way those concepts are combined yields a true belief. All that strong externalism could deliver in the way of environmental truths would be whatever followed from the fact that a particular natural kind or individual concept was possessed by someone: and this will be no more than the environmental *existence* of a certain natural kind or individual. Thus from the fact that I have the concept *water* it follows (granted strong externalism) that there is water somewhere in my environment. But that is just about all that follows; certainly we cannot make any comparable inferences from my other *water*-involving beliefs. It may reasonably be doubted whether a thesis so circumscribed in its scope could have any interest as a general answer to the sceptic. The sceptic may indeed be quite happy to concede this tiny victory to the externalist, secure in the knowledge that all the other battles – and hence the war – are going his way.

Third, even if strong externalism were universally true, it is powerless against a slightly modified sceptical argument – unless, that is, it is made implausibly extreme. Strong externalism fixes content by way of historically established causal connections with the environment – how mental states originally got to have their content. It does not suppose that the contents of a subject's mind will suddenly change if a new environment takes the place of the old: the content conferred by the old environment will linger on. But then the following possibility must be faced: last night while I slept I was whisked away to another galaxy where I was hooked up to electrodes that feed in the same neural inputs as I typically receive when I sit at my desk and write, as well as those corresponding to all my other usual activities. The electrodes will then elicit internal states that were historically connected with the usual environmental things, not with electrode stimulation. So the moderate strong externalist will say that my contents will stay the same – the world will seem the same to me – when I wake up in my new environment. Perhaps in due course my seemings will acquire a different kind of content (it depends on the degree of *plasticity* allowed by the strong externalist), but to begin with at least they will remain as they were on earth. And now, of course, the sceptic sees his chance. For he will argue that nothing in my experience can exclude this possibility: I might *now* be on the receiving end of those electrodes. In other words, there is no entailment from '*now* I have these experiences' to '*now* the world is thus and so'; at best we have only 'at *some* (formative) time the world was thus and so'. But then I cannot now know that my environment is *currently* as I take it to be; and this radically conflicts with what I customarily take to be my present epistemological position. (The same argument can be given in respect of knowledge of other minds.) On each day that I exist I cannot know that my environment is then as it seems, since it is always logically possible that I have been shifted to a new environment just when my experiences are adjusting their content to the old one. There are, at best, only limited periods when things are really as they seem – the times at which my contents are being established; for the rest of the time there may be radical mismatch. This is not, I take it, a very impressive anti-sceptical result. The entire epistemological thrust of the sceptic's argument is left intact by this position, it seems to me. We are about as badly off epistemologically as we ever were. The only way to strengthen the anti-sceptical upshot of strong externalism is to adopt a very extreme version of the thesis, namely that a change of environment produces an *instantaneous* switch of contents. As soon as I wake up in that other galaxy I start seeming to see (and in fact seeing) electrodes not furniture; despite the complete identity of my internal states, it instantly seems to me that things are not as they were. It is enough for a radical change of content that a given (constant) internal state be elicited just *once* by a new outside stimulus. This is, of course, a deeply implausible thesis with no real theoretical motivation behind it, and I take it that it will attract precisely no one. But it is what is required if the sceptic is to be prevented from raising his damaging sceptical possibility. Besides, this extreme thesis lands the strong externalist squarely with the next severe problem.

This fourth difficulty is that the price of defeating scepticism about the external world (or other minds) is scepticism about one's own mind. The sceptical focus merely gets shifted to a new place, where it does not belong. This is a point that has come up before (in my discussion of introspection and transparency in section 4), so I do not need to repeat what I said there. The point, it will be recalled, is that the content of experience becomes as epistemologically inaccessible to the subject as the sceptic claimed the environment to be. If I am a brain in a vat, then that is how it seems to me; but I cannot *tell* if that is how it seems to me, since I cannot tell if I am a brain in a vat. I am as ignorant of my representational contents as I am of the reality those contents purport to represent. I have therefore to admit that there are a large number of logical possibilities about how my experience currently represents the world and that I am powerless to choose among them. Asked to select which among these is the true way things seem to me, I have to confess that I am clueless. If I could select the true description of reality, *then* I could tell you how things seem to me – what my perceptual phenomenology is – but that is precisely what I cannot do. My experience becomes as opaque to me as the world outside me, as subject to Cartesian doubt as it is. A thick veil has thus been drawn between the knowing subject and his own sensory states.[127] Those states have been linked to reality, but they have in consequence lost their link with the subject. The epistemological distance between the subject and the world has been projected inwards. The case is somewhat analogous to scepticism about testimony and an externalist reply to such scepticism. The sceptic questions my right to rely on the testimony of others, pointing out that things might be quite other than my informant tells me. The externalist replies that there is nothing to worry about since *however* things are they fix the content of what my informant says. The sceptic then redirects his misgivings towards what the informant says: he wants to know how I can rule out all the alternative semantic possibilities concerning the content of my informant's utterances. For I can only know *what* he says, and hence use his assertions as reliable indicators of how the world really is, if I *already* know how the world really is. Thus the externalist makes no real progress with the original sceptical challenge, while adding a new sceptical problem to the old one, viz. scepticism about semantic content itself. In a similar way, strong externalism about seeming makes introspection as cut off from content as content originally was from the world (according to the sceptic). Essentially the same epistemological problem remains, only now it operates at another level.

It may be tempting now to try to reverse this argument. Instead of agreeing that our experience is opaque to us because our environment is, why not declare our environment transparent because our experience is! That is, I now know with certainty exactly how things seem to me – this is fully transparent to introspection – so I now know with equal certainty whatever is a conceptual precondition of this seeming, namely that my environment is thus and so. Since I am infallible in my belief that I have experiences as of red round objects, I am equally infallible

---

[127] I am using the metaphor of a veil in an epistemic sense, not a perceptual sense; I am saying that our reasons for crediting ourselves with particular experiences become as inconclusive and liable to error as our reasons for forming beliefs about the external world.

in my belief that there *are* red round objects in my environment with which I have been in causal-epistemic contact. So if a sceptic challenges me to rule out the possibility that all my experiences as of red round objects are illusions, and that I am in reality an isolated brain in a vat, then I can reply that this *could* not be so given the character of my experience: for I am infallible about this, and hence about what it entails. I can therefore be absolutely certain, with all the certainty Descartes ever required, that I am not being radically deceived about the world (or about other minds). I can be as secure in my worldly beliefs (at least generally) as I am about my own pains or the fact that I am a thinker. Not even God, with all his infinite ingenuity and power, could trick me into representing the general nature of my environment incorrectly; for he cannot trick me into forming false beliefs about how things *seem* to me, and I can *deduce* from this how reality really is, by a priori philosophical reflection on the individuation of content. In effect, I can achieve the anti-sceptical result Descartes needed God to vouchsafe by exploiting considerations about what determines content. Ah, the wonders of analytical philosophy!

It is an optimistic man who believes that Cartesian scepticism may be refuted in this way. To believe that it can be so refuted is to believe (in effect) that we can know the external world (or other minds) by *introspection*: we can use introspection (plus a philosophical theory) to determine what it has always been supposed to be the office of perception to determine. Consider singular thoughts about perceptible material objects. The optimistic thesis is that simply by introspecting I can tell whether (say) there is a cup in front of me – because I am infallible about the content of my thought and this content *includes* a particular cup. To put it mildly, it is surely preferable to go the other way and allow that I am fallible *both* about the cup *and* about the existence of my thought about it. Equally, I think, we should dismiss the suggestion that the givenness of my perceptual experience permits me to infer with certainty what *kinds* of objects are contained in my environment; it would surely be better (though still not good) to give up on the transparency of experience. This optimistic reply to the sceptic is altogether too cheap and easy. And anyway it relies on strong externalism about seeming, which we have seen to be false on independent grounds.

There are two contrasting attitudes that may to taken towards philosophical scepticism. One is that it is just an irritating conundrum, based on conceptual confusion, entailing ludicrous consequences; accordingly, the proper response to it is a diagnostic sneer. The other attitude is that scepticism reveals something deep and permanent about our epistemological predicament, that it is indeed already latent in our epistemic practices, however disturbing to those practices its results may prove to be; accordingly, the proper response to it is respectful containment, if that is at all possible, or rueful acceptance, if containment is not possible. I myself incline towards the latter attitude.[128] The appearance/reality divide seems to me genuine and hard to bridge, and this cannot but shake our customary epistemological complacency. I am therefore not eager to embrace a philosophical theory that makes scepticism look *obviously* misguided or misconceived, as externalism does (and verificationism did). We should not, I think, rush into accepting any philosophical theory that makes scepticism go quickly away, counting it a merit of the theory that it shows the sceptic up as a sophist and a dim-wit. Rather, we should view with considerable reserve any theory that has such immediately anti-sceptical consequences, for it is liable to have underestimated the problematic nature of our true epistemological predicament. And especially so if the theory offers no convincing story about how scepticism could have *seemed* so convincing in the first place. What I have just been arguing is that the force of scepticism is not diminished by the correct version of externalism. The sceptic was not arguing from a mistaken theory of content, after all. He was not wrong about the fundamental contingency of the link between appearance and reality. His argument is thus as good as it has always seemed.

To allow that the sceptic's putative possibilities are genuinely logically possible is not to question the correctness of 'naive realism' as a theory of perception. For naive realism is a thesis about the relation between experience and object *when the object is there to be perceived*. I do not question the thesis that when (as we say) we see an object our experience represents it as having the very objective properties that it in fact has; I do not, that is, question the 'directness' of perceptual acquaintance. Knowing that the perception relation holds is one thing; its correct analysis is quite another. I do not, therefore, believe that strong externalism is required for naive realism. Causal links are necessary between features of experience and properties in order that the one should count as a *perceiving* of the other, but it does not follow – and is false – that such links are necessary if experience is to have the representational features involved in such causal interactions. Seeing is necessarily causal, visually representing is not. What I do believe, however, is that naive realism requires *weak* externalism. This is because naive realism requires a certain identity thesis: namely, between what fixes the content of experience and the objective properties of perceptible things. Weak externalism delivers this identity thesis, because it says that specifying the content of experience involves reference to the very same items (viz. properties) as external objects may instantiate. Now what I want to claim is that only such an identity thesis can sustain naive realism; and since this thesis is essentially equivalent to weak externalism, we can have naive realism only if we can take

[128] Those with similar inclinations include Barry Stroud, *The Significance of Philosophical Scepticism*, and Thomas Nagel, *The View From Nowhere*.

weak externalism. The intuitive point here is that direct experience of propertied objects requires that how things (phenomenologically) seem *incorporate* how they objectively are; there must be no gap between the content of experience and objective properties of things. How things seem must be precisely as they are if direct perception is to be possible. Experience must represent objects *as* having the very objective properties that the objects themselves have, nothing less. But then I think it follows that naive realism depends upon the identity thesis definitive of weak externalism. Suppose weak externalism were not true, so that the content of experience could be specified otherwise than by mention of objective properties, say in terms of supposed sense-data properties (properties experiences themselves may instantiate). Then an experience could count as a perception of an object (perhaps an 'indirect perception') even though none of the object's properties entered the content of the experience, the perceiver's seemings somehow falling short of including external properties. But then it could not be the case that the experience genuinely reveals or presents the objective properties of things; naive realism would fail. Therefore, naive realism requires weak externalism. (I think an analogous conclusion holds for naive realism with respect to thought.[129]) Perceptual contents (their constituents) cannot be mere signs or simulacra of objective properties if naive realism is to be true; they must *be* objective properties. Not resemblance but coincidence. Putting it formally, naive realism requires that from 'x looks *F* to y and x is *F*' we may infer 'there is

---

[129] That is, thought can latch directly onto reality only if it contains worldly constituents (which is not to say if it contains *only* worldly constituents). This externalist thesis naturally prompts the question how thoughts differ from facts for an externalist, given that they share their constituents: how does the externalist stop thought collapsing into reality? The answer lies in firmly distinguishing predication from instantiation. Consider an object x and a property F. These two entities may be related either by the predication relation or by the instantiation relation or by both. Instantiation without predication is ignorance; predication without instantiation is error; both together give you true belief. So x and F are constituents both of the fact and of the thought, but what relates them is different in the two cases – either the objective instantiation of F by x or the mental predication of F on x. Internalist theories distinguish the constituents of thoughts and facts, keeping the two apart in that way; externalist theories identify the constituents but sharply distinguish between the relations of predication and instantiation. Any tendency to conflate these relations will be liable to undermine the viability of externalism and make internalism seem compulsory. For an externalist, we might say, a concept is a property considered as standing in the predication relation to an object, not a separate kind of entity altogether. What the mind brings to content are not new terms to relate but a new relation between the old familiar terms: it applies the relational mental act of predication to the nonmental entities already present in the world. Predication really is a relation between the judging subject and various objects and properties – as instantiation is a relation between the latter two sorts of items alone. A naive realist theory of mental predication is a theory that takes the relata of that relation to be objective worldly items. Such a theory will only be able to distinguish thought from reality if it steadfastly insists upon the utterly different character of the instantiation relation and the predication relation. Perhaps some insidious temptation to conflate these two relations is part of what makes externalism hard to accept for some people? If so, their rejection is founded on a logical confusion.

some P such that x looks P to y and x is P', where 'F' is some predicate constant and 'P' is a (second-order) variable over properties. Of course, this sort of inference is implicit in our ordinary way of describing experience and its objects, so (on my view) our ordinary way is committed both to naive realism and weak externalism. Naive realism requires that properties play this dual role: they are instantiated by objects, and they are constituents of experience (*not* instantiated by experience). These two types of property-involving relations – instantiation and constituency – are quite distinct, but properties need to stand in both of them to the appropriate entities (objects and subjects) if the world is to be directly perceived. Any metaphysical theory that cannot find a single category of items capable of standing in both sorts of relation will thus be incapable of allowing for perceptual directness. In particular, any theory of the nature of properties needs to respect these conceptual demands, if naive realism is to be preserved. Properties must enter into minds and be exemplified by objects.[130]

Joining these reflections to our earlier discussion of substantialism, we can now deduce the following result: naive realism requires that the mind not be a substance. Naive realism entails weak externalism, which entails anti-substantialism; therefore naive realism entails anti-substantialism. Contraposing, if the mind were a substance, then naive realism would have to be false.[131] Intuitively this is because naive realism requires the mind to reach out into the world, but no substance can do this. The conceptual connection here exposed links two sorts of philosophical error in an illuminating way: the error of substantialism, and the error of retreating from naive realism into some sort of 'indirect perception' theory. Assuming a substance conception, we find ourselves understandably perplexed by naive realism; we then adopt a revisionary theory of perception that preserves the substance conception – some sort of resemblance theory, say. Substantialism thus encourages us to hunt for perceptually operative intrinsic features of experience, specifiable without reference to objective properties; but then naive realism has been effectively abandoned. Unpuzzled acceptance of

[130] Thus consider nominalism about universals, i.e. the reduction of properties to predicates. This view has the consequence that the content of mental states comprises predicates, bits of language; but is this workable for the perceptual contents of nonlinguistic creatures? Are their experiences really *as of* certain predicates? Or again, mentalism about properties might be advanced in order to make us comfortable with the idea that thought can incorporate properties; but can this theory give a satisfactory account of what it is for an object to instantiate a property objectively? In my view, realism about properties is the best way to satisfy the various desiderata here: they are not linguistic and they are not mental – they are mind-independent and objective. They thus allow facts to obtain independently of minds, and they allow minds to represent such mind-independent facts. You need realism about properties in order to secure both realism about the world and naive realism about our ways of representing it. Properties are just as mind-independent as individuals, in my book.

[131] That is, only if the analogue of relationalism about space were true of the mind would it be capable of 'direct acquaintance' with things in the world.

commonsense naive realism presupposes rejection of the perennially tempting substantialist model (which I do not say is part of common sense); only if the mind is not (metaphysically) like a material object can it get into direct contact with external material things. Conversely, dissatisfaction with naive realism will feed substantialism. It is not surprising, then, that many philosophers (Locke, Descartes, Berkeley) have held substantialism in combination with a rejection of straightforward naive realism; for the two ideas slot into each other, setting up a field of mutual reinforcement. It is as if one starts off commonsensically with naive realism, observes that it requires weak externalism, notices that this conflicts with substantialism, feels the insidious pull of substantialism, and then argues back to the rejection of naive realism (I suppose these steps are gone through subliminally). The reasoning here is impeccable, the mistake being to submit to the substantialist pull. It is this pull that threatens to cut the mind off from the world, with all the epistemological consequences of that severance.[132] Scepticism motivated by a rejection of naive realism may then have its roots in substantialism, in which case the roots are insecure. However, scepticism need not be so motivated, and therefore weak externalism does not inevitably count against it. You can be both a sceptic and an externalist anti-substantialist – which is what I am, more or less.

(iv) *Externalism and psychological explanation* Representational states are commonly cited in (what appear to be) explanatory contexts. This is true both for propositional attitudes and perceptual states. These states are cited in the explanation of behaviour and in the explanation of further mental occurrences: we explain why someone did something by citing contentful states of the person, and we explain why someone formed a particular belief in a similar way. Such explanations – *content-based* explanations, as we might call them – can be found (it

---

[132] There are significant points of contact between what I have been saying here and McDowell's discussion of externalism and epistemology in 'Singular Thought and the Extent of Inner Space', though also various divergences. He offers a diagnosis of the Cartesian requirement of mental autonomy in terms of a wish to conceive the mind as an object of scientific study in something like the way physical substances are. This has not been my own diagnosis of why internalism can seem attractive, though the notion of substance occurs in both diagnoses. I don't think the tendency in question stems from a specifically scientific (or scientistic) motivation; I think modelling minds on material objects is a much more primitive and unreflective urge than McDowell's account suggests. I think this urge can be felt without wanting to do a 'physics of the mind' – as I think it is by novices in the philosophy of mind. It is part of the naive picture of the mind that seems to take a grip on anyone who has not struggled to see through it. It is part of what those in its grip insist to be simply common sense. Presumably a relationalist about space could view space as part of the subject matter of physics, though he would be denying its 'self-standingness'; and isn't field theory part of physics, though it dispenses with the idea of a material substance as substratum? Aspiring to make psychology like the natural sciences seems insufficiently intimately related to a commitment to mental autonomy for the former to explain the latter: the aspiration is neither necessary nor sufficient for the commitment. (Clearly, however, the issues here are not straightforward.)

seems) both in commonsense folk psychology and in theoretical scientific psychology. Content thus appears prima facie to have explanatory relevance; it presents itself as not merely explanatorily epiphenomenal. The question then arises of whether these appearances might not be deceptive: does content really have any deep explanatory or theoretical utility? And if it does, what is the nature of this utility? How, if at all, does content help us illuminatingly explain – and devise worthwhile theories of – what happens with psychological subjects? Might there not be some other alternative way of describing their states that does a better explanatory job? Must psychology ultimately be content-based? What is the real theoretical *point* of characterizing states of subjects in terms of representational content?

These questions cannot be satisfactorily answered unless we have a reasonably clear conception of the individuation of representational contents: of what their identity and distinctness hinges on, what a taxonomy of contentful states is responsible to. Only then can we ask what useful explanatory purpose classifications by content serve. Given *these* principles of individuation, how can states so individuated have the explanatory role we commonly take them to have? I have been largely concerned in this chapter with the question of individuation, arguing for a qualified externalist position. The question for me, then, is how this position bears on the issue of the explanatory utility of content: specifically, how are strongly external mental states explanatory (if they are) and how are merely weakly external mental states explanatory (if they are)? It should be clear already that the answers to these questions will not be entirely straightforward, given the (apparently) sui generis character of these modes of individuation. Certainly it is hard to see how contentful states could have the sort of explanatory relevance enjoyed by the intrinsic primary qualities of material substances. We identify representational states by reference to items that (intuitively) lie outside the subject: what is the explanatory point of this kind of extrinsic identification? Why do we not stick to what goes on *within* (or *at*) the subject? Suppose, for example, that I adjust my telescope, and you explain this action of mine by saying, 'Colin thought that galaxy might be interesting to look at', pointing to some distant galaxy in the spangled night sky. What do you think you are *doing* explaining my action, which is located right here on earth, by reference to my relation to some far distant celestial object? Why don't you just cite whatever internal state of mine caused me to adjust the telescope as I did? Why bother to identify my explanatory states in this indirect and extrinsic way? Externalism thus presents us with a prima facie puzzle – a puzzle not presented by internalist modes of individuation. It looks already as though there is going to have to be something rather special about psychological explanation if external individuation is to be integral to it. And since folk psychology is up to its neck in content, it looks as though *its* theoretical rationale (if it has one) is going to be rather special too. The worrying background question is whether it will have to be *too* special – so special indeed that it is disqualified from being what it appears to be, viz. a respectable style of explanation. This is a large question, requiring us to delve deeply into the philosophical foundations of content-based psychology, and intersecting with allied questions about the scientific credentials of mental content – a large enough question to demand a chapter to itself. The present chapter provides only some preliminary (but essential) materials to work with in addressing this large question; in the next chapter, then, I shall treat of it at some length. We shall have our work cut out.

2

The Utility of Content

1   The vernacular of commonsense or folk psychology includes such locutions as 'John believes that literature is dead', 'Bill desires that opera be banned', 'Susan sees that the lamp is lit.' These locutions exhibit a familiar and recurrent form. First reference is made to a particular *person*; then some *attitude* is ascribed to that person; finally a *content* is specified for that attitude. Assertions of this form tell us who has what attitude towards which proposition. By making and receiving such assertions we come (it seems) to understand other people: what they do, why they want such and such, what made them hope for so and so, and so forth. Varying the three elements in the *person–attitude–content* structure gives us a seemingly powerful system for describing the minds of others (and our own), a system both antique and ubiquitous. Thinking of this system as a (tacit and unformalized) theory, we can say that folk psychology is a theory that centrally employs an explanatory ontology of persons and contentful attitudes; with these basic theoretical resources it sets about its explanatory and descriptive work. The theory is, as we might say, *content-based*.[1]

The question arises, however, as to whether folk psychology is really a defensible or legitimate or useful theory: is it a *good* way to understand the workings of minds?[2] The question in fact divides into three subquestions,

[1] Two terminological remarks. The phrase 'folk psychology' is not one that I relish, because of its somewhat derisive overtones, but it has become established and it is a convenient name for the body of principles and assumptions we commonly bring to the task of understanding others. Nor do I intend my use of the word 'theory' to imply 'mere theory', as when 'theory' is contrasted with 'fact'. I simply mean an organized system of concepts that feature in descriptions and explanations. I am not assuming that anything that can be called a 'theory' is ipso facto in principle falsifiable – that will depend upon substantive questions about the theory, not upon whether we choose to call it a theory (cf. 'number theory'). So I am not begging any questions about the security or meritoriousness of our ordinary ways of understanding minds.

[2] Recent discussions may encourage the idea that this is a new question. It is not, of course. A negative answer to it was the basis of the movement in psychology, dating back to the beginning of the century, known as 'behaviourism'. J. B. Watson was an 'eliminative materialist' of sorts. (This is not to say that no new reasons for this position have been offered in recent years.)

according to which of the three elements in the familiar form we choose to focus on: (i) is the ontology of persons a good ontology? (ii) is the stock of attitudes a good stock of explanatory relations (assuming that they are relational)? (iii) are propositional contents a good sort of theoretical entity? Conceivably these three questions could receive different answers. We might, for example, jettison the ontology of persons (replacing it, perhaps, with an ontology of cognitive systems or modules), while retaining the old attitudes and their contents.[3] Or we might replace (or regiment) the attitudes, keeping the persons and contents. Or again, we might keep the persons and the attitudes and replace the contents, ascribing a new and unfamiliar content to the attitudes of persons. And of course we might just junk the lot. This last sweeping option might itself come in two strengths: either we abandon the characteristic *form* of vernacular psychological locutions, or we retain this form but clothe it differently. Eliminative behaviourism, for example, takes the former more drastic line. The latter less drastic line would be favoured by those who think that folk psychology provides the right skeleton for psychological theory but query the way that skeleton is commonsensically fleshed out; they would prefer a theory that trades only in such locutions as 'Visual module *m* computes that the binocular disparity is *n*.' This latter lines preserves the *form* of folk psychology in that it still employs a content-based mode of description. The question of the theoretically viability of folk psychology is thus more complex than it might at first appear; we always need to be told which *aspect* of it is being put in question.[4]

In this chapter I shall be principally concerned only with question (iii), whether psychology should be content-based. I want to know what the rationale for adverting to content of *any* kind might be, not specifically the kind of content we find reflected in the vernacular following the familiar verbs of attitude. It is important to be clear about this at the outset because certain arguments against content-based psychology apply only to the kind of content we find in the familiar quotidian belief–desire psychology of persons – and not obviously to any other possible kind of content. We need to know whether it is content as such that is being objected to or just the particular kinds of content-ascription encountered in the folk-psychological vernacular.

---

[3] This type of view is not uncommon in scientific psychology inspired by the computer analogy: (extant) computers are not persons, they are assemblages of functional units. Cognitive psychology typically gets by with an ontology of systems and subsystems; persons as such play no role in the theories. The sortal term 'person' seems not to be of interest to psychological theories of perception, memory, etc.

[4] Contemporary discussions of the scientific credentials of folk psychology are often rather undiscriminating in what they take to be in question, as if all of it is to be tarred with the same brush. But maybe some parts will stand up better than other parts. Old proverbs about the way to a man's heart are one thing; the general use of propositions to characterize mental states is quite another.

One more distinction before we proceed. Attacks on the theoretical virtue of folk psychology may take one of two forms, one more radical than the other. The less radical form contends only that folk psychology is an unsuitable model for scientific psychology: in some or all of its aspects it is hopeless as a framework for psychological science. The more radical form asserts that, not only is folk psychology scientifically lamentable, it is also defective as a system of understanding in the less hygenic world of the shopping mall, the battlefield and the bedroom. That is, it is a bad theory *tout court*: it simply gets people's psychology wrong, credits them with states that they just don't have.[5] On this more radical view, folk psychology should be banned from all public (and private) places, not just the laboratory. These two views are logically independent so long as we maintain a distinction between truth and scientific truth; so long, that is, as we do not infer outright falsity from unsuitability for science, i.e. go in for scientism. Maintaining that distinction, we will want to allow room for the idea that folk psychology is a perfectly legitimate way of understanding persons but not a way that can be converted as it stands into science (on some preferred conception of what it is to be genuinely scientific). It is rather like our ordinary talk of tables and chairs: true and useful but not of intense interest to the physicist.[6] However, one should not rest sanguinely and uncritically upon this distinction, dismissing every allegation against folk psychology merely as questioning its scientific utility, leaving its autonomous truth whole and intact; for it *may* be that the respects in which it is claimed to be unsuitable for science are respects in which it is unsuitable for any other kind of truth-seeking enterprise. We must therefore look at each allegation on its own merits, assessing its impact both on folk psychology as proto-science and as avowed nonscience. A proof that beliefs simply do not *exist*, say, could hardly be confined to the question of scientific eligibility; while a proof that there can be no *laws* of belief might well be so confinable. In what follows my attention will be chiefly on the question of science; for I take it that if content-based psychology can be

---

[5] A standard model here is primitive animism: rocks and trees simply do not *have* the kinds of states animists attribute to them. Similarly, the weather and volcanic eruptions are just not manifestations of the anger of the gods – for there are no such gods.

[6] Or again, like our talk of colour and other secondary qualities. There need be no conflict here, just a divergence of interest. It can be useful to compare the debate about commonsense and scientific psychology with the debate about the commonsense conception of the physical world and the conception supplied by physics. What looks like a straight conflict can sometimes turn out to be a peaceful difference of concern. See my *The Subjective View* on the latter debate. There I asked why we represent the world as coloured; here I am asking why we represent organisms as representational. In both cases there is a threat that the ascribed properties are going to turn out to be epiphenomenal. However, I give rather different answers in the two cases. Still, the problems are not dissimilar: we find ourselves attributing certain kinds of properties to things but we can become perplexed about what the point of these attributions is.

vindicated in this respect, then it will be secure also in the wider world. I begin, then, with some recent attempts to discredit content-based folk psychology as a basis for a science of mind. As will become clear, I do not myself find these attempts very convincing, and I will not spend much time signalling my disagreements with them – no doubt they deserve a more extended discussion than I shall give them. What I want to concentrate on is an objection to content that I *do* find disturbing and challenging; it is this objection (the 'causal objection') that I shall try to rebut at some length.

2 *Paul Churchland* has made a bold attempt to undermine the theoretical pretensions of folk psychology.[7] His case against it comes in two stages: first, he insists that folk psychology is an empirical theory; second, he argues that it is a *bad* empirical theory, as judged by the usual standards of theoretical virtue. It has three chief failings as a theory: it is severely limited in its explanatory scope; it is stagnant and infertile; and it is not integrated with the other sciences of man and beast. The explanatory limitations or lacunae are said to include: mental illness, creativity, intelligence, sleep, skills, vision, memory, learning – indeed all the things that scientists of the mind are endeavouring to find out about. If folk psychology were a complete theory of the mind, then we would not need to undertake these enquiries – they would already be the common property of ordinary folk: but we do, so it is not. The stagnancy and infertility are said to be apparent from the fact that folk psychology has scarcely changed since the time of the ancient Greeks, while almost every other theory of nature has matured and changed as science has progressed. The lack of integration shows the theoretical isolationism of folk psychology, its misalignment with our other theories – in biology, neuroscience, and so forth. Taken together these failings add up, Churchland claims, to a severe indictment of folk psychology as a framework for developing a systematic science of mind. In particular, the dependence on ascriptions of propositional content impedes the development of such a science.[8]

Let me make the following brief replies to these criticisms. The charge of explanatory incompleteness is not, of course, an argument for the *falsity* of folk psychology; it is only a reason for supposing that folk psychology does not contain the *whole* truth. Nor is this incompleteness any reason by itself for thinking that

---

[7] See his 'Eliminative Materialism and the Propositional Attitudes'.

[8] See also Patricia Churchland, 'A Perspective on Mind–Brain Research'. She is right to stress that this is the key issue for the viability of folk psychology. However, this should not be confused with the question whether the 'sentential paradigm' for mental processes is correct: see my next chapter on why rejecting the sentential theory is compatible with preserving the propositional form of folk psychology.

what completes the job will overturn what we already have in folk psychology. If this were a good objection to folk psychology, then it would be a good objection to almost any scientific theory, since theories are seldom finished and complete (Darwinian theory, for example, would be in deep trouble by these exacting standards). It is, of course, true that folk psychology does not contain all the *answers* to the questions it raises; but the issue is whether it raises the right *questions*, formulated in the appropriate vocabulary, and whether its categories will survive the answering of these questions. Churchland's incompleteness point does not entail the denial of the claim that folk psychology is basically on the right lines here. Indeed, theoretical incompleteness can be seen as an invitation to further fruitful development – the growing edge of an open-ended research programme. The completeness of a commonsense theory is what would be suspect.[9] My own view would be that folk psychology basically sets the explanatory agenda in the problematic areas Churchland mentions, so the final theories will in all likelihood have to persist in its categories, even though new theoretical concepts will need to be introduced into the explanations.

Secondly, the allegation of stagnancy seems to me unjustified. The constancy or longevity of a theory is not in itself, of course, any reason to suspect it: a really good theory may be *expected* to resist falsification over the centuries. The reason folk psychology has lasted so long, and changed so little, may be that it is basically sound, not that it is scientifically decadent and inherently indifferent to reasonable canons of theory-acceptance.[10] A more serious point is that folk psychology has not, despite its longevity, generated a very impressive psychological science: it has not proved itself a scientifically fecund basis for psychological theory. Perhaps if the psychologists ceased trying to shape their theories after the pattern of content-based folk psychology they would move forward far more rapidly? Now this criticism seems to me entirely misplaced. The fact is (as all the textbook histories of psychology say) that psychology as a science has only existed for about a hundred years, so that there was no real opportunity since the Greeks to sophisticate it into solid science. There was

---

[9] That is, if folk psychology somehow *purported* to be a complete theory of the mind, then we would be right to protest at its arrogance and smirk at its limitations. But it seems to me that folk psychology is quite candid about what it does not know; it does not *claim* to have the answers to all the questions it raises – the function of dreaming, the cause of schizophrenia, why we can't remember everything. Folk psychology does not in fact try to get much beyond what is needed in the conduct of everyday life; it does not advertise itself as a finished scientific psychology. So I see no force in the complaint that it is incomplete: it offers the beginnings, and it does not exaggerate what it has to offer.

[10] Arithmetic has not changed in essentials for a long time too, but we don't think that shows it to be smugly conservative – it is just a correct theory of numbers. Should we automatically start to question relativity theory if it resists falsification into the 3000s? Human beings, as a species, got to have propositional attitudes very early on, and they soon latched onto the fact that they had them and that they influenced their behaviour: why should that not be so?

simply no one putting in the effort. The theory itself therefore cannot take the blame. Whether it is because of the relative youth of the discipline or the intrinsic difficulty of its subject matter that it has not progressed more rapidly is hard to say: but it is certain that the centuries of alleged 'stagnation' cannot be put down to failed effort – rather to no effort. And if we enquire into the actual history of the science of psychology, what we discover is the exact opposite of Churchland's version of events. For most of the period in question psychology was dominated precisely by the *repudiation* of folk psychology, not by its infertile acceptance. After the initial introspectionist period the controlling philosophy of psychology was precisely *eliminative behaviourism* – the total rejection of the 'mentalism' of commonsense psychology. And I think it would be widely agreed now that this behaviourist period (by no means over even today) was in fact itself a period of relative stagnancy and infertility: behaviourism did not prove the royal road to understanding the workings of mind (the explanation of behaviour) – quite the opposite. The orthodox contemporary view, indeed, is that things got moving again once psychologists relaxed the dogmatic behaviourism they had derived from logical positivism and went frankly 'mentalist'. That is, the discipline took on life and excitement when psychologists, encouraged by computer science and linguistics (and perhaps a bit of philosophy), started speaking in terms of information processing, symbol manipulation, tacit knowledge, and so on.[11] Some of the most advanced work today seems plainly content-based, employing as it does algorithms defined over propositional representations – I am thinking particularly of recent work on vision.[12] I would say that scientific psychology has taken folk psychology more seriously in the last thirty years than it did for most of its early history, and the result has been considerable advance, compared to the period of anti-commonsense eliminative behaviourism. So, contrary to Churchland's claim, I think that infusions of folk psychology have benefited psychology not retarded it.

Thirdly, the charge of isolationism is hard to sustain. We should distinguish two relations in which content-based psychology might stand to disciplines (or subject matters) that do not themselves deal in content: reduction and integration. It does not follow from the fact that content-based psychology is not *reducible* to a science (say biochemistry) that does not employ content that it cannot be *integrated* with such a science. And what is generally required of a reputable theory is integration with allied theories, not reduction to them. It is reasonable to expect

---

[11] Chomsky's 1959 'Review of B. F. Skinner's *Verbal Behaviour*' is commonly regarded as the point of turnaround in psychology.

[12] See Marr, *Vision*. Fodor has consistently urged the content-based character of much contemporary psychology: see, e.g., *Psychosemantics*, where he argues that scientific psychology vindicates the basic structures of folk psychology.

evolutionary biology to be integrated with biochemistry (say), so that the two theories fit harmoniously together; but it is a far more dubious project to wish to *reduce* the notions of evolutionary biology (fitness, survival, selection, etc.) to notions of biochemistry. Similarly, a content-based psychologist will want his theory to be consilient with what is known of the neurophysiological hardware, but to insist on achieving total reduction seems distinctly supererogatory. To give an example: Marr's tripartite division of theoretical tasks into the computational, the algorithmic and the implementational (the hardware) does not require him to deliver a reduction of the first two levels to the third; it requires only that the algorithms devised to carry out the computations should be ones that the brain can empirically carry out – and, where possible, be ones for which we know the hardware mechanisms. There would be an objection to some proposed information-processing algorithm if it was known that the brain *could* not, given its hardware, do what the algorithm required; but it is no objection that we cannot *translate* talk of algorithms into talk of neural properties.[13] Integration does not require reduction (or if it does, we have yet to hear the argument). I think that Churchland's isolationist charge roundly conflates these two require-ments on psychological theories, and that content-based psychology has not been shown to flout the reasonable integration requirement (I don't mind agreeing that it flouts the *un*reasonable reduction requirement). The 'growing synthesis' of the life sciences need not consist in a steady *assimilation* of them all to the content-free zones.

I may now be asked whether I am saying that the categories of folk psychology are absolutely immune to scientific revision – a most dogmatic position! No, I have not been saying that; I have merely been objecting to certain arguments that purport to show that such revision is imminent or desirable, that there is substantial cause for concern over the framework of folk psychology. Asked whether I believe there is even an abstract possibility that folk psychology might be proved false, I would reply thus: almost anything is *possible*, if that means logically possible. In this sense it is also possible that there are no material objects and so nothing for physics to be true of – that is, this is the kind of possibility of (legitimate) interest to the philosophical sceptic. But it is not a possibility that *physics* needs at present to take terribly seriously. Similarly, there may be a remote logical possibility that the fundamental categories of folk psychology do not (as they say) carve the mind at its natural joints; but I have not seen reason in Churchland's discussion to take this seriously as a *real* possibility, one that

---

[13] Here I am just making the excessively familiar point that software specifications do not reduce to hardware specifications. Software and hardware have to *fit* each other, but they do not need to be identical (cf. suits and their wearers).

describes a serious scientific option for us at present.[14] I have seen no reason to suppose, for example, that commonsense decision theory is simply wrong about the basic principles of practical reasoning. Mere abstract possibilities come cheap and easy, and are not to be inflated into lively theoretical alternatives.

Stephen Stich has castigated content-based psychology on somewhat different grounds.[15] His basic argument is that formulating our psychological generalizations in terms of content is less comprehensive than formulating them in a content-free way (i.e. syntactically); and we should, other things being equal, prefer theoretical concepts that allow for greater inclusiveness, so long as there are interesting regularities there to be captured by those concepts. Attributions of content have a built-in relativity to the theorist, according to Stich, so that where the subject of the attribution differs in certain respects from the theorist an attribution of content will not be feasible. In the case of subjects with exotic sets of beliefs, or brain-damaged subjects, or immature subjects, or animal subjects – in these cases we will find ourselves unable to ascribe concepts sufficiently like our own to make a definite attribution of content. Yet, Stich says, it may be that there exist important cognitive regularities, applicable both to these conceptual fugitives and to ourselves, the normal ascribers of content. These regularities can, he thinks, be captured in terms of asemantic syntactic descriptions of internal structures. So we should drop the whole apparatus of content, with all its parochiality, and go ecumenically syntactic, thus covering every subject with the right causal profile. No longer even in the business of ascribing concepts, we shall not need to perplex ourselves wondering *when* a given concept may be ascribed to a subject. Instead, we can go cleanly syntactic in our psychological generalizations.[16]

---

[14] We must be careful here not to confuse the empirical possibility of discovering interesting new psychological natural kinds with the alleged possibility of discovering that the old psychological kinds are spurious. We might indeed discover that we need to postulate states and structures in people that folk psychology has no inkling of, as with recent connectionist theories; but it does not follow that the old notions of belief and desire correspond to no psychological reality. Physics discovers new forces and particles, but it does not thereby repudiate the old average-size wet goods. Always remember: any lump of the world can be classified in ever so many ways, each of them legitimate. Folk psychology does not claim to have all psychological natural kinds at its disposal (it does not claim to be a complete science); what it claims is that it has *some* of them (in one sense of 'natural kind').

[15] See his *From Folk Psychology to Cognitive Science.*

[16] This is the psychological analogue of the following position on language: we should abjure all semantic descriptions of sentences, thus avoiding problems of vagueness and indeterminacy and restrictions to what is translatable into our language, and simply describe sentences in entirely syntactic terms. Where Stich advocates a 'syntactic theory of mind' this analogous position embraces a 'syntactic theory of language'. The rationale in both cases would be basically this: we don't really need the semantic descriptions for scientific purposes, and they cause trouble, so let's forget them. One can see this kind of position as an extreme reaction to Quinean scepticism about meanings and concepts; it attempts to get on without even such etiolated semantic notions as that of 'stimulus meaning'. Instead of getting *Word and Object* we are given *Word and Word*.

Now I shall not attempt to rehearse Stich's detailed reasons for these bracing contentions; I shall assume, at least for the sake of argument, that his motivating claims are broadly correct – in particular, his claim that there are mental regularities capturable syntactically that cannot be captured in terms of content. What I want to question is what *follows* from this about the theoretical viability of content. That a theoretical concept admits of borderline cases (that it harbours a degree of vagueness) does not by itself count against its theoretical utility: consider the concepts of digestion and respiration, or star and planet. Producing actual or possible objects for which it is unclear whether these concepts are satisfied (plants and bacteria, celestial bodies of various sizes and densities and positions) does not undermine their utility in describing objects that *do* clearly satisfy them. Similarly, producing a subject for whom it is unclear whether he has (particular) beliefs does not (*of course*) discredit the notion of belief as applied to subjects that undisputably do have (such) beliefs. A vague concept can still wield theoretical power. What matters about content, then, is that it should pull its theoretical weight in application to the *central cases* – that it should do some worthwhile explaining within its undisputed domain. Now in the case of Stich's conceptual fugitives – the weird, the damaged, the callow, the brutish – it seems to me perfectly reasonable to declare them exceptional or borderline cases, and hence not to *want* to include them under our content-based generalizations. For we wish a theoretical apparatus that covers the central cases, and exhibits them *as* central, not an apparatus that blurs important distinctions among psychological subjects. Stich will reply to this point that the interesting psychological natural kinds are precisely ones that exceed the domain of content-based psychology – that there are real natural psychological similarities between subjects that cannot be caught in the net of content. To speak of central and peripheral cases here, he will say, is to beg the question in favour of content and against syntax. Now there are two replies we can make to this accusation. The first is that we are not in fact confronted with an exclusive choice: we can retain our content generalizations for the relevant subclass of central or typical subjects, while taking in the fugitives syntactically (as well as the content-endowed) – we simply use both types of generalization. We thus mark both similarities *and* dissimilarities.[17] The second reply is that the similarities Stich stresses must be seen against the background of other countervailing *dis*similarities. The brain-damaged patient may assent to the same sentence as you, so that there is one causal similarity between the two of you,

---

[17] Stich cannot plausibly deny that there are similarities within the normal cases that make these cases dissimilar to the fugitives. And the point of a taxonomic scheme is precisely to catch significant similarities between objects, as well as dissimilarities to other objects. Logically speaking, what we have is a semantically specified species falling within a syntactically specified genus. Why give up narrower groupings just because you want to recognize wider ones? You can have both.

but there will also be a host of other dissimilarities, relating to assent to other sentences and to behaviour generally. It would be different if Stich's fugitives were globally just like us in their causal profiles, but this is precisely what is not true. Consequently, a descriptively adequate psychological taxonomy will want to capture the dissimilarities as well as the similarities, and this is what the content-based taxonomy permits (by Stich's own hypothesis). The fact, upon which Stich heavily relies, that there are *some* psychological similarities between the fugitives and us – similarities that the content-based taxonomy cannot capture – does not show (what the argument against content requires) that there are not *also* significant dissimilarities that that taxonomy *does* capture. And it seems obvious enough that there are such dissimilarities. Only the mistaken idea that we cannot avail ourselves of both sorts of taxonomy could lead one to think that we must abandon content entirely and stick exclusively to syntax. I myself would suggest that the class of undamaged normal sane adult human agents is a sufficiently natural class of subjects for us to want some way of registering the psychological similarities that unite subjects into this class; and content-based generalizations seem perfectly suited to that task – they thus mark out what ought to be marked out. Subjects that are similar to this class in certain limited respects can then be brought under wider content-free syntactic generalizations, if this seems theoretically desirable – but with no prejudice to the independent utility of the first content-based mode of classification. This seems to me no more parochial than marking out the digestive systems of mammals (say) from those of other animals. Far from it being a disadvantage of content-based psychology that it groups psychological subjects in this selective way, it seems to me to be a positive virtue. I think, therefore, that Stich's argument from maximum coverage fails to banish content.

Hilary Putnam has suggested that the notion of content is unsuitable for science because it *is* suitable for something that *isn't* science.[18] He distinguishes between what he calls functional psychology and interpretation theory. And his thesis is that content has its proper home in the latter enterprise, not the former. The two enterprises are distinguished by a series of contrasts: functional psychology is algorithmic, formal, operationally local, subpersonal, continuous with the natural sciences – everything a proper psychological science aspires to be; interpretation theory is heuristic, informal, holistic, personal, normative – discontinuous with the natural sciences (though not by that token 'unnatural'). Putnam argues that the notion of sameness of content (synonymy) belongs distinctively with interpretation theory, and is therefore infected (or blessed) with all the unscientific features proper to that mode of understanding. Decisions

---

[18] See his 'Computational Psychology and Interpretation Theory'.

about sameness of content therefore require the employment of radically unformalizable notions such as rational intelligibility and what it is to be 'human'. Putnam's position here may be compared with that of Wittgenstein (though he does not himself make the comparison); for Wittgenstein held that sameness of meaning depends ultimately upon sameness of 'form of life' – as we might say, *the* unformalizable notion.[19] The doctrine is not intended in a Quinean spirit: there is no attempt by Putnam to besmirch and extrude the notion of content. Rather, Putnam is anxious to assign the notion to its proper (and respectable) theoretical place, viz. interpretation theory. And since this is its proper home, it will be inherently unsuitable for science – that is, for functional psychology as Putnam characterizes it. Accordingly, functional psychology must treat its postulated internal symbols as semantically uninterpreted.

I have two main objections to Putnam's argument. The first is that he confines himself to the conceptual content of propositional attitudes such as belief, and to the meanings of words in a public natural language. Now it may well be (I do not wish to deny it) that this level or kind of content belongs to interpretation theory in Putnam's sense – so that there are no precise algorithms for assigning such contents. But it does not follow that *any* notion of content *must* behave in that slippery way; so it does not follow that cognitive psychology cannot fashion a regimented notion of content that is *not* similarly bound up with the notions of personhood and intelligibility and hermeneutics. Indeed, it looks very much as if such a notion is already in place. Animals are commonly regarded as information processors and hence as bearers of a kind of representational content: they perceive, remember and perhaps even think. The vision of frogs, say, is as susceptible as that of human beings to a content-based study. And such notions of content are certainly not governed by any principle of *humanity*. Similarly, human nervous system – or the subpersonal cognitive machinery embodied in them – are commonly described in terms of content: 'computing that p', 'sending the information that q', 'filtering out a signal that r', etc.). Again, such ascriptions do not seem as hermeneutically unrigorous as Putnam claims that ascriptions of belief proper are; they are not even bound up with *consciousness*, to start with.[20] Of course these appearances *may* be deceptive: perhaps it is really an

---

[19] Wittgenstein says: 'It is what human beings *say* that is true and false; and they agree in the *language* they use. That is not an agreement in opinions but in form of life' (*Philosophical Investigations*, 241). There are also obvious affinities between Putnam's position here and that of Davidson: see Davidson's 'Radical Interpretation'.

[20] Interestingly, Putnam does not attempt to confine content to beings with consciousness; his point is not that consciousness is bound up with content and that *it* cannot be pressed into the straitjacket of 'functional psychology'. But if he did try to link content and consciousness, then he would need to show why the link is necessary. I think that content can exist without consciousness (and vice versa): aboutness does not logically require conscious aboutness. I discuss this further below.

error to describe animals and nervous systems in terms of content; or perhaps this kind of description is to be seen as strictly parasitic upon higher-level ascriptions of propositional attitudes to persons. But if so, we need to be told why – especially since there seem to be going theories that proceed as if these descriptions are literally true. So we should at least be open to the possibility that some kinds of content have the features necessary to qualify them for a place in Putnam's functional psychology. In fact, as I shall argue later, I think that the notion of content can be about as naturalistic and scientific as the notion of biological function, since it has its roots in that notion. So if functional psychology can admit biological concepts, then it can in principle work with *a* notion of content, though not perhaps the kind of content that arises from the accretion of an interpretative overlay upon the biological foundation.

But, second, it seems to me that Putnam's equation of scientific psychology with his conception of functional psychology is tendentious. Who *says* that scientific psychology must have the kind of formality Putnam demands? Do accredited theories in psychology actually exhibit such formality? It may be that certain philosophers of psychology like to think of cognitive psychology in this super-rigorous way, but that may simply not be an accurate reflection of the actual practice of the discipline. And I would say that large tracts of experimental psychology just *do* make essential use of the notion of content: studies of perception, memory, reasoning – not to speak of social psychology.[21] If these kinds of content are really part of interpretation theory, then the proper conclusion to draw is that scientific psychology is itself enmeshed in interpretation theory – and only a misplaced ideal of scientific purity could make one deny this. Psychology is thus like economics and anthropology and history in this respect: all these disciplines employ notions that call on a background understanding of what it is to be a rational agent – however holistic and normative that understanding turns out to be. The correct moral is thus that Putnam's functional psychology is not what real psychology should attempt to be. Psychology can be rigorous without being rigorous in *that* way. Science has many mansions.[22]

The psychology of sensation provides a useful parallel here. Many of us have felt compelled by the thesis that an attribution of sensation – say, of pain or colour experience – can be understood only by someone who himself has sensations of the same (or a similar) kind. There is, we might say, an element of *empathy* in knowledgeably making such attributions: to interpret a subject as having

---

[21] Cf. Burge, 'Individualism and Psychology'.

[22] We do not want to find ourselves simply defining psychology in such a way that content cannot feature in it; we need to reflect the way the science of psychology is actually conducted. And psychology may not in fact fit the paradigms of the scientific that psychologists themselves enunciate in their philosophical moments.

particular sensations the interpreter must make tacit appeal to his own sensations. This makes the attribution of sensations importantly different from the description of the physical world, including the nervous system of the possessor of the sensations attributed. Now one might be tempted to conclude from this that there can be no psychological science of sensations, since any such would-be science would differ in the respect noted from the paradigm of the physical sciences. But this would be a mistake, I think: for the subjectivity of sensations does not prevent the formulation of theories and laws about sensations. The student of colour vision, say, or of pain, can do proper science in respect of these subject matters, even though to grasp the theories she produces she needs to employ empathy in understanding the terms that refer to those sensations. Only a misplaced standard of what it takes for a body of theory to count as a science could rule such psychological theories of sensation 'unscientific'; indeed, the claim begins to look uninterestingly verbal if we are advised to make this ruling. Content is somewhat similar in that its location within interpretation theory need not disqualify it from serving a useful scientific purpose – the purpose, in fact, that it seems to serve in current psychological theories (e.g. in the study of errors of syllogistic reasoning). The right response to Putnam's argument is not intolerantly to banish content from the science of psychology, but to recognize that scientific psychology is less like physics (or 'functional psychology') than some philosophers of psychology have encouraged us to believe.

3   I come now to what I take to be the most serious and challenging argument against content-based psychology. It is an argument that applies to any kind of content, and it strikes right at the heart of the idea that propositional contents can be genuinely explanatory. The argument puts the very coherence of content-based explanation into doubt. Although I think the argument can be turned, I shall state it as forcefully as I can, because I want to disturb any lingering complacency that may exist in the presence of the argument: it is not easily refuted, and it brings much into question. The argument proceeds from certain principles about causation (so let us call it 'the causal argument') – specifically, about how mental causation must be seen to work. And its conclusion is that content and causality do not mix: content can play no (nonredundant) causal role in producing the effects of a given mental state, either behavioural or mental. In a word, content is causally epiphenomenal.[23] The argument for this claim

---

[23] We can compare the role of colours in the folk psychology of perception. We commonsensically cite the colours of objects in explaining why people see those objects as having certain colours. But this kind of purported explanation can seem shallow or illegitimate once we reflect seriously on the nature of colour: the causal efficacy of colours then comes under doubt, as does the role of ordinary colour

presupposes externalism, either weak or strong. According to externalism, contentful states are identified by reference to entities that lie outside the subject's body (including, of course, his head): these extrinsic entities are the constituents of such states. Now this implies that contentful states are (as we might say) extrinsically relational: they essentially consist in relations to extrinsic nonmental items (objects, properties, etc.). They thus involve certain 'correspondence relations' between the subject (or his intrinsic states) and entities that exist beyond the confines of the subject. For example, for John to have the concept *square* (and so to be capable of believing that the box is square) is for John to stand in a certain relation to the *property* of being square. So when we ascribe that concept to John we report him as standing in this extrinsic correspondence relation to that objective property. And now the causal objection to citing such contents in psychological explanations is just this: if such explanations purport to be causal, then these correspondence relations cannot themselves be implicated in the causal transaction being reported.[24] This is because what happens at the causal nexus is local, proximate and intrinsic: the features of the cause that lead to the effect must be right there where the causal interaction takes place. Causation is the same with brains and minds as it is with billiard balls. Their effects depend upon local properties of these entities. The causal powers of a state or property must be intrinsically grounded; they cannot depend essentially upon relations to what lies quite elsewhere. The question then is how correspondence relations to what exists outside of the subject's body can be causally relevant to changes initiated from within the body. To put it less tendentiously, how can contentful states have their

predicates in a developed science of perception. So we might wonder whether colours are a component of the folk psychology of perception that we wish ultimately to keep. In a proper science of colour perception we might replace ordinary talk of the colours of objects with talk of wavelengths and so forth, rather as some wish to replace contents with purely intrinsic 'syntactic' properties of subjects. And the motivation in both cases might be the conviction that colour ascriptions and content ascriptions fail to describe things in terms of their causally relevant properties. This causal lack might then be traced to the relationality of the properties in question. One can see, at least, that a parallel issue arises for both, and that parallel options present themselves. My final view will be that content can be saved for science, but I doubt that colours can be – certainly they cannot be saved in the same way.

[24] This line of thought can be found in many writers. See, especially, Field, 'Mental Representation', Loar, *Mind and Meaning*, Fodor, *Psychosemantics*, Pylyshyn, *Computation and Cognition*, McGinn, 'The Structure of Content'. My way of putting the point in the text may not be exactly the way these writers might individually prefer to put it, though I think what I say is in the spirit of their various formulations. Basically the point could be stated thus: the reference relation, as between symbol and object, does not contribute to the causal powers of the symbol – it is not what empowers the symbol to bring about its effects. The causal mechanism whereby the symbol has an impact on the world does not somehow incorporate the relation of reference. The relation of reference is to the symbol what the country of origin of a car is to its engine, i.e. not part of the causal machinery. Intentionality is not what makes the world go from one state to the next. Content is not a *mechanistic* feature of the world.

effects *in virtue of* the extrinsic relations that constitute them? Surely, if the external relata of these relations were not to exist, this would not necessarily alter the causal power of states of the subject to bring about the same bodily movements. At best, therefore, the extrinsic relations definitive of content are causally redundant, thus inviting an application of Occam's razor.[25] The causal *mechanisms* do not incorporate these relations, and causal explanation consists in describing (however crudely) the operation of such mechanisms. The case of content is thus just like the cases of knowledge and perception: here too the extrinsic factor has no role to play in the causal processes in which states of knowledge and perception may be involved.[26] Logically, the opponent of content will say, citing content in explanatory contexts is no different from citing mental states in would-be explanations against a background of general epiphenomenalism. Suppose one held that mental states in general have no causal powers – that they are causally quite inert. Then it would seem clearly wrong to cite mental states in explanatory contexts, all explanation being causal explanation. Nor would it help in this case to say that this is really just another way to identify the genuine underlying causes (brain states, presumably), since the question would then be 'why cite causally relevant features by citing causally *ir*relevant ones?' Causal

[25] There are two positions here. Either we can allow that content ascriptions serve obliquely to specify the cause, or we can deny outright that they manage to cite anything causal: they are partially causal, or they are not causal at all. On either assumption, the requirement that explanations cite only causally relevant properties has the result that content is epiphenomenal, since even the former position has to concede that content exceeds what is legitimate. In other words, content ascriptions should be replaced with a direct specification of the causally operative properties of the subject. The case is exactly analogous to making ascriptions of knowledge in explanatory contexts. If our aim is to pare down our psychological descriptions of organisms to the minimum necessary to explain what needs to be explained, then it looks as if content ascriptions (like ascriptions of knowledge) are at best excess baggage. That, at least, is the position we need to refute if content is to be made scientifically secure.

[26] We assign truth-values to mental states, and some ascriptions of mental states directly entail that they have a certain truth-value: but does the assignment of truth-values to mental states play any part in characterizing their explanatory potential? It is certainly very hard to see how any such contribution could possibly be causal: how could the causal potential of a belief depend upon whether it is true? Surely if (counterfactually) the belief were false, its causal powers would remain the same. So truth (and falsity) are not legitimate concepts in any theory of mental states that sets out to detail the causal properties of mental states. And this implies that whether a belief counts as knowledge or an experience counts as a perception will not be of interest to a theory of the causal properties of the mental states so specified. The point about extrinsic content (i.e. reference) is precisely parallel: it too involves an assignment to mental states of properties that cannot plausibly be reckoned to the causal structure of the state. Generalizing: the extensions of mental states do not contribute to their causal workings (consider the extensions of concepts, i.e. the sets of objects they apply to). Assigning extensions to mental states – whether truth-values or sets or properties or objects – cannot then be justified by observing that these extensions are implicated in the causal machinery of the states. (Isn't this point really just perfectly obvious?) The question must then be faced as to what does justify such assignments.

explanation aims to delineate the causally relevant properties involved in a causal transaction, but the property of having a certain (extrinsically individuated) content cannot be such a property, on pain of externalism about the causal nexus. Causal processes, we might say, are methodologically solipsist, but content is not; so contents cannot be causes.

This kind of point has been expressed by different authors in slightly different ways: that mental causes must be supervenient on internal states of the subject; that only the 'shape' of a mental symbol can enter into its causal activities, not its semantic relations; that characterizations of causal mental processes must respect a 'formality constraint'; that the cognitive operating system is causally a 'syntactic engine'; that mental algorithms can be causally sensitive only to local features of their inputs; that truth conditions cannot play any role in causal-role or functional psychology; that it is a kind of category mistake to attribute causal potential to meanings; that a causal-explanatory taxonomy of mental states must be narrowly individuated, i.e. be governed by methodological solipsism.[27] What these various formulations have in common is the idea – intuitively compelling as it is – that mental explanations must cite local causes. Just as the causal powers of a pain depend only upon its intrinsic features, so too do the causal powers of a belief or a perceptual experience. Just as we would think it decidedly peculiar to identify a pain state by reference to some extrinsic relation when giving an explanation in terms of that state, so we should think it equally odd to do the same thing with representational states. In so far as psychology is concerned to uncover the causal laws and mechanisms of mind, then, it had better not reserve a theoretical place for content. Folk psychology violates the first principle of scientific theories: viz. do not postulate epiphenomenal theoretical entities.

I fear that those who are already impressed by the causal objection will find what I have just said a wearisome reiteration of the obvious and established; while those who refuse to be impressed by it will not now be suddenly struck with the power of the objection. I hope, though, that those new to the subject will at least feel that a genuine challenge has been laid down: that there is something here that needs to be answered if we are to persist in good conscience with our content-

[27] I have culled these formulations from a number of writers: Fodor, Dennett, Stich, Loar and others. Burge, in 'Individualism and Psychology', effectively concedes that content, as it is individuated in folk and scientific psychology, goes beyond the causal features of contentful mental states, since he agrees that causation is 'local' and content is not. But he does not square up to the question what theoretical purpose might be served by content if it is *not* the delineation of local causal factors. What controls the selection of psychological natural kinds if it is not their causal profiles – and is this selection scientifically reputable? (Compare the analogous question about colours: they are inherently relational with respect to perceptual reactions, so they cannot be local causes, so what role can they play in a science addressed to the world's causal structure?) That is the challenge I am trying to meet. I think it can be met, but I want to insist that it needs to be.

based psychological explanations. How is it *possible* for content to be explanatory? Must psychological causation be regarded as radically different from other kinds of causation? If so, how is it to be conceived as working? What exactly is going *on* here? Before I give my answer to these pressing questions, let me discuss one type of response to the causal objection that has attracted some, and which seems to me not to work.

This response concedes the force of the causal objection, but tries to meet it by appealing to a special sort of relation between intrinsic states and what they represent.[28] The response is most readily understood if we assume an internal system of symbols with semantic properties, but it does not strictly depend on this assumption. Since only the 'shape' (syntax, orthography) of internal symbols can be relevant to their causal powers, not their semantic relations to items in the world, we need, if we are to save content for psychology, to find a way of *linking* shape with semantics. We need, that is, to suppose that content is somehow reflected in intrinsic features of the symbol: that distinctions of content are mirrored by distinctions of shape. Let us call the claim that there are such shape/content links the *encoding thesis*. The encoding thesis says that semantic properties are perfectly matched by syntactic properties – semantics is coded into syntax. As binary codes can conserve the information carried by the codes of natural language, so syntax can code and conserve every item of semantic information relating to a given symbol.[29] Distinctions of reference between singular terms, say, get encoded as differences of syntactic shape. There exists an adequate translation scheme from semantic descriptions of mental symbols to syntactic descriptions of those symbols; so we can always reconstruct a content attribution from a suitable syntactic description of the symbol in question (and vice versa). And it is in virtue of this one–one correspondence between semantic and syntactic properties that content gets a causal foothold. For whenever a content enters into a causal explanation we know that there exists some intrinsic syntactic property of the underlying symbol that is turning the wheels of the causal mechanism. In other words, content attributions can occur legitimately in causal explanations

---

[28] See Fodor, 'Methodological Solipsism Considered as a Research Strategy in Cognitive Psychology', and Pylyshyn, *Computation and Cognition*.

[29] Sometimes a partial encoding thesis is adopted, as a concession to twin earth cases; this thesis holds that only 'narrow content' is encoded internally. This already retreats significantly from folk psychology, since that psychology individuates content widely; the resulting position is thus deeply revisionary of our usual ways of ascribing content. And the new notion of narrow content is apt to spiral away into ineffability, as it does in Fodor's *Psychosemantics*. His position *seems* to be that narrow content is not specifiable using ordinary 'that'-clauses, so that scientific psychology cannot follow folk psychology in the way it characterizes mental states. Fodor's vindication of folk psychology thus ends up looking pretty hollow: the kind of content we can save is not the kind spoken of in our ordinary ascriptions of belief and desire – indeed, it is inexpressible using embedded 'that'-clauses. Some vindication!

because they are guaranteed to have syntactic *proxies*. In answer to the question how extrinsic relations can feature in the mental causal nexus, the encoding thesis says: strictly speaking, they don't; rather, it is the syntactic properties for which they stand proxy that so feature. It is the mapping between these two levels of description that explains and legitimates the use of content in psychology.

There are, I think, two main problems with the encoding thesis as an answer to the causal objection. We can present the first problem as a dilemma. Either content is coded into syntax or it is not. If it is not, then it has a chance of doing some work not already covered by syntax; but the causal objection then deprives it of any hope of doing such additional causal-explanatory work. But if it is, so that it does its causal work by proxy, then it seems redundant to invoke it – we could simply stick with syntax. The second horn of the dilemma is an application of Occam's razor: keep your theoretical entities down to a minimum, compatibly with preservation of explanatory power. The encoding thesis, by guaranteeing a translation from content to syntax, invites the elimination of talk of content altogether in favour of syntactic talk. At best content-based theories become mere notational variants of syntactic theories, if the encoding thesis is true. The case is comparable with epiphenomenalism about mental states in general: holding an encoding thesis does not restore explanatory dignity to mental states if it is really the underlying brain states that are doing all the explanatory work. If it is the shapes of mental symbols that turn the causal cogs, then surely we can get by with predicates of shape; we do not need to concern ourselves with what these predicates may translate in the way of semantics.[30] Consider an analogy. We come across a race of people who explain dissolvings of solids in liquids by appeal to wholly extrinsic relations to items quite extraneous to the substances involved. For example, they say that salt dissolves in water because salt is R to the Eiffel tower, where R is a relation that every solid bears to some extraneous landmark (it is all part of some strange cosmic myth). We are not presumptuous enough to question their cultural lore, but we do drop hesitant hints about the explanatory utility of R and the Eiffel tower in accounting for why salt dissolves in water. They nod and smile, then tell us that things are not quite as they appear: it may look as if their explanatory apparatus is quite inappropriate to the job, but in fact

---

[30] There are two views the encoding thesis may take about the relation between semantic and syntactic properties: they are identical or they are distinct. The distinctness view, which is more natural and plausible, has the problem that semantic properties do not need to be referred to in a causal psychology, and are not referred to by syntactic predicates. The identity view allows that semantic properties are referred to but only under syntactic descriptions, so that semantic predicates can be dispensed with. Either way no talk of semantic content is permitted; the talk will be exclusively of syntax and its causal powers. But this is like trying to 'save' the correspondence theory of truth by claiming that correspondence is actually reconstructable from the purely inter-sentential relation of coherence.

(they assure us) *R*-relatedness to the Eiffel tower is coded into the molecular structure of salt – and so for all the other solids they identify thus extrinsically in explanatory contexts. We frown a bit, shuffle our feet and eventually ask them why, if that is so, they don't just cut out the extrinsic stuff altogether and go right for the molecular structure – after all, it can do all that *R* and the Eiffel tower can do and it doesn't look as strange. History does not record their reaction to this suggestion, but we can be sure that some of the more reflective among them went away and gave the matter some serious thought. Just so, the encoding thesis about content invites its theoretical elimination: by selling content short it makes it good for nothing. In a regimented psychological theory, in which all unnecessary baggage has been stripped away, we will not find attributions of content, only bloodless descriptions of syntactic shape. The lesson is that content will have to do something *more* than syntax does if it is to be reserved a secure place in that finished psychological theory. And the problem we are having is that by doing more content seems to absent itself from the causal nexus.

The second problem concerns the inherent plausibility of the encoding thesis. For, construed literally, it looks highly *im*plausible: the semantics of a language is simply not coded into its syntax. Consider natural public languages like English: there is nothing *like* a one–one correspondence between meaning and syntactic shape. The same shaped words can have different meanings (ambiguity), and the same meanings can be carried by differently shaped words (synonymy) – and this is even before we get onto indexicality in which the breakdown becomes systematic. The relation between syntax (orthography) and semantics is conventional and flexible; mutual covariation is not the rule. To this observation it may be replied that a less literal construal would be more charitable. By 'syntax' is meant whatever intrinsic states underlie the causal dispositions associated with an internal symbol – presumably brain states at some level of description. Let us accept this more liberal notion of the syntactic. Then we still have all the problems stemming from twin earth cases: we still have distinctions of content cut finer than distinctions of causal role. So any strongly external kinds of content there are will not gain entry to psychological theory on the authority of the encoding thesis. That leaves only the weakly external contents, and their right of entry is severely restricted too: even if the intrinsic causal role of a mental state does uniquely determine its weakly external content, the correlation between causal basis and content is just that – mere correlation. The one is a quite different species of animal from the other. The internal may *correlate* with the external – there is some function from one to the other – but the arguments and values of that function are not items with the same kind of structure or nature.[31]

[31] Syntax itself has no 'directedness' to the world, no intentionality; but semantic relations essentially consist in such 'pointing beyond'. So the idea of a syntactic explication or reduction of

In roughly the same way there is a function from material objects to regions of space – for every object there is a unique place at which it is located (at a time) – but to speak of encoding here would presumably be to stretch a point. To justify places in some explanatory theory would not ipso facto be to justify material objects, despite the fact that no object lacked a place; and to justify internal causal bases in a psychological theory would not ipso facto be to justify weakly external contents, despite the fact that for every such content we could point to a unique intrinsic basis. Encoding has to mean more than the existence of such a function; it has to mean genuine *mirroring*, some sort of recapitulation of the distinctive features of that which is mirrored. But correspondence cannot be captured by what lies on one side of the correspondence. I think, then, that the encoding thesis is not the answer to our problem.

4   I want to build up to the answer to our problem that I favour by first considering the application of mathematics to the physical world in explanatory theories. For this is a procedure that bears a striking analogy (at least prima facie) with ascriptions of content in psychology, as several writers have observed.[32] In particular, it looks all but impossible to give a causal justification for exploiting relations to numbers in physical theories. On the face of it, we routinely refer to numbers in explanatory contexts, as when we say that the water turned to steam because it reached 100 degrees centigrade. Physics is shot through with such numerical reference. But it cannot really be supposed that reference to numbers helps in characterizing the causal mechanisms at work in producing a particular state or event. There are two reasons why such a supposition would be doomed. First, numbers themselves are abstract and hence cause nothing; and neither are properties of numbers capable of causal relevance (that 2 is even could not be causally relevant to the instantiation of any physical properties by physical objects). Second, and more germane to our concerns here, numbers are extrinsic to the causal transactions they are invoked to describe: they are not parts of the cogs within the causal mechanism – they exist somewhere else entirely (perhaps in platonic heaven). So even if numbers were not abstract, they would still be

content seems a contradiction in terms; certainly it is a million miles away from the folk psychological notion of what a belief is *about*. The trouble is that the encoding thesis concedes far too much to the causal objection to stand a chance of holding genuine full-blooded content in place. For nothing wholly intrinsic would ever be recognizable as the reference relation.

[32] See Field, 'Mental Representation', Davidson, 'Reality without Reference', Churchland, 'Eliminative Materialism and Propositional Attitudes'. My use of this analogy stresses the role of the worldly constituents of propositions as indices of mental contents. (Compare the numbers that compose the ordered triples that are employed to specify spatial coordinates.)

causally extraneous and hence not justifiable in the way causally intrinsic entities are.[33] They cannot be justified in the way atoms are. The question must then arise what explanatory role numbers *are* fit to play, if any. Why do we refer to them in our theories?

Once this question has been asked we can imagine becoming seized with doubt about the utility of numbers in explanatory theories. Impressed by the causal inertness and extraneousness of numbers, we begin pressing such questions as these: How can number-based physics be legitimate, given that physical processes are driven solely by intrinsic states of the physical system? How can water's turning to steam *depend* upon its standing in some extrinsic relation to the abstract object 100? Numbers cannot jiggle molecules! Since physical processes have 'access' only to the intrinsic 'shape' of what they operate on, how can numbers ever make a difference to what happens in the physical world? How can numbers figure as physical inputs into causal sequences? Isn't it a sort of category mistake to press numbers into causal-explanatory service? Doesn't number-based physics violate a plausible principle of 'methodological solipsism'? Are not numbers otiose, epiphenomenal, dispensable? Should not physics accept a 'formality constraint' which does away with reference to numbers? Perhaps number-based physics is an obsolete remnant of 'folk physics', which has been only incompletely abandoned? It may be a convenient way to talk about the physical world, but it cannot be taken seriously as an indispensable component of a finished physics. Maybe physics stands in need of radical conceptual overhaul?

Faced with these questions someone might advance an encoding thesis. Relations to numbers are coded into intrinsic physical states of objects, so that they stand as proxies for those states. There is thus a one–one correspondence between numerical relations and conditions of the causal mechanisms. Only if there were no such correspondence would numerical differences *make* no difference. But, again, such as encoding thesis would run into much the same problems as before: if it is true, then it renders numbers otiose after all, since what does the coding can in principle do everything that that which is encoded does (and without the misleading appearance that the latter does more). In a properly regimented theory, reference to numbers would not need to occur,

[33] Suppose you identified numbers with inscriptions of numerals. Then numbers would be concrete and be capable of entering into causal relations, but presumably it would be mistaken to think that they entered into the very causal processes they are used to describe: the inscription of '100' on a piece of paper is not part of the causal process involved in making water turn to steam at 100 degrees centigrade. Why? – because of extrinsicness. Field emphasizes the causal extrinsicness of numbers in *Science Without Numbers*, as well as their abstractness. He enunciates the principle: 'underlying every good extrinsic explanation there is an intrinsic explanation' (p. 44). This principle is then used to motivate his nominalist programme. The same principle could be invoked with respect to extrinsic content and psychological explanation.

being replaced by reference to the actually operative physical states the numbers were used to identify in the old formulation. At best numbers feature merely as convenient ways of picking out the fundamental theoretical properties; they have no indispensable role in theories of the physical world. Mere instrumental utility is the best they can hope for.

Now it is not my aim here to advocate any particular view about the role of numbers in physics (and other sciences). I am concerned, rather, to exploit the parallel with content-based psychology in order to arrive at a better understanding of what is going on in that latter area. And the point I have been making is that a very similar dialectic arises for the two cases. The same pattern of moves and countermoves comes naturally for both. This is, in a certain way, comforting for the adherent of content: if all that is wrong with content-based psychology is that it resembles number-based physics, then there can't really be all *that* much wrong with it. Would that all our theories had such troubles! However, any complacency we may feel as a result of the parallel is apt to turn to panic once we start taking the idea of a number-free physics seriously, as Hartry Field has done.[34] Indeed, one of his reasons for trying to implement this nominalist programme is the requirement of explanatory intrinsicness, which numbers violate.[35] Suppose then that the nominalist programme were well-motivated, and that it could be comprehensively carried out (as Field has given us reason to suppose). Then pursuing the parallel we would expect similar developments with respect to content-based psychology, since the same basic motivations *seem* to apply there too. Just as we must rewrite physics without making reference to numbers, so we must rewrite psychology without making reference to content. Thus the analogy, so far from encouraging complacency about content, should promote extreme anxiety about its ultimate fate. The causal objection ditches both numbers and content in the end; *it* is not refuted by their demonstrable indispensability. Science without numbers; psychology without content. The parallel with numbers turns out to be a wolf in sheep's clothing.

But let us complacently suppose instead, at least for present purposes, that Field's nominalist programme is *ill*-advised, that numbers are here to stay, that they are indispensable in physics. Would number-based physics *then* provide a

---

[34] See his *Science Without Numbers*. When I first started thinking about this I thought the parallel with numbers already showed that the causal objection had to be unsound, but now it does not seem to me so easy. Field's view is essentially that the causal objection *is* sound for numbers; so it would be suspect for me simply to rely on the received idea that not all theoretical entities need to be causal since numbers are not but do an indispensable theoretical job in science.

[35] Field's nominalism about numbers seems closely akin, in motivation and form, to his 'syntacticalist' proposal in 'Mental Representation'. Perhaps his idea of the 'conservativeness' of mathematics is mirrored by the 'conservativeness' of content?

good model for content-based psychology? Could it be that contents play the same *sort* of role in psychology that numbers play in physics?

I think that the parallel is at best partial. Although number-based physics might provide a model for how theoretical indispensability need not rest on causal involvement, the *way* in which numbers figure in physics is importantly different from the way we want content to figure in psychology. The numbers used in measurement index physical facts according to a choice of scale; choose a different scale and you will assign a different number. There is thus, in the numerical indexing relation, a conventional or stipulative element – *which* number gives the temperature of an object is essentially arbitrary. But (I would insist) the assignment of content to psychological subjects is not in this way arbitrary, unless we are prepared to take on a very radical form of content indeterminacy: namely, that it is a matter of mere stipulation which objects and properties I assign to you (or to myself), as constituents of propositions, in describing you (or myself) psychologically.[36] My present demonstrative thought's being about that tree is just not the conventional affair that my coffee's being 98 degrees centigrade is – so I am prepared to assert. This is no doubt connected with the fact that there are various *natural* relations in which we stand to the constituents of content – centrally (but not only) causal relations (them on us, we on them). Numbers, by contrast, are not naturally related in these ways to what they are used to measure. And the attribution of content is constrained by these natural relations, unlike the assignment of numbers. Thus we do not think of hot objects as *about* the numbers that index them; we do not impute number-directedness to measured objects – mathematical intentionality, arithmetic meaning. We simply *impose* numbers on the world, applying mathematics to a reality that exists independently of numbers. But this is not the way we tend to think about content: we *find* that a subject has various contentful states – we do not have the idea of a mind existing independently of the imposition of content upon it.[37] Intentionality is (in some sense) a natural phenomenon, but the mathematical indexing relation has the look of an artefact. Furthermore, it seems strained to regard content attribution as analogous to measurement as such – to see the

[36] Davidson does not recoil from this consequence of the comparison in 'Reality without Reference'; indeed, he welcomes it. I am not that tough(-minded).

[37] It seems constitutive of the mental realm that it be populated by states with specific contents, i.e. targeted onto an array of propositions. The mental (qua mental) is not thinkable apart from such targeting, with the concomitant targeting onto the world. But it does not seem similarly true that the material world is constitutively targeted onto the world of numbers: the measurement relation between material things and abstract entities does not seem to *constitute* what it is to be a material thing. Brentano said that the essence of mind is directedness to the world; but it is not similarly attractive to say that the essence of matter is directedness to numbers. (Note that where the latter relation seems least arbitrary, i.e. in counting, the reference to numbers is dispensable in favour of quantifiers and identity.)

psychological *point* of extrinsic content as analogous to the mensural point of numbers. It is true that in both cases we exploit a normative structure (logic, the number system) to aid our theories of the empirical world, but it is hard to see how the constituents of propositions can play the same sort of *mensural* role as numbers – that is not *why* we go in for these extrinsic descriptions.[38] Referring to external objects and properties in the ascription of content is not a kind of measurement. (Note that we are not now trying to explain why we ascribe propositional *structures* to states of subjects; our question is why we *fill* those structures with extraneous items. So the point of applying logic to minds does not transfer directly to the point of assigning extrinsic worldly items to minds.)

It is difficult for me to continue with this insistence on the important differences between content and numbers without myself proffering some more positive account of what the point of content *is*. For without such an account some people may be prepared to overlook these apparent differences, counting them as so much uncritical folk psychology; they may claim that we need to *revise* our naive conception of content so as to bring it into line with the analogy – this being our only hope for finding *some* role for content. After all, acknowledging the essential arbitrariness of content is better than giving up on it entirely. However, I do not myself believe that we are forced into this fallback position; for there is an account of content that preserves and explains the disanalogies with numbers just gestured at.[39] It comes next.

5   The account I favour lays heavy stress on the *teleology* of mental states. It is not an account that originates with me; indeed I was slow to come round to it.[40] I

---

[38] Remember that the objects and properties assigned are just your ordinary objects and properties, the mundane things you talk about when you are not doing psychology: and they don't look much like measuring instruments in that latter context. Constituents of content are not in the same business as calculational aids: one doesn't do sums with them.

[39] I have not considered the suggestion that ascriptions of content have their point in enabling us to exploit other people's beliefs to arrive at knowledge of the world, i.e. semantic notions pull their weight in a theory of testimony. This suggestion has its own troubles, but even if correct it would not provide what *we* are seeking, since it locates the point of content in the enterprise of getting to know about the *world*, not getting to know about the *mind*. That is, such a theory of testimony, enabling us to read facts about the world off facts about minds, would not be of interest to the psychologist qua psychologist; for he is interested in developing illuminating theories of the mind itself. Or, alternatively, he is interested in the explanation of the subject's behaviour, not in what the subject can teach him about physics and history and where the rest-rooms are. If content is to be of concern to the psychologist, then it must have its point in telling us something important about psychological subjects themselves, not merely in helping us find out about the nonpsychological world. I discuss this kind of proposal in 'The Structure of Content'; see also Field, 'The Deflationary Conception of Truth'.

[40] The earliest statement of the view I know is Dennis Stampe, 'Toward a Causal Theory of Linguistic Representation'. See also Dretske, 'Misrepresentation', Fodor, 'Semantics, Wisconsin

think that was because I failed to see what useful work the teleological account might do for us; I didn't see which itch was being scratched. It looked to me like reductionism for its own sake. (And it *is* a lot to come round to.) In any case, it now seems to me that the account derives its primary motivation from scepticism about content-based psychology; it enables us to find a theoretical rationale for externally individuated content. In particular, it provides a convincing way around the causal objection. That, at any rate, is what I intend to propose (I do not know that other writers have seen the teleological account is quite this light).[41] The general idea is going to be that teleologically based taxonomies of mental states are not straightforwardly causal, yet they perform an important theoretical function, of which content partakes. I thus concede the force of the causal objection but insist that there can be more to explanation than simply the citation of causes.[42] What the causal objection forgets is that mental states have an environment-directed purpose, and that specifying that purpose tells us something important about them.

Let us start with the notion of *relational proper function*.[43] The proper function of some organ or trait or process is what it is designed to do, what it is supposed to do, what it ought to do. Proper functions can come about either through the intentions of a designer or through a mindless process like natural selection. A hammer has the proper function of knocking in nails in virtue of the intentions of its makers and users; a heart has the proper function of pumping blood in virtue of (roughly) the selective pressures that have shaped the physiology of organisms. The proper function of some item is not defined dispositionally or causally: what something does (or is disposed to do) is not always what it is supposed to do. The notion of proper function is normative in the sense that it is defined in terms of

Style', David Papineau, *Reality and Representation*, and especially Ruth Millikan, *Language, Thought and Other Biological Categories*.

[41] I do not wish to commit myself to the full reductionist ambitions of the teleological theory; in fact, as I shall suggest, it is only part of the truth about content. My central thesis is the more limited one, that the extrinsicness of content can be connected with the world-directed functions of mental states, and derives its rationale from that connection. I would quite like to see the teleological theory, in conjunction with other ideas, developed into a set of necessary and sufficient conditions for content, but I do not want to stick my neck out any further than is necessary for the purpose at hand. A more wishy-washy attitude towards the teleological theory seems prudent in the current state of understanding. Still, I do think it is a *good* theory.

[42] More precisely, teleologically charged predicates can be used to identify states that are in fact causes but these predicates do not themselves cite aspects of the underlying causal mechanism. Mental events and states can be brought under both causal and teleological descriptions, but these specify quite different properties of what they describe; and extrinsic content is bound up with the latter type of description, not the former. The power of content ascriptions to illuminate is therefore dependent upon the interest of teleological information about states of organisms. This should become clearer as we proceed.

[43] I get this phrase from Millikan's book. What follows more or less summarizes her account.

what an item *should* do, not what it actually does or is disposed to do. In the case of evolved organisms function is always in fact ultimately relative to survival (or gene reproduction): the function of an evolved characteristic is always ultimately to enhance reproductive capacity, as Darwin taught us. Generally this means that it is to enable the organism to cope with its given environment: to locate food, evade predators, protect itself against heat or cold, and so on. An organism must be designed (by natural selection) according to the environmental constraints; indeed the given environment is the chief *architect* in constructing a species of organism, since it does the selecting of characteristics. And here is where the relationality of proper function comes in: proper functions are generally defined *relatively* to some environmental object or feature. Thus the function of the chameleon's pigmentation mechanism is to make the chameleon the same colour as its immediate environment; the function of a lion's teeth is (inter alia) to tear the flesh of its prey; the function of the antelope's leg muscles is to enable it to flee from the lion's teeth; the function of the peacock's tail feathers is to attract and impress the peahen; the function of the bee's dance is to help other bees locate nectar; and so on. In each case we specify the function of the characteristic in terms of a relation to some environmental item. This is not a bit surprising, given that the very reason why the characteristics in question *exist* is that the organism is subject to environmental pressures of various kinds. We might indeed think of an organism's phenotype as a kind of sculpture wrought by the environment over evolutionary time (he is a slow and methodical worker but he gets results). The environment is the matrix out of which organisms take shape; an organism is a sort of complex reflection (or refraction) of a particular environmental niche. Thus it is that function is an environment-relative notion (in the case of evolved organisms). As we might say, function is typically extrinsically defined, i.e. by reference to items extraneous to the organism in question.[44]

Now there is clearly a lot to be said about the general notion of biological relational proper function, but I think I have said enough to convey the core idea – enough, at least, to predict where I am heading with the notion. For we can now see that relational proper function can be used to impose a taxonomy upon traits of organisms that is differently based from purely causal taxonomy. To classify by function is not to classify by causal mechanism. Each function is indeed subserved by some causal mechanism, but the *principles* which guide the

---

[44] A function-based biology thus essentially includes features of the environment in its theoretical apparatus. A science of biological adaptation is concerned with relations between organisms and the world: adaptiveness is always adaptiveness *to*. Paraphrasing Brentano: functions are always directed at something beyond themselves.

two taxonomic schemes are theoretically quite distinct.[45] In fact, there is a failure of unique determination both ways round: the same causal mechanism can subserve distinct functions in different environments in which the organism has evolved; and the same function can be subserved by distinct causal mechanisms in different organisms. There is what something is *designed* to do, and there is *how* it does it: and these are not at all the same thing. What natural selection must do is to install a causal mechanism of some kind which carries out the function selected for in a specific environment, but that function is not interdefinable with the mechanism. The skins of animals, for example, may serve different functions depending upon their environment (land or sea, say), though they can be made of the same materials; and the same function may be performed by different material kinds of skin. The teleological taxonomy thus contains information about the trait that is not contained in a nonfunctional description of the causal mechanism; roughly, information about what the trait is *for*. And so specifications of relational proper function have explanatory utility – the kind appropriate to biological understanding. Knowing what something is for tells us why it does what it does, and it enables us to derive predictions about what else we can expect it to do (in normal conditions). Functional understanding enables us to impose a systematizing and explanatory theoretical structure, of a quasi-normative kind, upon the brute physiological mechanisms we find in the bodies of organisms. It enables us to make *sense* of the causal transactions involving organisms that we observe and conjecture. Much of this understanding already belongs to folk biology, of course: the functions of the limbs, of the stomach, of the sex organs are all pretty much understood by most people, so that a good deal of lore about relational proper function is a (perhaps tacit) part of our ordinary ways of thinking about ourselves and others. But scientific biology expands and refines these homely functional conceptions, fitting them into a systematic theory, occasionally surprising us with some novel and unexpected revelation about why organisms are built the way they are. Relational proper function is thus an established part of commonsense and scientific biology. It is, we might say, the basic biological notion.

It is not difficult to see how this idea might be applied to traits of mind as well as to traits of body. The mind and its characteristic powers and properties are evolutionary products too, and as such may be expected to exhibit functional

---

[45] I have not said what it is that confers a particular function on a trait, i.e. what governs functional taxonomies. There is controversy about this – and indeed the question is not easy. Is function a backward-looking historical fact about the trait, or is it a forward-looking fact concerning what effects the trait has in certain ideal circumstances? I want to remain neutral on such questions here. It suffices that function is not definable in terms of actual causal properties of the trait, i.e. in terms of causal mechanism or actual causal role. Millikan has a good discussion of this.

features: mental states will have their own distinctive relational proper functions. On general grounds, then, we may anticipate environment-directed functions on the part of such states as desire, belief and perception; they too will play their part in helping the organism adapt itself to the environmental contingencies. This is as true for our minds as it is for the minds of fish and frogs. We are all products of evolution: each species having a particular type of mind as well as a particular type of body. This, presumably, is not (or ought not to be) in dispute – nor is it, thus far, of any great relevance to the *content* of mental states. Where the teleological theory gets interesting is in its claim that *the relational proper function of representational mental states coincides with their extrinsically individuated content.* That is to say, content is an upshot or concomitant of function; the relationality of the former reflects the relationality of the latter. It is not merely that mental states have both content and function; the two are intimately connected, integrally related.[46] The attraction of this claim is most easily and strikingly appreciated in the case of desire. Consider the desire for water, caused (we may safely suppose) by the organism's need for water. What is the biological function of that desire? Why, to bring about the introduction of *water* into the interior of the organism – to make it drink water. The desire may not of course succeed in fulfilling this goal – its actual causal career may not match its original purpose – but that, nevertheless, is what the desire is there *for*. It exists in order to have certain environment-directed effects. But now we cannot help but notice a remarkable coincidence: in giving the environmental relatum of the relational proper function of the desire we mention the very environmental item that the desire is *about*. Amazing! The content of the desire contains water (the liquid itself) as a constituent, this being what individuates that content, and that very substance is *also* constitutive of the desire's having the biological function it has. The environmental component of the desire's function makes, as it were, a second appearance as a constituent of the desire's content. But (the teleological account insists) this concidence cannot be mere coincidence: the double appearance of water must reflect a systematic conceptual or theoretical connection – function fixes, and is fixed by, content. In the case of cognitive mental states, such as perception, where the 'direction of fit' is reversed, we find a parallel coincidence

---

[46] Thus, which proposition, externally individuated, is correctly assigned to a mental state as its content is constrained by the relational proper function of the state; content and function do not float free of each other, each going their separate ways ad libitum. Function, we might say, is criterial for content in something like the standard sense of that (somewhat obscure) notion – strongly presumptive though not perhaps absolutely indefeasible. So there might be possible cases in which function and content come apart, but these would be necessarily exceptional. I suppose it is conceivable that human beings should have a death-wish whose function was to keep them alive – say by causing them to withdraw themselves from some of the riskier ways of living. But this could not be the general case.

of content and function. Take the frog's visual states in respect of bugs: their function is clearly to indicate the presence of bugs, so that the frog's need of bugs can be satisfied by its acting appropriately; and, remarkably enough, the content of these experiences is also bug-related. A sensory state fulfils its function of indicating *Fs* by representing the world as containing *Fs*; and it fails in discharging that function when what it represents is not how things environmentally are.[47] We have here a very basic biological duality: a need of the organism in respect of the world (to eat it, to escape it, to mate with it), and a sensor that will indicate to the organism when the environment is the way it is needed to be (or not to be). Evolution must install mechanisms which perform these interlocking functions of sensitivity to need and sensitivity to what in the world will meet the need: desire and perception are the solutions it has come up with, at least in 'higher' organisms. The teleological theory sees in these basic relational functions the deep roots of content. Belief comes into the picture as a way of guiding behaviour in the light of perception so as to satisfy desires. Thus

---

[47] How we interpret the word 'indicate' here determines the status we can claim for the teleological account in which it is embedded. If we wish to develop an account of mental representation that does not take the meaning of 'represent' as given, then we shall have to interpret 'indicate' in such a way that indication does not presuppose representation. The natural idea is to take it in the nonintentional sense it has when we say that clouds indicate (mean) rain, i.e. as just regular causal sensitivity. This is the strategy of Dretske in 'Misrepresentation'. On this strategy, representation proper emerges as the 'logical product' of function and causal sensitivity, teleology and detection. But we might renounce such analytic ambitions and take 'indicate' to mean simply 'represent'. This would, of course, preclude us from explaining the meaning of 'represent' in terms of 'function of indicating/ representing', but it would not stop us making other claims for the account. Suppose we agree that perceptual states have relational proper functions, and that a complete theory of an organism tells us the functions of its traits. Then we can specify the relational function of perceptual states simply by saying what they are supposed to represent: their relational functions just are specified by *using* intentional notions. So if we omit the intentional relations we omit one whole class of functions, and that is to omit something that counts theoretically. On the other hand, if the representational relations are *not* their relational functions, then we have not yet found a place for content. In other words, we do not need to be teleological reductionists about content in order to give a teleological reply to the question what the *point* of speaking of intentional relations is. But, also, the account that presupposes grasp of 'represents' is not thereby trivial even as an account of the conditions under which a state has a particular content. The account says that S represents P iff the function of S is to represent P. But it is not inconceivable that what S represents is not what it is *supposed* to represent; the alleged coincidence here is not guaranteed by logic or the meaning of the terms on either side of the biconditional. So the biconditional still expresses a substantive nontautological thesis. And it lays down noncircular conditions for the ascription of contents to states: viz. ascribe the content the state is supposed to have and no other content. The teleological account can therefore be philosophically nutritious even when it takes 'represents' or 'refers' as primitive. (Compare the biconditional: an object is red iff it is disposed to appear red in normal conditions.) Still, I think it is reasonable to expect that we can do a little better than that with the account: for we can get some insight into what 'represents' *means* by judiciously combining the idea of function with the (nonintentional) notion of indication or detection or lawlike connection. We have, then, a number of options, and which we choose will depend upon what we want to do with the account.

the function of the belief that there is water here is to combine with perceptions of water to guide behaviour in the satisfaction of the desire (and hence need) for water: the desire can only cause the right goal-satisfying behaviour if it is controlled by beliefs about the current state of the environment. In this way, then, the functions of mental states are absorbed into their content, thus incorporating the worldly items that the functions themselves concern. Teleology is what originally brings the world into the mind. It spans the divide.[48]

What I have just said is the merest sketch of the general shape of a teleological theory of content; other authors have done much to fill out and deepen the sketch.[49] But I think I have said enough to give a sense of how the theory answers the causal objection and locates content in a wider (and eminently respectable) context. The fundamental point is that staring at the causal mechanisms that underlie contentful states will never reveal the functions such mechanisms serve – and *this* is why content cannot be recovered from causal basis.[50] The causal mechanisms whereby beliefs and desires and perceptions produce their effects are indeed methodologically solipsist, while content is essentially not – so content cannot be saved on the strength of what it takes for the causal wheels to turn. But the biological function of a trait, mental or bodily, cannot be revealed by examination of the causal mechanisms either: functional taxonomy is not methodologically solipsist – it reaches out beyond the confines of the organism and the causal processes that control its behaviour. So if we rest content on function, we locate its point in a theoretical structure that inherently (and gladly) traffics in extrinsic relations to the environment. Correspondence relations emerge as a special case of relational proper function. And just as no sane person thinks that functional taxonomies must be reconstructable in terms of intrinsic causal taxonomies in order to be theoretically justifiable, so we should not make

---

[48] Let me emphasize that I am not simply *identifying* reference with relational function. On the contrary, I think substantial further conditions have to be met before we have anything describable as genuine intentionality – in particular, the states which have these functions need to be embedded in a network of states that exhibits a rational structure. The function has to attach to something which is itself propositional: only in the context of a proposition does relational function become reference. A similar point needs to be made about causal theories too: they cannot supply conditions sufficient for reference without the assumption that the causal relation holds between an object (or property) and something propositional in form: only in the context of a proposition do causal relations constitute reference. The theory of intentionality cannot be separated from the question what makes something propositional. Relational functions need to subtend propositional structures before they can qualify as relations of *reference*.

[49] Millikan's is the most thorough treatment I know.

[50] If we think of the mechanisms as syntactic in character, then the point is that gazing at syntax (shapes) will never reveal the world-directed functions of these mechanisms; this is *why* semantics is not legible from mechanism. Content transcends syntax *because* function transcends mechanism. We cannot discover what a sentence is *for* just by scrutinizing its syntactic form. Hence content will not be vouchsafed by the mechanisms of mental causation.

that unreasonable demand of content-based taxonomies – they being one kind of functional taxonomy. The purpose of a causal mechanism is not contained in the way it works, but it is no less respectable for that. (We now see why the analogy with number-based physics is only partially correct: for it is not part of the *function* of traits of inanimate physical objects to bring them into a specific relation with a particular number. This is the sense in which attributions of content are natural and nonarbitrary, whereas assignments of numbers in measurement are conventional and stipulative. Hence there *is* a fundamental difference in the rationale for number-based physics and content-based psychology; the two sorts of assignment are quite differently motivated.)

It is important to be clear about how exactly I am using the teleological account in motivating externally individuated content. I am emphatically *not* using it to give a complete theory of how propositions come to be assigned to states of subjects. Specifically, I am not suggesting that propositional *structures* come into play on the basis of relational proper function, that the propositionality of mental states is emergent on their function alone. To make that suggestion would invite the following obvious and crushing objection: traits of organisms can have relational functions and yet not have propositional content – *most* traits, in fact, are like that. Hearts, for example, do not represent what they are designed to do. That objection is, of course, entirely sound: but it does not count against what I have said. For what I have been concerned with is not how states get to be propositional but how they get to be *relational*, i.e. identified in terms of extrinsic worldly descriptions. To put it differently, my question has been: *granted* that mental states have propositional structure, why do we insist on filling that structure with extraneous items? Why do we not just stick with internal sentential structure and let correspondence relations go?[51] Of course it is a perfectly good question why we ascribe propositional structure to mental states, but it has not been my question. I have assumed that propositionality is well-motivated and then gone on to ask how we might justify relating states of subjects to the world. What do such relations buy for us that is not already covered by assignments of suitably structured propositional entities? Why go beyond syntax? A full theory of why we ascribe the extrinsically individuated propositions we do to states of subjects would be (notionally at least) a bipartite theory: it would explain the assignment of propositional structures, and it would explain why those structures are related to the world in the particular way they are. Let me now indicate, then,

---

[51] I have not been trying to motivate just any kind of content; my concern has been to motivate content as an externalist understands it (the way *I* understand it). My efforts will not appeal to people who do not think of content in this way. A thoroughgoing internalist will not need to answer the question I have set myself, because internalism is consistent with a purely causal account of content. On the other hand, if the teleological story sounds plausible this will lend support to the externalism it helps legitimate: it will make externalism look nice and predictable.

how the teleological theory of the relationality of content might mesh with a theory of the internal structure of content. This is, in effect, the question of how relational function comes to be aboutness or intentionality – how teleology turns into truth conditions.

It is surely not far off the truth to say that the recognition of propositional structure in the mind of another is connected with the acknowledgement of *rationality* in their mental processes and plans of action. Under what conditions we acknowledge the presence of rationality is an interesting and difficult question, but it seems clear enough that propositional ascriptions are coeval with such acknowledgement. Essentially we come to see that mental transitions within the subject need to be described by invoking the normative apparatus of logic – the subject, we see, comes to be in that state because it *follows* from this other state. Psychological structure comes to be interpreted within logical structure. Causal transitions are seen as pieces of reasoning. Once propositions are ascribed to the subject we can begin to exploit the power of logic to predict his internal transitions and outer actions. Propositional psychology is applied logic. The ascription of propositional structure, then, is essentially a matter of describing transitions *between* mental states; it is keyed to relations *among* states of the subject. But if propositional psychology were keyed simply and wholly to capturing logical transitions, then it is hard to see how we could motivate anything beyond internal sentences (or other structures with the right combinatorial properties): why not limit ourselves to the (etiolated) notion of rationality permitted by purely syntactic theories of mind? Instead of saying that the subject goes from one contentful state into another, we could say instead that he goes from one sentential state into another.[52] This is why motivations for propositional structure do not immediately deliver motivations for extrinsic content.

Content arises, I suggest, at the intersection of rationality and teleology. Prismatically, as it were, rationality takes proper function and bends it into extrinsic content. Less metaphorically, when mental states with specific relational functions enter into certain transitional relations with other such states – the kind that invite logical description – then the upshot is representational content: reference, satisfaction, truth conditions – the structures of intentionality. Put the other way about, when sententially structured states come to be seen as having particular relational functions, they are then taken to have content. Reasoning

[52] One lesson of Field's 'Logic, Meaning, and Conceptual Role' is that a notion of rationality can be characterized that does not depend upon an appeal to referential truth conditions. So we cannot use the bare idea of rationality by itself to motivate extrinsic content. My suggestion, putting it in Field's terms, is that truth conditions result from embedding the subjective probability interpretation in a teleological context: the sentences have their conditional probabilities, but they also have their relational functions.

processes take us to syntax; teleology gets us from there to semantics; and then semantics feeds back to our understanding of reasoning. For vividness think of it developmentally: the infant (or our evolutionary ancestor) has mental states with functions that relate her to the environment; in due course these states begin to interact in complex ways, thus inviting logical description; at this stage the states come to have propositional contents in which the environmental relata of the functions figure. Neither the horizontal relations between mental states, nor the vertical relations that link these states to the world, suffice on their own to confer content; but together they mesh and bond to bring content into the world. A content-based psychology therefore rests on two foundation stones, *both* of which are needed if the theoretical structure is to be held securely in place. As a result of coordinating these two bases, the notion of rationality comes to be invested with genuine semantic significance and the notion of biological function gets set against a background of logical relations. Extrinsic content is the interlocking (better the fusion) of logical structure and proper function. Both together are necessary and neither alone is sufficient. My focus in this chapter has been on the contribution of function to content because my question has been how externalism about content can be squared with the apparent explanatory utility of content; I have not been concerned (except in the last two paragraphs) with the question of the utility of ascriptions of propositional *structure* – a question which it is widely agreed is not very hard to answer. (So if you think this latter question *is* hard to answer, then accepting my answer to the former question will not be enough on its own to convince you that propositional psychology is the right way for psychology to go; you might wish to accept relational functions for mental states but decline to embed them within propositional structures. Teleology without content: that might be your preferred conception of psychology.)

What is the basic form of psychological explanation according to the teleological account of content? To answer this we need to expose the structure of the explanatory mental properties, as the teleological account sees them. Suppose we explain why an organism performs some action by attributing a constellation of contentful states to the organism. The theory I have been outlining takes the explanation to involve three distinguishable elements. First, we are citing a cause, adverting to a causal mechanism, asserting the operation of a causal nexus: this element lies well within the limits of the organism.[53] Second, we are

---

[53] We do not, though, describe the mechanism – how it brings about what it does. That will be up to the neuroscientists and their colleagues. So in an important sense the *explanation* is not causal, if a causal explanation is one that describes how a causal mechanism works. The explanatory property – namely, a state with a certain content – is just not a 'mechanistic' property, any more than functional properties in general are. Reasons are not causally explanatory qua reasons, though reasons may in fact be causes. The causal mechanisms are in the head (literally), but reasons themselves are not in the head, since their contents are not. But in the same way the property of having the function of

attributing rational or logical relations to the causal states in question, locating them within a normative pattern: this element involves horizontal relations between mental states of the organism. Third, we are describing these causal-logical states in terms of their relational functions, saying what they are for, what they ought to achieve: this element introduces vertical relations between states of the organism and aspects of the environment. It would therefore be quite misleading to characterize such explanations as 'purely causal', as if they did not significantly differ from explanations of events in the inanimate world. Each of these elements, moreover, is robustly factual, firmly rooted in reality: there is nothing instrumentalist or fictionalist or second-class about such explanations – any more than biology itself is any of these things. The general form of the teleological component might be schematized as follows. Suppose a trait t of an organism x has the function of making x R to y, where y is some environmental item and R some relation between x and y. Let 'P' stand for the property of having this relational function. Now suppose that x performs some action e and we want to explain e by reference to x's being P. Then when we say that x did e because it was P what we say is that e occurred because x has a trait t whose function it is to make x R to y. And if the explanation is good, then this will adequately explain why e occurred: it will exhibit e as ensuring (or helping to ensure) that x got to be R to y. This schema applies both to content-based explanations and to nonpsychological teleological explanations. Citing the content of a mental state is giving its function, and this will explain why the organism did what it did: it drank the water because (causally) it had a desire whose function it is to bring about water drinking. Equally, we can explain why the chameleon changed colour by saying that its skin contains a device whose function it is to make the chameleon the same colour as its immediate environment, and this device caused the change of colour. (No doubt more interesting explanations can be contrived: I am only illustrating the general principle.) In both cases, giving the function of the causally operative trait tells us what the point of the explanandum event was – it fits it into a pattern of purposes. One advantage of this form of explanation is that it enables us to predict an organism's behaviour (in the broadest sense) without knowing the detailed workings of its causal mechanisms. For, if we know the needs of the organism – what it requires of the environment in order to flourish and survive – then we can generally infer

---

pumping blood to the muscles is not in the heart, since it involves a relation between the organ that is the heart and the muscles; the mechanism of that function, however, *is* right there in the heart. Functional properties of this kind are not causally explanatory either – if this means that they figure in the mechanisms that bring about the effects. We might more perspicuously say: explanation by reasons is not a species of mechanistic explanation, i.e. an account of the causal mechanisms whose operation led to the behaviour being explained. Cf. Arthur Collins, 'Action, Causality, and Teleological Explanation'.

(assuming a principle of normal functioning) that it is guided by states with specific functions: it does this thing because it has states whose function it is to enable it to do just that. In this way we infer that people have desires for food and sleep and sex – and we explain their behaviour accordingly – as well as imputing various beliefs about, and perceptions of, the world around them. Organisms tend to have the functional states they need to thrive and endure. Our ordinary attributions of content thus rely on a system of folk biology – a set of principles linking needs, functions and contents. This system obviates the necessity to have a look at what is going on inside people and other animals: we can explain and predict their behaviour without knowing the hidden mechanical details. And that is all to the good, since we don't typically *have* any notion of the internal workings that produce behaviour. Abandoning the functional taxonomy, and with it content, would therefore deprive us of this advantage, leaving us in blank ignorance of the springs of action, as well as gratuitously denuding organisms of their biologicality (and I hope none of us wants to do *that*).

In sum: the teleological account of world-directed content offers the hope of a naturalistic underpinning for content-based psychology, thus protecting it from scepticism about the legitimacy and point of ascriptions of content. Extrinsic content inherits the good repute of the teleological framework within which it is embedded. It is thus engaged in a worthwhile and productive line of business. It is not, after all, theoretically epiphenomenal. Moreover, the account is independently plausible and attractive. Content turns out to be not high-flown metaphysics but earthbound biology, as natural as you like. Nature extends beyond the head. There is nothing sinister about worldly correspondence.

6   I shall round off this chapter by drawing out some consequences of the approach to content I have been recommending. I expect these to put the approach in a good light.

(i) *Psychology and biology*   It is not infrequently said that psychologists should always remember that their subjects of study are biological organisms, whether rats or monkeys or human beings. Psychology should be seen (and heard) as a department of biology. I have argued that content-based psychology has become entrenched, and should be persisted in, because of its intimate connection with biological notions, notably relational proper function. This, I think, gives a rather strong and definite sense to the doctrine of the biological character of psychology. The mind, like the body, has evolved to have traits with environment-directed functions, and these functions have duly inserted themselves into propositional content. Conceiving mental processes purely syntactically, by contrast, fails to acknowledge the way that function has entered into the fixation of mental states: the mind may as well not be a biological system so far as purely syntactic descriptions of it are concerned. I suspect that the computer model of mind has been partly responsible for undermining (in some people's minds) the status of content in psychology – somewhat ironically since it was intended to rehabilitate the conception of mind as a symbol-manipulating device. Reflecting on the symbolic manipulations of computers, one is hard put to find a secure place for extrinsic content – for computers really do have the look of purely syntactic engines. Operations defined over intrinsic properties of symbols seem all there *is* to computational processes.[54] Content looks adventitious. If the teleological account of content is right, this is not hard to explain. For computers are not biological entities – so they do not have *original* teleology.[55] Being artefacts of their biological creators and tools of their biological users, they become derivatively invested with representational states; but this kind of derivative intentionality is apt to seem flimsy and metaphorical – too projective to be true. The reason is simply that their relational proper functions are also derivative and projected. *Because* they do not have inherent teleology, they do not have inherent intentionality; so their entitlement to literal factual content attributions is apt to appear weak and negligible. But then, if we insist on viewing the mind (or brain) on the model of the computer, thus forgetting or downplaying its biological character, we will also be prone, and reasonably enough, to regard content attribution as suspect and merely imposed from outside. An organ without original teleology can be nothing but a syntactic engine. The computer has the structure of rationality (a system of logically describable transitions among symbolic states) but it lacks the (original) teleology to give this dry husk real content. Accordingly, if we want to recognize semantics in the mind, we must treat the computer model with due reserve: it lacks the biological dimension that gives semantics a firm foothold. We need a properly biological psychology if we are to keep content solidly in place. Never forget that minds evolved to solve survival problems.[56]

(ii) *Content and science*   To what extent can content-based psychology be a

---

[54] Cf. John Searle's argument that computer programmes are purely syntactic recipes that cannot be used to bake semantic bread: see his 'Minds, Brains and Programs'.

[55] I learnt this phrase from Daniel Dennett.

[56] It is significant that computers are commonly used to model cognitive states, not affective or conative states. But this must strike us as biologically unrealistic, since beliefs exist in order to help organisms satisfy their desires, and hence their needs. So machines will have to model this whole psychological structure before they can realistically model any part of it. I myself would say that desire is the more basic propositional attitude, theoretically and developmentally. And desire is where teleology gets its initial grip on minds. Accordingly, artificial intelligence work should start with desire and work out from there to thought. Intentionality begins with wanting, I suggest, not with thinking. To simulate intentionality properly you need to simulate the entire biological system in which it is found, not attempt to slice off the cognitive part and hope to find real intentionality in that part considered by itself.

science? If our paradigm of science is physics, then content-based psychology can look pretty alien to science; its conceptual apparatus seems far removed from anything we find in the physical sciences. But if our conception of what it takes to be scientific is shaped by the science of biology, then content-based psychology will not look as alien and sui generis as it did before, assuming the teleological view of content. If the conceptual apparatus of content-based psychology is just a specialization of the conceptual apparatus of biology, though a rather special kind of specialization, then certainly it will have its roots in a discipline accurately described as a science. (Biology may not itself look like much of a 'science' if physics is our paradigm.) In so far as biology is concerned to discover laws, so too might content-based psychology have this concern, though the character of these laws may differ significantly from the kinds of laws sought by physics. One notable difference here stems from the normative character of the notion of function. If we know that the function of some trait is to bring about a certain state of affairs, then we know that it *ought* to bring that states of affairs about – that this would be for the trait to operate correctly, as it is supposed to. Thus the heart *should* pump the blood at a certain rate and so keep the organism alive. But it would be a version of the naturalistic fallacy (the 'converse naturalistic fallacy') to try to deduce from such a normative law (viz. 'hearts are supposed to pump blood') that a corresponding descriptive law obtains (viz. 'hearts do, as a matter of causal or nomic necessity, pump blood') – for that would be to try to deduce an *is* from an *ought*. Under normal conditions of well-functioning, of course, the normative law yields a corresponding descriptive law; but to say this is to build into the descriptive law a normatively defined initial condition. Nothing like this holds in physics, since it lacks the normative element proper to biology.[57] In much the same way, content-based psychology trades in normative laws; given a desire for water (and appropriate beliefs), an agent should seek water (other things being equal). Whether he in fact does what he should, given what he wants, is another matter, and not one that can be simply deduced from the original normative principle. It is true that in both cases we are concerned (at least in part) to use normative laws to make actual empirical predictions – we

---

[57] Here, then, we have the ideas of loose laws and normative principles, where the normativity is what explains the looseness. Where there are ideals looseness is sure to follow, the world being the place it is. Both themes – the looseness of psychological laws and their normative involvements – are to be found in Davidson's writings (e.g. 'Mental Events'), but the kinds of looseness and normativity he has in mind seem not to be teleologically based. One might, however, try to forge a connection here: the function of the belief-forming mechanisms is to generate beliefs that follow from other beliefs, so that it is a norm (ideal) of mental functioning that the norms (laws) of logic be respected. Your mind is not functioning as it (biologically) ought to if you do not believe what you (logically) ought to (within certain limits). This property of the mental has no 'echo' in physical theory (at least if we exclude biology from the domain of physical theory).

apply the norms to the actual course of nature – but this should not obscure the fact that the kinds of principles we are operating with are not straightforward empirical causal laws. There is thus plenty of scope for slack between what ought to happen, given a certain function, and what does in fact happen – a kind of slack not encountered in the physical sciences. But this asymmetry should not induce us to deny outright that content-based psychology can be a science – on pain of tarring biology with the same brush. Strict descriptive laws there may not be; scientific generalizations there may be.[58]

(iii) *Twin earth and teleology* Consider the skin of the organisms populating twin earth. Suppose it contains pigments chemically just like those of organisms on earth: these pigments cause the skin to darken under the impact of light and so forth. On earth we would say that the function of these pigments is (roughly) to protect organisms from light rays emanating from the sun – to prevent sunburn, we would say. But now suppose that twin earth orbits, not around the sun, but around a *twin sun*. The skin of organisms on twin earth has never been exposed to light rays from the sun, only to rays from the twin sun. Nevertheless, what happens locally at the skin – the causal mechanism that operates there – is indistinguishable from what happens at the skin of earthlings. Question: what is the function of these pigments on twin earth? I think we would naturally say that their function is to protect the organisms from rays emanating from the twin sun – to prevent twin sunburn, we would say. We would say this because the relation implicated in the function is a relation between the organisms and their environment – which contains the twin sun, not the sun.[59] In other words, function is environment-dependent; these functions are individuated by reference to the surrounding world. As we might put it, such functions are not 'in the body' – they are strongly external. You cannot then be an 'individualist' about relational functions like these. Teleology, here, is a contextual matter.

It is the same with functions that relate to natural kinds. The function of earth kidneys is to process water (H_2O); the function of twin earth kidneys is to process retaw (XYZ). The function of earth bee dances is to indicate the whereabouts of nectar; the function of twin earth bee dances is to indicate the whereabouts of ratcen. And so on. The relevant traits have in fact evolved to cope with what is actually there in the environment, not with qualitative doubles of what is there.

[58] Cf. Millikan's paper, 'Thought without Laws: Cognitive Science without Content'.

[59] If you find it more natural to say that the function is to protect the skin from light rays of certain sorts, so that no mention is made of the specific celestial source of these rays, thus picking out the same function on earth and twin earth, then change the example so that the proximate natural kind is varied between the two planets – suppose that on twin earth *twight* rays are what cause the pigments to operate.

The actual environment does the selecting, so it gets to individuate the function selected.[60]

But now we can hardly fail to be struck by this structural parallel between function and content: they both seem context-sensitive in the same sort of way. The teleological theory offers a neat explanation of this parallel: content just is a special case of function. The desire for water, say, is associated with the function of obtaining water; but the desire for retaw is associated with the function of obtaining retaw. The content differs because the function differs. And so for the other propositional attitudes in which the concept *water* features. Twin earth cases for this kind of content are thus *predictable* from the teleological theory plus the context-dependence of functional specifications. This seems like a pleasant confirmation of the teleological theory.

It might be objected that I am describing functions in too fine-grained a way. Instead of saying that the function of skin pigments is to prevent sunburn (or twin sunburn), I should say that their function is to prevent burns from *any* fiery celestial body that sends down light rays of the kind organisms need to be protected from. And similarly for the other cases mentioned. Then we could say that the functions are *in*variant between earth and twin earth. But if we did that, then we obviously could not explain the agreed differences of content in terms of functional differences. I would make two replies to this objection. First, I think we do in fact naturally employ the more specific mode of functional description, and that there seems nothing particularly objectionable in this practice – indeed it seems rather well motivated in view of our general conception of how natural selection works.[61] We can, of course, though perhaps with some contrivance, fashion less specific descriptions of function, but these need not be taken to oust the more specific descriptions: what we in effect have is a sort of nesting of

[60] The detailed principles controlling the way function ascription is dependent upon the environment will no doubt be fairly subtle, and different kinds of function may be tied more or less strongly to the actual environment. We need, in particular, to allow for weakly external functional descriptions in order to deal with cases in which the function fails to be fulfilled in the organism's actual environment. As a conceptual point, indeed, we need to allow for functions that exist and yet never succeed in being fulfilled, even for the ancestors of a given organism. God could equip a species with an organ designed to melt ice into liquid water but then never let the temperature fall below zero (He finds it a bit hard to keep track of everything He does). There is no reason in general to believe that the individuation of functions is going to be any simpler than the individuation of contents – which is one reason why function is a good way of thinking about content. The difficulties match.

[61] It is part of our unreflective folk biology, how we actually operate with the notion of function. Of course, we may find reasons for doing it differently in scientific biology – we might prefer a notion of 'narrow function' there. And so we have the question whether folk biology provides a sound starting-point for scientific biology – specifically, with respect to its individuative predilections. I can see the journal papers now: 'Methodological Solipsism Considered as a Research Strategy in Evolutionary Biology', 'A Syntactic Theory of Biological Function', 'Wide Function: Does Biology Need It?'.

increasingly specific functional descriptions. It is an interesting question what general principles govern this sort of nesting, but I do not see that any reason has been given to distrust or extrude the specific functional descriptions naturally evoked by my twin earth cases. Second, it seems to me that the availability of the less specific functional descriptions comports with a feature of twin earth cases that we *want* registered, so that the teleological theory is in fact doubly confirmed. For it is also clear that there is *a* level of psychological description with respect to which thinkers on earth and twin earth *are* indiscernible: that level which makes us want to say that things *seem* the same to the two groups of subjects. Beliefs about water and beliefs about retaw present themselves to their subjects in phenomenologically similar ways, despite the difference of content. We can account for the difference in terms of specific function; and we can account for the similarity in terms of less specific function. The specific function of the belief is to combine with the desire for water to obtain *water*; the less specific function is to combine with the desire for water to obtain *whatever nourishes as water does* – this including retaw. Thus the teleological theory can capture the commonalities as well as the divergences of content.

We also get a rather natural account of weakly external content. I said in chapter 1 that it is logically possible to have perceptual contents such as *square* in the complete absence of square things. I even went so far as to agree with the Cartesian tradition in holding that someone could enjoy the same contentful experiences as us normally placed people even though he was esconsed in a stimulation machine cut off from ordinary objects and their properties. The reason this is possible, according to the teleological account, is that traits can (logically) have functions which they never in fact fulfil. The function of perceptual experience is to indicate the incidence of environmental features, but there is no logical guarantee that it will succeed in performing this function. You cannot deduce a fact from a norm. The conditions under which perceptual experiences are supposed to occur need not be the conditions under which they actually (typically or invariably) do occur. Of this more in (viii) below, on scepticism.

(iv) *Normativity again* We cannot, it seems, recover the content of a representation (conceptual or linguistic) simply from the way it is actually used or is disposed to be used. This is fundamentally because representations can always be used incorrectly; and if they are, then the mistake will be rated to the content of the representation. Thus it is with Saul Kripke's example of plus and quus.[62]

---

[62] See his *Wittgenstein on Rules and Private Language*. Quus and plus are different arithmetical functions that agree in their values for given arguments up to some point but diverge thereafter; and the question is what makes it the case that someone refers to one of these functions with '+' and not the other, given that he has never reached that point of divergence. In effect, this is the question what fixes the extension of the reference relation, i.e. the determination of extrinsic content.

The general point here is that we can partition the totality of uses (actual or potential) into two sets, the correct and the incorrect, those that accord with the content of the representation and those that do not; but this partitioning cannot be effected without employing a notion not definable simply from the notion of a bare use, actual or dispositional, viz. the normative notion of using a representation as it *ought* to be used given its content. It is thus a condition of adequacy upon any account of content that it provide for this distinction among uses – as simple dispositional theories do not. Here the teleological theory scores valuable points. For it is similarly true that proper function is not definable dispositionally: what a trait or organ is supposed to do cannot be deduced from what it is causally disposed to do.[63] You cannot deduce a norm from a fact. This is simply because of the possibility of malfunction, defect, error. Among all the things a functional trait does we can distinguish between those that it is designed to do and those that it does otherwise than by design, between the things it is supposed to do and the things it does by mistake. The heart is supposed to pump blood to other organs of the body, but it can go wrong and break a blood vessel. The skin is supposed to protect us from viral infestation, but viruses occasionally get through. Cell multiplication is supposed to aid repair of damaged tissue, but it can turn cancerous. The desire for water is supposed to bring an adequate supply of water, but it can lead to too much drinking. And if it is the function of a sign to be used to indicate the presence of Fs, it is possible for the sign to be used otherwise than as it is supposed to be used, in the presence of Gs. This is as true for signs of human languages as it is for signs in the bee's nectar-indicating dance. Suppose a certain zig-zag movement has evolved with the function of causing other bees to fly due west for a mile; it is supposed to be produced when and only when the dancing bee has just found nectar at that locale. But suppose the bee has a systematic genetic defect (or acquired defect) that causes it to produce that zig-zag dance when the nectar is a mile due east: it is disposed to zig-zag that way when it returns from a successful expedition a mile eastwards. Then it is clear that this defective bee is using the zig-zag dance incorrectly – making other bees fly to barren places, wearing them out, impairing their survival prospects. (They would correct him if they could.) By not dancing as he is biologically supposed to he is violating a norm of bee nectar-signalling. Thus there is room here for a distinction between *is* and *ought*, and hence the rudiments of a normative notion of content. The basic point is simply that the notion of proper function, being normative, provides a basis for the kind of distinction between correct and incorrect that we expect from a theory of content. Semantic

---

[63] This point is stressed by Millikan. So Kripke's sceptic, given the kinds of facts he allows appeal to, would find himself questioning the factuality of ascriptions of function. We, on the other hand, might prefer to cite function precisely as a *reply* to his scepticism about content.

normativity grows out of functional normativity, on the teleological view. Teleological theories thus have the right *form* to account for content, unlike purely descriptive dispositional theories.[64]

(v) *Dual componency* I have concentrated in this chapter (and in the previous one) on the extrinsic aspect of content. But I have not supposed that this exhausts content; I have not denied that content also has a wholly intrinsic component, tied to causal role.[65] In the case of strongly external contents I would want to distinguish three aspects of content, graded according to their degree of involvement with the environment. First, there is the aspect of content that is fixed by specific environmental relations – the aspect that differentiates earthian natural kind concepts from twin earthian ones. Second, we have an aspect of content that is only weakly external – the observational stereotype (or some such) in the case of natural kind concepts.[66] Third, we have the causal role aspect of content, the bit that is quite internal – the power of the mental state to interact with other mental states in a certain way. In the case of weakly external contents, however, we need only the two levels: the extrinsic relation to an existent item, and the intrinsically grounded causal role of the representation.[67] The important

[64] Clearly, a lot more would need to be said here to make it plausible that meaning can be illuminated by consideration of function. The general conception that seems to me attractive is that meaning and content can be seen as intelligibly growing out of function when certain other conditions are met. As a rough analogy, we might compare Wittgenstein's idea that sensation language is connected developmentally with the nonlinguistic expression of sensations and comes to be used in the place of these natural expressions (see *Philosophical Investigations*, 244). What I mean is that we might come to understand the nature of content better if we see it as *succeeding* mere function, as building upon it – as Wittgenstein thinks we shall better understand pain language if we remember its prelinguistic origins. In neither case do we want to say that there is *no difference* between what comes first and what grows out of it. Propositional content, we might say, is what 'issues from' function and indication (or some such) – which is not to say that it can be reductively analysed in such terms. At any rate, we want to recognize a conceptual connection without taking it to be equivalent to an outright reduction.

[65] See my 'The Structure of Content'. In fact, my earlier emphasis (in chapter 1) on the constraining role of behaviour in the ascription of content was a (not-so-)tacit acknowledgement of the need to invoke 'internal' factors in the conditions of content ascription. We need to recognize that content is something that has distinctive behavioural effects, as well as pointing outwards to the world. Representations have a role within the subject as well as mapping onto worldly states of affairs, and this role requires a (causal) basis within the subject. My aim in this chapter has been primarily to defend and explain such aspects of content as cannot be accounted for in terms of internal causal considerations, i.e. everything that involves the representing of specific states of affairs (as opposed, say, to how the representation makes an impact on the subject's behaviour).

[66] See Putnam, 'The Meaning of "Meaning"' on stereotypes for natural kinds.

[67] We need the third level once we distinguish strong and weak externalism, since we now have two modes of worldly determination as well as the causal potential of the representation. Suppose, for the moment, that we think of the representation as a syntactic structure, so that its causal profile is fixed by the shape of this structure. Then we can capture the extrinsic components of content by indexing the structure either singly or doubly – singly if the content is like *square*, doubly if it is like *water*. Formally, of course, we could pack the double indices into an ordered pair and then say that the full

theoretical division is between the extrinsic vertical relations to the world and the intrinsic causal horizontal relations between mental states themselves (as well as peripheral inputs and outputs). Now the point I want to make here is just that the teleological theory suggests a particular conception of how these two components interlock. Internally there is the causal mechanism; externally there is the relational function of this mechanism. The mechanism is designed to discharge the function, though the function cannot.be read off its intrinsic features (remember the skin on twin earth). The relation between the two aspects of content is thus like the relation between any causal mechanism and its biological purpose: intimate, but not too intimate. Underlying a desire (say) is a causal mechanism that brings about behaviour that results in the satisfaction of the desire (if things go as planned) – this is the intrinsic causal component of content. The mechanism was installed to fulfil a certain purpose, to direct the organism to a particular environmental feature – this is the extrinsic relational component. The mechanism interacts with other mechanisms as one mental state combines with others to get behavioural results. Since the extrinsic component is fixed by what the mechanism is supposed to do and not by what it actually does (or is disposed to do), the operations of the mechanism can veer away from their allotted function, thus pulling causal role away from extrinsic content. Consequently we get a certain looseness of fit between causal role and extrinsic content. This explains how it is possible for a content to behave abnormally with respect to what it represents. A desire with a particular content may operate in the mind in a way that is quite inappropriate to this content – it might even operate in a way appropriate to the content of some other desire. This yields a certain kind of irrationality – most vividly in cases of weakness of will. These are cases in which the causal dispositions and powers of an attitude fail to operate as the content of the attitude dictates: instead of fulfilling the function contained in that content they operate (in concert with other mental states) to produce behaviour that militates against its fulfilment. Mental causation fails to respect mental content; mechanism lets down function. Habitual irrationality thus resembles a defective heart – literally.[68] The reason we do not revise our ascriptions of

content consists in the causal role plus the indexing ordered pair – thus preserving the essential form of the original dual component theory. The basic point is to distinguish the extrinsic relations of the representation from its dispositional relations with respect to other representations and to input and output. The three-level characterization just adds extra fine structure to the basic duality of content.

[68] Your decision-making mechanism is working as it is supposed to if the desire you judge to be your 'strongest' is the one you act on, i.e. you do what you think is best all things considered. It is malfunctioning if your strongest desire fails to cause its own fulfilment, thus manifesting weakness of will. Practical rationality consists in your strongest desire causing its own fulfilment; irrationality is the breakdown of this causal mechanism. The decision-making mechanism fails to fulfil its function in much the same way the digestive system can fail in its function: both are cases in which what ought to happen, biologically, fails to be brought about because of some defect in the system.

content or hearthood to get a closer fit with actual causal role is that we recognize that functional ascriptions are not determined by actual causal role – only by *ideal* causal role. The two components of content interlock or harmonize only to the extent that proper function and actual causal performance do – which is to say, only up to a point.[69]

(vi) *Subpersonal content* This is the kind of content routinely attributed by cognitive scientists to information-processing systems of which the subject has no awareness: for example, the visual modules investigated by Marr and his associates.[70] It is the kind of content ascribed in such sentences as 'the binocular disparity module has just computed that the retinal images were produced by an object at depth *d*.' I want to make two points about this kind of content attribution. One is that the teleological theory suggests a sharp sense in which such attributions are not parasitic on personal-level content attributions. The view with which the teleological theory here conflicts is that it makes no sense to attribute subpersonal content unless this is seen as somehow derivative from the kind of content consciously possessed by persons; so that in describing a visual module in contentful terms we must be treating it *as if* it were a conscious person – a manner of treatment that can be at best metaphorical or instrumentalist. But the teleological theory requires only appropriate relational functions and a sufficiently rich pattern of horizontal connections in order to warrant literal attributions of content; and subpersonal systems seem well up to that mark. Subpersonal intentionality could therefore come into the world before conscious beliefs and desires. And this seems to me a desirable result because I think evolution discovered subpersonal content before it worked up to producing conscious beliefs and desires. Content, I would say, is a relatively primitive evolutionary achievement; more primitive than consciousness, or belief/desire practical reasoning. Indeed, personal-level content should, I think, be seen as a more sophisticated later development which depended for its upsurge on a prior level of subpersonal content. The teleological theory helps one see how this might be a possible position.

The other point I want to make is that the teleological theory explains how it is possible to make empirical discoveries about the kinds of representational

[69] This possibility of disengagement is additional to that present in twin earth cases: causal role can come apart from content by virtue of the normative character of content as a teleological notion, but also by virtue of the extrinsicness of content with respect to causal role. Identity of causal powers is therefore doubly insufficient for identity of content; and this shows that the taxonomy of content cannot be (fully) explicated in terms of causal powers. We need, accordingly, to make a rather radical break with the idea that causality is what content is all about – either causal relations within the subject or causal relations between the subject and the environment. The notion of causation is just too broad and undiscriminating to do what is wanted here.

[70] See Marr, *Vision*.

contents there are. That is, in investigating a cognitive system a psychologist may find himself devising representational primitives that do not feature in the personal-level propositional attitudes of the subject – which, indeed, the subject himself could not even master. For example, Marr introduces representations of 'generalized cones' into the repertoire of the ordinary person's visual system – a technical notion that it takes a bit of mathematics to grasp. The question arises how this can happen: on what basis are such contents introduced? The answer suggested by the teleological theory is as follows: the psychologist has uncovered a mechanism whose biological function it is to indicate the incidence of this abstract environmental feature. Typically a complex biological system is made up of subsystems each with specialized functions; by investigating how the system is constructed one may discover new functions not anticipated by the global function assigned to the whole system. The functions of the blood provide a good example, as does the visual system. In the same way, the content-based psychologist will disassemble a complex information-processing system and find that its subsystems have functions in respect of features of the environment that are not represented at the personal level. He will then find himself attributing novel representational contents to the subsystems, building up an empirical theory of the whole system as he goes. And, of course, it may be a deep and difficult theoretical question what sorts of content are required to give an account of the overall workings of the system. The point I am making is that this is because it is in general a nontrivial question what the function of biological mechanisms is. To arrive at the right description of a function (and hence a content) one may have to articulate features of the environment whose theoretical salience is not apparent to casual inspection. In this way one's theory of functions must go hand in hand with one's theory of the world. This is *why* one can make startling empirical discoveries about the constituents of subpersonal content; and also why we are not limited to concepts drawn from the personal level.

(vii) *Radical interpretation*   Radical interpretation is knowledge of other minds writ explicit. Both are folk psychology gone empirical. We manage to apply the principles of folk psychology to each other with apparent ease; in ordinary messy unsystematic life we smoothly and confidently attribute contentful states to one another. But this facility is apt to appear facile (in the pejorative sense) when scepticism about other minds is raised – or the question pressed how radical interpretation is possible. What assumptions ground our easy habit of crediting others with representational states, and are these assumptions defensible? It seems to me that the epistemology of (third-person) folk psychology should be approached on the basis of a prior understanding of what contentful states *are*. Here, as elsewhere, metaphysics precedes epistemology. To know how we know things we need to know what those things are. Thus we need to know, as radical interpreters, what it *is* to have a representational state – specifically, what it is for such a state to have the content it has. Then we will know *what* it is we know when we know that someone grasps that content – and only then. The principles of radical interpretation must tell us where to look to ascertain what someone believes, desires, etc.; but they cannot direct us to the right place unless they are informed by an account of what having such a state *consists in*. Suppose you were some kind of internalist about content, so that for you the fixation of content is completely world-independent (I am not accusing you!). Then you would naturally look to the internal facts in radical interpretation, not to the extrinsic relations between subject and world. On the other hand, an externalist of the causal variety will attempt to descry the native's contents in the causal transactions between the subject and his environment.[71] The data for interpretation need to be geared to the *nature* of the states we are trying to interpret. A thoroughgoing causal externalist will deny that internal data, no matter how comprehensive, could possibly warrant a scheme of content attribution. (I stress this point because it typically goes unstressed.) The question for us, then, is how radical interpretation should proceed under the teleological theory.

And the general shape of the answer is not far to seek. Since folk psychology is embedded within folk biology – attributions of content follow attributions of function – the empirical basis of the former will partake of the empirical basis of the latter. The prior question, then, is the epistemology of folk biology: how we commonsensically assign functions to organisms. Once we have a handle on this we shall be in a position to transpose it (plus some) to the third-person epistemology of content. For to ascribe a content to another we shall need to know the function of the state that subserves that content. Thus if we know that some mental state has the function of fulfilling the organism's need for water, then we have a pretty shrewd idea that the state in question is a desire for water. Or if we are apprised that a perceptual state has the function of indicating the presence of square things (i.e. of being caused by and only by square things), then we are evidentially well placed to infer that it has the content *square*. Data for content come from data for function.

Now it is not my aim here to offer any very detailed proposal for radical interpretation, either of content or of function in general; I am concerned only to

---

[71] This is Davidson's approach: see 'A Coherence Theory of Truth and Knowledge'. Any environmentalist about content will adopt essentially the same line: the interpreter must first gather data about the composition of the native's habitat and then use this to infer what the native is thinking – what he thinks is what he is environmentally caused to think. (Incidentally, this procedure seems to allow that others could have a different conceptual scheme from us – so long as they lived in a radically disjoint environment from ours. Consider the case of the native brain in a vat; or suppose *we* were in the vat and they were roaming around the world the way we are now.)

expose the basic structure of an adequately conceived theory. One standard approach to these matters seeks to discover what a representational state is about by identifying its typical cause. For a number of reasons we have (implicitly) rejected such an approach. At best the typical cause of a mental state can provide a defeasible clue to its function; but it will lead us radically astray given that such causation is merely part of the success conditions of the function in question – since success is not guaranteed. No, what we require, in the ascription of function, is basically knowledge of the organism's *needs* – what the conditions of its thriving are – and some way to link these needs with the functions of specific traits and organs. In practice I think we proceed by correlating presumed needs and patterns of behaviour to yield knowledge of function. We observe which kinds of behaviour (in the broadest sense) promote the gratification of needs (in the broadest sense) and then we attribute a corresponding function to the mechanisms that produce that behaviour. For example, we know that human beings must not get too hot (they need to keep a steady temperature or they sicken and perish); we observe that they sweat when they get hot and that this cools them down; so we infer that the function of sweating is temperature control. Animals need to eat regularly; hunger pangs drive them to seek food; so the function of hunger pangs is to make animals seek food. Similarly, we know that human beings need sex; we observe them in discoteques making eye contact and asking each other to dance; so we infer that they (then) desire sex, i.e. *sex* enters the content of their present desires. Moving to the higher cognitive faculties, we know that people need to avoid bumping into solid objects all the time and bruising themselves; we observe that their sense organs enable them to perform this impressive feat; so we infer that they see and believe that objects are disposed around them thus and so. That is to say, we take it that generally behaviour conduces to need satisfaction (and we can tell when it does not), and then we ascribe functions that serve to mediate need and behaviour. This is the way folk biology gets empirical grip on organisms, and hence how folk psychology gets *its* grip on their minds. Attributions of content have to be sensitive to horizontal relations too, of course; but when it comes to the relational aspect of content radical interpretation is a matter of triangulating function from need and behaviour.

No doubt much more could (and should) be said about this conception of radical interpretation; my aim here has only been to sketch the gross architecture of a position.[72]

(viii) *Scepticism*   If you crave a refutation of scepticism, then the teleological theory will disappoint you. What the theory does do, however, is offer an

---

[72] I mean what I have just said to supplement the account of interpretation I gave in my 'Radical Interpretation and Epistemology'.

explanation of why scepticism is coherent; it explains the conceptual background to the sceptic's outlandish possibilities. To refute scepticism with regard to the senses we would need a demonstration that our experiences are generally veridical. Strong causal externalism would give us such a demonstration, but (as I argued in chapter 1) it is false. Does the teleological theory contain the materials to construct the needed demonstration? Well, it tells us that the content of a perceptual state is fixed by its function; and its function (we said) is to occur in the mind just when the environment is a certain way – so to indicate the incidence of an environmental feature. In other words, it is the function of (for example) an experience as of something square to be caused to occur in the mind by square things, and only square things, located in the environment of the perceiver: the experience is thus *supposed* to have a particular causal history, *designed* to result from a certain causal sequence. But now, if content is so fixed by function, then the relevant question for scepticism is whether the function is *necessarily* fulfilled: could our experiences have just the functions they have and yet never (or seldom) successfully perform these functions? The answer to this question depends on the force of the 'could'. No, if 'could' means 'as a matter of natural history'; for organisms whose traits systematically fail in their functions do not make good vehicles of gene reproduction – they quickly come to a sticky end.[73] But this is not the 'could' of interest to the sceptic: he is concerned with the 'could' of logical (or metaphysical) possibility. And I think in *this* sense of 'could' the answer is clearly Yes. All it takes is for some other agency to perform the need-fulfilling functions so dismally discharged by systematically erroneous perceptual experiences. And of course this is just what the classical sceptical possibilities tacitly assume: Descartes' evil demon can only successfully deceive us if he keeps us from perishing, and the scientific supervisor of the vats in which our brains float and bob has the task of ensuring that they stay healthy. These external agencies do for us what our experiences do in a normal environment, viz. keep us going, cater to our needs. To be so situated is not to *lose* one's biological functions (at least those relating to the brain); it is to keep them but have them fail systematically. Thus you *could* have the same experiences as a normally situated person and yet those experiences never (or seldom) be veridical – which is precisely what the sceptic requires. You simply need outside help – someone to give you what veridicality normally does.

According to the teleological theory, the sceptic's possibilities are like the following possibility. The teeth of a lion are designed to tear the flesh of its prey.

---

[73] A persistently hallucinating organism, constantly out on LSD, will not survive long in jungle conditions; LSD is a chemical substance whose (long-term) presence in the brain would be summarily selected against. Veridical perception is what natural selection prefers, the steady unclouded eye (at least while the organism is awake and moving).

If a lion fails to use her teeth in that way, she starves and dies; survival normally depends upon her teeth fulfilling their function. Does it follow that a lion logically could not survive unless her teeth fulfilled their function? Of course not, since her dietary needs might be otherwise met: she might be fed antelope broth by a conscientious zoo keeper or drip-fed by a mad medical expert. She has the teeth, they have their flesh-tearing function, but they never in fact get to fulfil that function. They might, indeed, be (or become) incapable of fulfilling their function, being too fragile for ripping into raw flesh; but this would not, in suitably hospitable circumstances, spell starvation and death – nor would it imply that the teeth no longer *have* their flesh-tearing function. As will be clear, this lion's teeth are like the experiences of the systematically deceived perceiver: both fail abjectly in their proper function but both still *have* that function. This is why it is a non sequitur to try to deduce the general veridicality of experience from the following two premises: (a) my experiences have the function of veridicality, which function they have so that I can survive; and (b) I survive. The conclusion does not follow simply because it is logically possible for me to survive without the survival function of my experiences being fulfilled. And this is just an instance of a general truth about survival and function. The sceptic who accepts the teleological theory of content is then trading on the logical gap between having a function and succeeding in fulfilling it – a gap to which I think he is fully entitled.

The teleological theory is therefore entirely consistent with scepticism with regard to the senses, unlike the strong causal externalism which ties perceptual content to the contingencies of the actual environment. I think this is a desirable feature of the teleological theory, and it brings out the radical difference there is between the two theories. Moreover, I think the teleological theory supplies an illuminating explanation of the conceptual assumptions implicit in the sceptic's possibilities; these possibilities emerge as theoretically well motivated, not merely(!) as intuitively compelling. In view of the other virtues of the theory, I venture to suggest that teleology is the best way we have at present of thinking about content. It gets more things right than any other theory I know of.[74]

---

[74] I mean just this – I know of no better approach. The whole issue of content is distressingly difficult, and it would be rash to endorse any theory as definitively correct. I think the teleological story still has a long way to go, but I think it is going in roughly the right direction – and it comes closer than any other available theory to meeting the requisite desiderata. Maybe we shouldn't quite believe it yet; we should just adopt it as our best working hypothesis. It accounts for a good deal, and I have yet to see it refuted.

3

The Basis of Content

1 Functions need mechanisms. If bodily organ o has the function f, then o must contain some mechanism m which enables it to discharge f. If it is the function of the heart to pump blood around the body, then the heart must contain some mechanism which will enable it to perform this function – as it turns out, a continually flexing muscle equipped with various chambers and valves. Let us say that the mechanism *realizes* or *supports* the function. The mechanism is a *good* realization of the function only if it discharges the function effectively, i.e. makes the organ do what it functionally should as regularly as is appropriate for the survival of the organism. The realizing mechanism must *fit* the function; it must be constructed in the right way to carry out its assigned job.

I argued in the previous chapter that the representational content of mental states should be understood (partly) in terms of biological function: specifically, the relational proper function of a mental state coincides with what the state is about. Now the brain is the organ of the body which harbours the states with these content-fixing functions; it is the mechanical basis of the mind's capacity to represent states of affairs. It must therefore contain mechanisms that discharge the functions that fix content. The question thus arises as to the character of the mechanical basis of content: what must this basis be like if it is to subserve the functions in question? The nature of the mechanism must be constrained by what it realizes; it must be suitable for the job assigned to it: so what can be the manner of its construction? How might such a content-supporting mechanism be designed and built? This is the question I want to address in this chapter.

The appropriateness of this question does not depend essentially upon accepting the teleological account of content. You can (and should) seek the mechanism of content even if you don't conceive of the mechanism as the realization of a biological function. For, whatever view you take of the roots of content, there must be *some* way in which content is supported by the brain; evolution had to install some sort of cerebral machinery, appropriately constructed, to serve as the basis of content. Some sort of mechanism *must* exist to enable representational states to do what they do. You can't make a representational system just anyhow; you need a proper plan, an effective design. You have to put the right equipment in the black box. You cannot make do with a void in the brain (though the converse is not inconceivable); and sawdust will not do the job either. A quick way to see this is to remember that a representational system will have a pattern of behavioural dispositions conditional upon the inputs received; but these dispositions must have a categorical ground capable of acting as their causal basis – and this will require a certain richness of intrinsic structure, a certain precision in the machinery. And so with the other characteristics of content: they do not come from nothing, they need an appropriately designed support system. So those who remain sceptical of the teleological account still have a motive for persisting with this chapter.

What *kind* of question is it that I am asking? And to whom would its answer be of interest? I am not intending to ask a question of traditional conceptual analysis, a question about the a priori necessary and sufficient conditions for possessing content. Nor am I intending to ask a question to which a transcendental argument would be the right form of reply (not that I have any general objection to such arguments). I do not suppose that we can excogitate merely from the concept of content what its realizing basis *must* be. Rather, I intend the question to belong to speculative empirical psychology: I want to know which (high-level) empirical hypothesis best explains the known features of representational systems such as ourselves. I am speculating about what sort of mechanism *might* underlie the possession and operation of contentful states. My procedure, then, will be to compare rival explanatory theories to see which does the explanatory work best. The best theory need not therefore be the one which is uniquely recommended on grounds of a priori necessity. But this theoretical status need not deprive the question of philosophical interest and bite – consign it to the specialisms of empirical psychology and neuroscience. For there are philosophical perplexities about content that can be resolved by showing how content might be mechanically realized, as will become clear as we proceed. If we are worried about how some feature of content is so much as possible, then explaining how it might be mechanically based can help restore tranquillity. In fact, as will become plain, we are here straddling the border between psychology and philosophy, taking from each whatever aids our understanding. There is little point in tormenting ourselves with anxieties about disciplinary boundaries. Let the illumination fall where it may and don't fret too much about its source. That, at any rate, would be my advice.

I have formulated the question as an engineering problem: how to construct a device that invites the attribution of content. And I think this is the best way to construe it. Such an engineering problem was faced by evolution in the dim distant past and is faced by workers in artificial intelligence today. Content has obvious adaptive advantages, so the genes had the task of building a machine that could instantiate content – and they succeeded. Designers of artificial intelligence want to replicate with ingenuity and forethought what evolution did blindly, the better to understand how evolution actually solved the problem. So far blindness seems to have had better results than forethought, but then it has had a lot longer. In any case, both are concerned with solving an engineering problem. What kinds of parts are needed and how should they put together? What design principles should be employed to end up with a machine that bears representational content? This is really a way of asking how actual content-bearing systems might bring the trick off. For, if we know how such a system *could* be built, then we shall have a workable hypothesis about how actual systems *might* in fact be built; and if we can narrow the range of possible designs down, on the strength of various empirical and other constraints, then we shall be in a position to determine the actual design of content-bearing organisms. To figure out how a given system is in fact engineered we ask how *we* might engineer it. My question, then, belongs to the field of what might be called *psychotectonics*, if the neologism may be forgiven: the discipline that investigates how psychological systems are constructed – how the edifice of the mind is erected from the ground up – by what design principles psychological capacities are engineered.[1] We might compare this question with an analogous question in biology, namely how to construct a device that is capable of subserving genetic inheritance. We know that some machinery must exist to support the transmission of characteristics from parents to progeny, and it is reasonable to ask how such machinery might be engineered to produce the known facts ('artificial inheritance'). By pursuing this question we might learn how it is actually done, as well as relieve any perplexity we may feel about the very possibility of what we observe concerning the phenomena of inheritance.[2] This would be an exercise in *biotectonics*, the study of the hidden architecture of biological systems (of course this study already goes by other names in biology: biochemistry, histology, cytology, etc.). And it is just conceivable that by asking how *we* might engineer a mechanism of inheritance we might come up with the idea of DNA and the double helix, the actual mechanism

[1] 'Tectonic' means 'of building or construction'. 'Psychotectonic' therefore means 'of the building or construction of minds'; it is a branch of what we might call 'natural architecture'. As neologisms go, I think this is quite a nice one. (Psychotectonics is not to be confused with dianetics or aerobics or psychokinetics or . . . psychosemantics.)

[2] In particular, it might relieve us of the need to invoke a *deus ex machina*: we would come to see that inheritance is not inherently miraculous. This has a clear counterpart in the threat of a *deus ex machina* of intentionality: a god who kindly points our thoughts (and desires) in the right direction for us, thus saving us from incurable intentional blindness.

for terrestrial organisms. The equivalent result in psychotectonics would be something worth having. Thus inspired, let us proceed with our engineering question – how minds are made.

I think it will be agreed that the tectonic proposal currently most favoured, at least within philosophy, is that representational systems are devices for the manipulation of *sentences* – minds are 'sentential engines'.[3] If you want to make a mind capable of representing states of affairs, then you construct a machine that stores and processes linguistic strings – structures with grammar, logical form, orthography, semantics. The mechanism of content is a Language of Thought, in the strict and literal sense of 'language'. This is how evolution solved the problem, and this is what the designers of artificial intelligence (or artificial intentionality) should now be aiming at. The best explanation of the characteristics of content is the hypothesis that we all have fancy word processors in our heads – devices that generate sentences, transform them, initiate transitions between them, and so forth.[4] Not only is it supposed that this is the best available explanation of content; it is also commonly alleged that there simply *is* no other serious theory in the running – the language of thought is the only remotely feasible format for mental engineering known to man. It may not be *necessarily* true, but it is currently the only place to go if you want to get the job done.[5]

What I shall be arguing in this chapter is that there is another theory to consider, a theory that has a strong claim to explanatory superiority over the sentential theory. To be bold: I think it is a *better* theory. This is the theory, familiar to many psychologists but alien to most (contemporary) philosophers, that thinking is based on *mental models*.[6] My aim in what follows is to advertise the virtues of the mental model theory from a philosophical point of view, thus

---

[3] See, especially, Jerry Fodor, *The Language of Thought* and *Psychosemantics*. The general idea that we 'think in words' is ancient and widely received. Many other contemporary philosophers and psychologists subscribe to this idea, though Fodor flinches least from its various commitments and consequences. He also tends to think of it in the engineering terms I favour. My discussion, however, will not be limited to his particular version of the idea, and it may be that he would not accept every aspect of the composite theory I shall be arguing for an alternative to.

[4] With this crucial difference, of course: these in-head user-seductive word processors do not need an independent thinking being to operate them. They operate autonomously, juggling their symbols around without the aid of antecedent intentionality. There must be no representational homunculus gazing rapt at the cerebral VDU.

[5] Thus Fodor: 'There must be mental symbols because, in a nutshell, only symbols have syntax, and our best available theory of mental processes – indeed, the *only* available theory of mental processes that isn't *known* to be false – needs the picture of the mind as a syntax-driven machine' (*Psychosemantics*, pp. 19–20).

[6] The chief exponent of this kind of theory in contemporary psychology is Philip Johnson-Laird: see his *Mental Models*. He acknowledges his debt to the seminal writings of Kenneth Craik – about whom much more soon.

clearing the way for its employment in empirical theories (where it already enjoys some success). I think the theory has important philosophical merits that have not been recognized, and its explanatory power as a theory of (the basis of) intentionality has not yet been adequately brought out. In particular, we need to be clear about precisely what it is intended as a theory *of*, and about how exactly it *can* serve as a theory of that of which it purports to *be* a theory. For there are prima facie obstacles in the way of its explaining what it sets out to explain — obstacles that call for conceptual care in surmounting them. The manufacturer of content should choose mental models as his basic components, but he needs to be careful how he slots them into place and sophisticated about how they function theoretically. The mental engineer needs the help of a philosophical adviser if he is to grasp the import of his own construction. It is not enough simply to build the machine; we need to be told how the machine *can be* a content-bearing system. We need to understand how the realizations of contents *could* consist in mental models, given the nature of both of them. I begin with a preliminary exposition of the theory; then I move on to proclaiming its merits.

2   The locus classicus of the theory of mental models is Kenneth Craik's renowed book, *The Nature of Explanation*, published in 1943. That book is remarkable for its boldness and its prescience, particularly in view of the intellectual climate prevailing at the time it was written. For this was the period of Behaviourism, and Craik's theorizing runs flat against the dogmas of that misbegotten scientific ideology: he is cheerfully up to his neck in internal structures and processes, constrained only by considerations of overall explanatory adequacy. In this respect, as in others, he anticipated the 'scientific revolution' that was to issue in what is now called 'cognitive science'. Craik's work draws upon philosophy, neurophysiology, biology and computer science (as well as engineering and electronics) to confect a striking and sophisticated theory of thinking. In effect, he is seeking an explanatorily adequate theory of cognitive competence of the kind later sought by Chomsky for language mastery and Marr for visual perception.[7] He begins by asking what thinking does, what its

---

[7] Chomsky's psychotectonic question is how the language faculty must be innately structured in order that language-learning should take place at the rate it does and with the features it has: how would you build a language acquisition device that does what human youngsters do? Marr's question is how the visual system must be computationally organized so as to enable it to generate full representations of the external world from the little patches of light that play upon the retinae: how would you build a visual device that could take these little patches and project them to full-blown visual percepts — what sort of internal structure would be required to perform this remarkable feat? Craik's question is how must the thinking faculty be constructed so as to enable it to do what thinking does: how would you make a cognitive device capable of solving problems about the external world?

competence characteristics are, and then asks what sort of mechanism – what sorts of design principles – would be capable of instantiating these characteristics. What kind of internal structure would be necessary and sufficient to confer the capacity to *think* on an organism? Only when we have a convincing answer to that question will we have a scientifically adequate *explanation* of thinking.[8] This search for appropriate mechanisms effectively initiates the artificial intelligence approach to psychological questions, as well as replacing the sterile strictures of Behaviourism with a properly rigorous 'mentalism'. For these reasons Craik is commonly regarded today as the father of the modern 'cognitivist' approach to psychological theory – and with considerable justice.[9] But he also proposes a quite specific theory of thinking within his general methodological framework, viz. mental model theory: and it is this with which I shall be mainly concerned here. Since this theory, and Craik's original statement of it, are not widely known among philosophers – and not widely understood generally – I shall start by quoting at some length from chapter 5 of Craik's book, entitled 'Hypothesis on the Nature of Thought', before going on to give my own gloss on the theory:[10]

'One of the most fundamental properties of thought is its power of predicting events. This gives it immense adaptive and constructive significance as noted by Dewey and other pragmatists. It enables us, for instance, to design bridges with a sufficient factor of safety instead of building them haphazard and waiting to see whether they collapse, and to predict consequences of recondite physical or chemical processes whose value may often be more theoretical than practical. In all these cases the process of thought, reduced to its simplest terms, is as follows: a man observes some external event or process and arrives at some 'conclusion' or 'prediction' expressed in words or numbers that 'mean' or refer to or describe some external event or process which comes to pass if the man's reasoning was correct. During the process of reasoning, he may also have availed himself of words or numbers. Here there are three essential processes:
(1) 'Translation' of external process into words, numbers or other symbols,

All three men suppose some initial state – linguistic ignorance, an incident patch of light, a problem to be solved – and some final state – speech, seeing, solving the problem – and they want to know what sort of machinery might take the subject from the initial state to the final state. And they share the assumption that substantial internal structure is going to be required to answer these questions.

   [8] I shall follow Craik in speaking of 'thinking', but our (and his) question is both broader and narrower than this verb suggests. Broader, in that we are concerned with any kind of content-based problem-solving, including subpersonal kinds; narrower, in that our concern is not with all the peculiarities of what we call thinking – so we are not trying to give a full theory of what thinking is (in particular, we are not concerned to explain how consciousness relates to the process of thinking). In a word, it is not the specific attitude itself that concerns us, but its being an attitude with content.
   [9] Or at least one of its fathers.
   [10] *The Nature of Explanation*, pp. 50–2.

(2) Arrival at other symbols by a process of 'reasoning', deduction, inference, etc., and

(3) 'Retranslation' of these symbols into external processes (as in building a bridge to a design) or at least recognition of the correspondence between these symbols and external events (as in realising that a prediction is fulfilled).

One other point is clear; this process of reasoning has produced a final result similar to that which might have been reached by causing the actual physical processes to occur (e.g. building the bridge haphazard and measuring its strength or compounding certain chemicals and seeing what happened); but it is also clear that this is not what happened; the man's mind does not contain a material bridge or the required chemicals. Surely, however, this process of prediction is not unique to minds, though no doubt it is hard to imitate the flexibility and versatility of mental prediction. A calculating machine, an anti-aircraft 'predictor', and Kelvin's tidal predictor all show the same ability. In all these latter cases, the physical process which it is desired to predict is *imitated* by some mechanical device or model which is cheaper, or quicker, or more convenient in operation. Here we have a very close parallel to our three stages of reasoning – the 'translation' of the external processes into their representatives (positions of gears, etc.) in the model; the arrival at other positions of gears, etc., by mechanical processes in the instrument; and finally, the retranslation of these into physical processes of the original type.

By a model we thus mean any physical or chemical system which has a similar relation-structure to that of the process it imitates. By 'relation-structure' I do not mean some obscure non-physical entity which attends the model, but the fact that it is a physical working model which works in the same way as the process it parallels, in the aspects under consideration at any moment. Thus, the model need not resemble the real object pictorially; Kelvin's tide-predictor, which consists of a number of pulleys on levers, does not resemble a tide in appearance, but it works in the same way in certain essential respects – it combines oscillations of various frequencies so as to produce an oscillation which closely resembles in amplitude at each moment the variation in tide level at any place. Again, since the physical object is 'translated' into a working model which gives a prediction which is retranslated into terms of the original object, we cannot say that the model invariably precedes or succeeds the external object it models. The only logical distinction is on the ground of cheapness, speed, and convenience. The *Queen Mary* is designed with the aid of a model in a tank because of the greater cheapness and convenience of the latter; we do not design toy boats by trying out the different plans on boats the size of Atlantic liners. In the same way, in the particular case of our own nervous systems, the reason why I regard them as modelling the real process is that they permit trial of alternatives, in, e.g., bridge

design, to proceed on a cheaper and smaller scale than if each bridge in turn were
built and tried by sending a train over it, to see whether it was sufficiently strong.'

It is absolutely clear from this passage that Craik intends his use of the word
'model' to be taken quite literally; it is not a mere stylistic variant of
'representation' or 'symbolic structure' (as it has tended to become in much
subsequent psychological literature). This is why the suggestion that thinking is
based on mental models is a genuine *theory of* mental representation, not just
another way of talking about the same thing: we construct mental representations
of the world *by* constructing mental models of it – this is the explanatory
mechanism of mental representation. Manipulating mental models thus
constitutes the working machinery of cognitive problem solving. A thinking
system, we might say, is a *simulation engine* – a device that mimics, copies,
replicates, duplicates, imitates, parallels reality. The basis of the intentional
relation consists in the relation of literal modelling. And the procedures that
operate on these models themselves model external processes: mental causal
processes replicate worldly causal processes, mental laws imitate physical laws.
There is a kind of isomorphism between the world and the mind (or its tectonic
basis). Not only, then, do mental models have the structure of what they
represent; they also *work* in the same way – their operations simulate the
operations of the thing modelled. The brain therefore does essentially what the
naval engineer does when he builds his model ships, though using its own special
materials of course. We all have a model builder labouring away in our heads,
working with whatever raw materials lie within the confines of the skull; more
soberly put, the brain has the capacity to generate structures that imitate external
states of affairs. It is these modelling structures that make thinking possible.
    There is some excuse for being reminded at this point of another celebrated
theory of representation, namely Wittgenstein's theory in the *Tractatus*. For
Craik's modelling theory and Wittgenstein's picturing theory certainly *sound*
strikingly similar. Consider these remarks from the *Tractatus*: 'A picture is a
model of reality' (2.12); 'A logical picture of a fact is a thought' (3); 'A
proposition is a model of reality as we imagine it' (4.01). And, most Craikian-
sounding of all:

'A gramophone record, the musical idea, the written notes, and the sound-waves,
all stand to one another in the same internal relation of depicting that holds
between language and the world.
    They are all constructed according to a common logical pattern.
    (Like the two youths in the fairy-tale, their two horses, and their lilies. They
are all in a certain sense one.)' (4.014)

Wittgenstein's idea, that symbolic representation works by the sharing of form, certainly seems closely echoed in the following passage from Craik:

'Without falling into the trap of attempting a precise definition, we may suggest a theory as to the general nature of symbolism, viz. that it is the ability of processes to parallel or imitate each other, or the fact that they can do so since there are recurrent patterns in reality. The concepts of abilities and patterns and formal identity in material diversity are all hard ones; but the point is that symbolism does occur, and that we wish to explore its possibilities.' (pp. 58–9)

We should not of course run away with the idea that the two theories are identical or differ only trivially – for one thing, Wittgenstein's emphasis on the sharing of *logical* form does not seem present in Craik's theory – but the theories are similar-sounding enough to make it somewhat surprising that Craik makes no mention of Wittgenstein, and this despite the fact that both men were working in Cambridge in the first half of the century. And it cannot be that Craik was generally ignorant of philosophy, for he gives ample evidence of being steeped in it; in fact he studied philosophy (in Edinburgh) as an undergraduate. I have not been able to resolve this historical puzzle to my satisfaction: either Craik had, by some miracle, never heard of Wittgenstein's picture theory; or he had but found it sufficiently impenetrable to deter him from enlisting Wittgenstein in his cause; or some other thing entirely. At any rate, the parallel (or convergence) seems interesting enough to be worth exploring further – though I won't be doing that here. (How, for example, does Craik's theory relate to Wittgenstein's distinction between saying and showing?)

Nor do the historical parallels end there. Ramsey too gave aphoristic formulation to (what sounds very much like) essentially the same idea when he said that a belief is 'a map of neighbouring space by which we steer'.[11] Here we find conjoined the two basic components of Craik's theory: the idea of modelling (maps being a species of model), and the idea that models guide us in our practical dealings with the world (steer us). Craik makes no mention of Ramsey either, but this is less surprising in view of the relative obscurity of Ramsey's remark (I do not mean its unclarity). Ramsey, for his part, does not mention Wittgenstein's picture theory either, but in his case we *know* that he was familiar with the *Tractatus* – for he reviewed it. I assume he was simply taking the derivativeness of his remark as obvious.[12] Anyway we seem to have the makings

[11] Frank Ramsey, *Foundations of Mathematics and Other Essays*, p. 238. David Armstrong, in *Belief, Truth and Knowledge*, professes to be a follower of Ramsey, but he shows no awareness of Craik's work (I do not intend this observation as knuckle-rapping).

[12] The steering component does not seem present in the *Tractatus*, just the mapping component. Wittgenstein is markedly unconcerned with the relation between action and thought in the *Tractatus* –

of a Cambridge tradition here; one might almost call it 'the Cambridge theory'. Its most well-known contemporary exponent, Philip Johnson-Laird, also works in Cambridge. There must be something in the air. (Perhaps I contracted it on one of my rare trips there. The air is certainly different from Oxford.[13])

Let us now leave these pleasant psycho-geographical speculations behind and take up the question how best to formulate Craik's theory. The modern contrast between analogue and digital codes, not invoked by Craik explicitly, will serve to get at the heart of the modelling theory. This distinction has been variously understood, but I will take it that the crux of the intended distinction concerns, not so much the intrinsic features of the elements of the code – whether they are discrete or continuous, for example – but rather the different *relations* such codes have to what they represent. An analogue code consists of symbols whose properties vary as a function of the things represented, while a digital code is such that its features are independent of the properties of the things represented – there is no rule whereby one can derive features of the symbol from properties of the thing symbolized or vice versa. In analogue codes properties of the represented states of affairs are somehow *reflected* in features of the code itself; but in a digital code this is not so – here the representational relation is essentially arbitrary. Thus magnitude covariation, as between sign and object, is the hallmark of an analogue code; whereas magnitude independence characterizes digital codes. Natural languages are digital (apart from phenomena such as onomatopoeia) because syntactic or phonetic features do not vary systematically with properties of the referent, and binary codes such as Morse are too. Atlases, on the other hand, are full of analogue representations because a scale is essentially a function from the region represented to intrinsic features of the map, and so too are pictures and graphs analogue. Analogue representations need not, of course, employ the same *kinds* of magnitude as the magnitudes they represent, as ordinary two-dimensional scale maps do; they can employ quite other kinds of magnitude so long as variation in one can be systematically correlated with variation in the other. Thus we could in principle devise maps that represent geographical size by means of brightness of colour or density of cross-hatching – we would still have a kind of magnitude covariation allowing us to read the values of one dimension off values of the other. For this reason analogue codes need not literally *resemble* what they stand for; the relation between sign and

---

a connection he is clearly obsessed with in the *Investigations*. Ramsey's formulation seems to straddle both these emphases: 'picturing plus use', as we might say. Craik and Ramsey agree that content must not be seen as a passive mirroring of the world; we must always remember that thought feeds into action (cf. my discussion of perceptual content and behaviour in chapter 1).

[13] They seem keener on the inner life in Cambridge, the fine-tuning of the soul; in Oxford the main business lies in behaviour, in polishing the surface. Not so?

object can be much more abstract than the notion of resemblance allows.[14] Analogue representation depends only upon a certain kind of identity of abstract structure (of the kind studied in mathematics under the heading of 'homology theory' – or so I am told).

It should be obvious enough how Craik's theory relates to the notion of analogue representation: a mental model precisely is an analogue representation. Craik's own phrase, 'similarity of relation-structure', seems to capture exactly the notion intended by the above characterization of an analogue code; indeed, we find Craik using the idea of 'analogy' in a number of places to hit off his basic thought (e.g. pp. 52, 53). What Craik adds to the bare idea of analogue representation is the insistence that mental models *function* in a certain way, that they are *working* models that permit simulation experiments to be performed on them. But still these models are to be conceived analogically not digitally; in fact, they must be so conceived if they are to count as genuine *models*, since digital representations (as we have characterized them) do *not* have the same 'relation-structure' as what they signify. Internal sentences would indeed be digital representations, but models are not sententially structured (more on this shortly). Perhaps a little bit of formalism might serve to crystallize the notion of an analogue model (if the pleonasm may be excused). Suppose we have an object or phenomenon or process D which consists of parts $x_1 \ldots x_n$, these parts having properties and relations $R_1 \ldots R_j$. Then a model of D (either mental or external) is an entity D' which consists of parts $x'_1 \ldots x'_n$, these parts having properties and relations $R'_1 \ldots R'_j$ – where there exists a systematic function mapping

[14] So the modelling theory is not like the old image theory, which does require literal resemblance. It might help in getting at the more abstract notion of an analogue representation to borrow the idea of 'second-order isomorphism' from studies of imagery. A first-order isomorphism holds between a representation of a square object and the object itself if the representation is itself square, but a second-order ismorphism consists 'not in the first order relation between (a) an individual object, and (b) its corresponding internal representation – but in the second order relation between (a) the relations among alternative external objects, and (b) the relations among their corresponding internal representations. Thus, although the internal representation for a square need not itself be square, it should (whatever it is) at least have a closer functional relation to the internal representation for a rectangle than to that, say, for a green flash or the taste of persimmon.' (The quotation is from R. Shepard and S. Chipman, 'Second-Order Isomorphism of Internal Representations: Shapes of States', p. 2.) This idea seems close to Craik's suggestion that a model is something that 'works like' what it models, only now at second order. Second-order isomorphism allows us to define an abstract notion of analogue representation which does not collapse either into a mere stylistic variant of 'representation' or into a sentential conception. For further discussion of this kind of notion, focused on the case of imagery, see various papers in Ned Block, *Imagery*, especially those by Stephen Kosslyn. But even if these attempts to define a precise notion of analogue representation are flawed, the important point is that some such notion exists and differs from the notion of a sentential representation. What I want to know is how far we can get with this notion in the theory of thought. At present the advice to follow is: think abstract, don't be too prosaic about what a mental model might look like.

instances of R onto instances of R' which preserves the magnitude relations between these instances.[15] In other words, there is some rule or law relating values of 'R' to values of 'R''' which preserves the 'structure' of these values. In the case of a simple map, this rule determines that if one region is bigger than another in geographical reality, then the area of the map that represents the former region is itself to be bigger than the area representing the latter region, though not by the same *amount* (similarly for maps that code geographical size as brightness or cross-hatching).

We can now express Craik's three stages of problem solving as follows. First, an external state of affairs is 'translated' into an analogue representation: in the simplest case this will involve the perceptual generation of a suitable model – the state of affairs outside causes the brain to construct an internal simulation of that state of affairs. Second, the model will be manipulated by various procedures and algorithms that transform it, relate it to other models, work experimentally on it – these procedures being themselves analogues of external processes. Third, there will be some appropriate output of these internal operations – either action (if the reasoning was practical) or a new belief (if the reasoning was theoretical). These are the three phases gone through by an engineer modelling a bridge, and these are the three phases involved in the brain's solving a problem by means of its internal models. (As an exercise, think how this three-stage account would apply to the problem of arranging furniture in a room.) Problem-directed thinking is experimenting on analogue representations generated and stored in the brain; as it were, conducting dry-runs on cerebral copies or replicas. Thinking before you act is running a simulation of the projected act in your head to see what will happen before you commit yourself to actually doing it. The hypothetical thinking of practical reason consists in experimenting on internal models and coming up with actual internal results: if the simulation experiment has untoward consequences for the agent's internal model of himself, then he will refrain from undertaking the external course of action so simulated (assuming he is rational). So, at least, the Craikian theory claims. It is a theory not wanting in audacity. It boasts a certain shocking simplicity.

---

[15] I am here idealizing to what might be called *total* models, i.e. models in which every part and property of the modelled thing finds a corresponding feature in the model. In reality, mental models will always be partial, selecting only a subset of the parts and properties of the thing modelled. The modelling relation is always of the form 'm models x in respects F_1 to F_n', where the list of respects will not be exhaustive. I am also idealizing to what might be called *veridical* models, i.e. models which simulate every feature of the modelled thing correctly. Again, reality at best approximates to this ideal (as professional simulators know); our representations have their erroneous spots. A total and veridical model of D would be a *perfect* model of D – it would capture everything and it would get everything right – but such perfection is only an ideal. Still, this idealization does not detract from the utility of the 'definition' of a model given in the text (cf. frictionless planes).

3   Some distinctions are now called for.

(a) I have set the modelling theory in opposition to the sentential theory; neither type of theory is a special case of the other – though both may be species of a wider genus (internal structure theories). The reason for the opposition is that sentences do not simulate what they describe and models do not describe what they simulate. Simulating and describing are toto caelo distinct kinds of relations, calling for quite different features in the items they relate. Sentences are digital; models are analogue. Sentences have grammatical structure; models have the structure of the worldly things they simulate, which is not grammatical (unless these things happen to be themselves sentences). Sentences have semantic properties – truth conditions, reference, sense; models do not – any more than maps or tree rings do. Sentences and models reach out to reality using quite different kinds of limbs or hooks; in no way are the two theories notational variants of each other.

This sharp division between the two theories is not, it must be said, to be found in Craik's own discussion; indeed, he seems to write as if *all* symbol systems were ultimately imitative, even natural languages (though it is hard to detect a clear view on the question). He might, then, regard a Fodorean language of thought as one kind of modelling theory, construing the internal sentences as sharing their structure with the things represented. I take it that this would be a plain mistake, since words simply do not replicate the properties of what they refer to. Names and predicates are just not imitations of objects and properties. An engineer cannot run his simulations on *sentences*; if he could, then he would not need to labour to construct proper working models.[16] To fix the difference in our minds, and to have a perspicuous formulation of the essence of the two theories, we can characterize the theories in the following way. We want to say what it is (tectonically) for a subject S to believe that p. The sentential theory says that it consists in the truth of this proposition:

$$(\exists s)(S \text{ bel* } s \ \& \ s \text{ means that } p)$$

where s is a sentence is S's language of thought and 'bel*' stands for whatever

---

[16] This is not, of course, to say that we cannot explain the meaning of sentences – overt or covert – in terms of associated mental models, pairing sentence and model to confer a semantics on the sentence. It is just to deny that sentences are themselves modelling structures. Putting it in terms of second-order isomorphism, syntactic similarity among sentences does not correlate with similarity among the states of affairs in the world that are described by those sentences; the word for square is not more like the word for rectangle than it is like the word for a green flash or the taste persimmon. Yet the semantics for these words might be determined by such an isomorphism at the level of the associated models. Conceivably this is what Craik really had in mind: for such a view does enable one to say, correctly, that all symbolism, including the linguistic, works by way of modelling – though at one remove.

relation it is that makes a propositional attitude the attitude of belief (it might be something like internal assent to s).[17] The modelling theory, for its part, explains what it is for S to believe that p in terms of the following condition:

$$(\exists m)(S \text{ bel*} \; m \; \& \; m \text{ simulates that } p)$$

where m is a model in S's internal system of models and 'bel*' is the same as before. Focus hard on the second conjunct of these two formulations and you will not be inclined to assimilate the two theories (I am sure *you* are not so inclined anyway). Different theoretical entities, different explanatory predicates: not the same at all.

(b) That first distinction, which I have (wittingly) laboured, is connected with a second, which is less easily appreciated. We need to keep two theoretical projects firmly apart: accounting for propositional content itself, and accounting for the tectonic basis of content. Propositional contents – the denotata of 'that'-clauses, if you like – are (trivially) propositional items, endowed with all the distinctive properties of propositions. The study of these items belongs to logical theory, or perhaps to linguistics. Mental models cannot be construed as *identical* with such items, nor can they in any reasonable sense be said to constitute them; for models are *not* propositional entities – they do not have sentential structure or logical form. The study of mental models belongs to psychology (or its psychotectonic branch). The modelling theory, to repeat, is in the engineering business, not the logical line: it purports to say how to build a device that invites the assignment of propositional items, not to say what these assigned items themselves consist in. A theory of the *ground* of a propositional attitude is not a theory of the *object* of such an attitude; the two theories belong to quite different (though connected) domains of enquiry. The mechanism that supports directedness towards a particular proposition is not to be confused with the target of this directedness. If we confuse ground and object, then we will think it compulsory to hold either a modelling theory of propositions or a sentential theory of the underlying mechanism. But neither alternative is forced on us if we steadfastly maintain the distinction. It is true that the sentential theory treats both object and ground as propositional in structure, but (as we shall see) this is not mandatory – which is a good thing for the modelling theory.

The most convenient way to articulate the distinction between ground and object is to invoke the relation of *indexing*, a relation that has come in handy in earlier connections.[18] In measurement, say of temperature, we index physical states of objects with abstract entities, viz. numbers; and there is no temptation here to suppose that the physical ground of the indexing relation somehow

[17] I get this formulation from Hartry Field, 'Mental Representation'.
[18] See Brain Loar, *Mind and Meaning*, for a discussion of indexing.

contains simulacra of numbers and numerical relations.[19] Similarly, in indexing states of a subject's head with propositions we are not thereby committed to inserting logical structure *into* the subject's head – finding shadows of propositions in the brain's crevices and nuclei. Rather, the modelling theory will maintain, we simply need some systematic rule for selecting an appropriate item from logical space as the index to be assigned to a given internal model – a rule or function that takes us from models to propositions. Maps provide a helpful analogy here. Corresponding to the analogue features of a map will be a set of propositions which describe what the map models: these propositions may be said to index the analogue features in question without sharing their analogue structure. The rule here is: for any analogue feature of the map, select the proposition that describes what that feature models. We might then say that the selected proposition is the propositional 'content' of the feature in question, the propositional object of which that feature is the non-propositional ground. Logically, it is the same with mental models: pick the propositional index that describes the state of affairs simulated by the model – this will then be the content of the mental state in question. Thus logical structure is not literally *in* the head (though it may be uniquely determined by what is), but that does not prevent it being correctly *assigned* to what is in the head.[20] Indices need not in general be *in* what they index. From this it immediately follows that you cannot hope to prove the existence of a language of thought from the necessity to find a

[19] There is, of course, a sense in which physical magnitude relations have the same structure as mathematical relations when we use the numbers to measure the magnitudes: if x is hotter than y, then the number that measures the temperature of x is bigger than the number that measures the temperature of y. But this sort of structural mapping does not warrant the idea that 'being hotter than' really is intrinsically an arithmetic relation, nor the idea that the state of having a certain temperature really is intrinsically an arithmetical object. These states and relations are in themselves just physical states and physical relations between such states – as it might be, motions of molecules. In measurement we map one system of relations onto another, but we do not have to think (what would be crazy) that these relations are somehow the *same* relations. For the nature of the entities in the two domains – the indexed and the indexing – is quite different. The virtue of the indexing idea is that it enables us to recognize that assigning propositions (with worldly constituents) to mental states need not be interpreted as implying that the persons to whom the propositions are assigned actually have proposition-like entities nestling in their heads. The cerebral machinery does not, then, need to be propositionally structured in order that it should map onto a space of propositions.

[20] In effect, this gives us weak externalism about the logical form of propositional attitudes. We need to advert to a logical form (a propositional structure) in order to specify the content of an attitude, as well as to specific objects and properties, but we should not infer that this logical form is literally a denizen of the cranium. Models populate the space within the skull, but they lack logical form since they are not propositional. So when you are reasoning logically no logical forms pass through your head, no causal machinery propels propositional structures through the system. You think in accordance with logic by virtue of your brain states being mappable onto extrinsic logical forms, not by being internally designed so as to have such forms as part of your cognitive architecture. The laws of logic may be inscribed on your heart, but they are not legible from the crevices of your brain.

structural ground for the propositional/sentential objects of belief.[21] We are therefore free to combine a sentential theory of the objects of the attitudes with a thoroughly asentential theory of their ground – as the modelling theory in effect suggests.

(c) Tectonic theories built around the notion of a model can be more or less ambitious. A modest version of the theory would give models a merely subsidiary or supplementary role in an account of mental representation. Other kinds of representational structure would then coexist with models, playing a more foundational role than models in the theory of content. Thus it might be allowed that mental maps have *some* role to play in spatial thinking but denied that they can by themselves subserve such thinking without sentential supplementation. In particular, a modest model theory does not claim that models can serve as the *basic* mechanism of content; it concedes that no amount of pure modelling apparatus can add up to propositional content. At best, then, models would form one part of a dual representation system, the other part being linguistic in character. The ambitious version of the theory, which Craik actually advanced and I have been assuming so far, claims that models can suffice on their own as realizations of content, without reliance upon any other kind of representational system. Models thus provide a *radical* theory of content, a self-sufficient foundation. The ambitious theory may allow a role for sentences as representational adjuncts, to be superimposed upon a bedrock of models, but it denies that sentences are strictly needed to order to lift an organism into the content-bearing bracket. Where a creature has a public language this may indeed seep back into its system of mental representation, but no such seepage is necessary in order that mental representation be possible. Even if having a language somehow confers greater richness on the models available to a creature, the mechanism of content is still essentially model-based – models do all the basic representational work. It is this ambitious form of the modelling theory which is philosophically most interesting, because only it claims to offer a completely nonsentential theory of how content is possible. Mixed theories may do useful empirical work, but they do not provide real alternatives to sentential theories as foundational accounts of content. I shall therefore carry on assuming that it is the ambitious theory that is at issue.

(d) At what theoretical level should our characterizations of mental models be

---

[21] That is, sentential machinery cannot be *deduced* from sentential (or propositional) indices. This is not to say that we cannot legitimately argue to such machinery as an inference to the best explanation. But I am in the process of suggesting that this is not in fact the best explanation. What might perhaps be deducible is the need for some (as yet unspecified) representational system to function as the basis of content. I sense in Fodor's *The Language of Thought* a tendency to slide from this latter kind of deduction to the much stronger thesis that the system in question must be sentential in character.

pitched? What sort of vocabulary should be used in specifying these models? Well, that obviously depends upon what theoretical levels we recognize. It is usual to distinguish three levels of description that might be given of a minded organism: (i) the hardware level, i.e. the physico-chemical neural nuts and bolts of the brain; (ii) the software level, i.e. the programmes and computations and abstract structures that constitute the cognitive system realized in the hardware of the brain; (iii) the personal level, i.e. the beliefs and desires and sensations had by the subject himself and typically available to his consciousness. I suspect myself that this tripartite layering of levels is rather too simple to capture the realities of mental processing – in particular, the software level may itself have to be subdivided into a hierarchy of levels operating in parallel – but I won't go into this question now. The point I want to make is simply that it is unlikely that descriptions of mental models will proceed at the personal level: for mental models are not acknowledged constructs of commonsense psychology. Rather, we will need to pitch our descriptions of them at the software level (or levels), developing suitable concepts to do so – as indeed is already the case in empirical studies in which mental models are invoked.[22] No doubt these software models require hardware realizations, and are constrained by the kinds of hardware structures known to exist. But we might envisage the same software models being realized in different kinds of hardware in different creatures, as computer programmes are commonly said to be variously realized in different kinds of physical machine. Interestingly enough, Craik himself is apt to characterize the models he conjectures in straight neurophysiological terms – patterns of neural excitation and so forth – but clearly there is no heavy commitment to this style of description in his general conception. Perhaps the contemporary tripartite division of theoretical levels was not clear in his mind, despite his having the conceptual materials to hand to make the requisite distinctions. He certainly had the idea of formal identity in material diversity, since this is the heart of his official theory; so he simply needed to apply this idea to the underlying mechanisms of thinking themselves. At any rate, there is considerable flexibility in the kinds of terms we might choose to characterize internal models, depending upon the tectonic level we are operating at; and no doubt it is an empirical question how in detail these characterizations might be framed. It is certainly not to be supposed that we already have available the necessary conceptual resources. Quite new concepts may well need to be devised.

[22] See Johnson-Laird's descriptions of the kinds of models implicated (according to him) in syllogistic reasoning: *Mental Models*. Work on images is also couched in these sorts of terms: see Block, *Imagery*. In fact, characterizations of models will occupy the same theoretical level as grammatical characterizations of sentences, while not actually being a *kind* of grammatical characterization: not hardware (physical), and not at the level of consciousness either.

With these distinctions made we can now turn to the explanatory capacities of the modelling theory.

4   The modelling theory is offered as an account of the (basis of the) content of propositional attitudes, both personal and subpersonal. But the kind of mental representation for which the Craikian conception seems custom-built is *images*. For images *seem* prima facie to be iconic, nondiscursive, analogue – as thoughts do not. It may therefore seem that the obvious contrast between images and thoughts, and the aptness of the idea of mental models for the former items, casts doubt upon the feasibility of a model theory of the latter items. Sententialism about thought would help capture the contrast perfectly, but models blur it: so it may be supposed. It is quite true, I think, that recent experimental work on image-dependent tasks strongly encourages the idea that images are internal models on which experimental manipulations are performed by the subject (or some subpersonal system within him).[23] Findings that correlate problem-solving response latency with the degree of rotation of an hypothesized internal analogue structure certainly invite interpretation in terms of internal processes that simulate the actual rotation of the imaged figure. But I do not think the aptness of the model theory for these representations need count against its aptness for propositional attitudes. It may appear to introspection as if images and thoughts have different sorts of structure, but that may just be because the models involved in thinking do their stuff subpersonally, whereas images seem to wear their iconicity on their introspectable face. The real question is whether we can give an explanatorily adequate *theory* of thinking in terms of models, not whether thoughts present themselves to us introspectively as based on models. Still, the objection from images at least poses a challenge to any attempt to explain propositional attitudes in terms of models: we will need to be able to register the contrast somewhere in the theory; in particular, we will need to show how models can support propositional contents as well as iconic contents. How can models explain the *distinctive* features of the contents of propositional attitudes? The distinction between ground and object, and the associated notion of indexing, turn out to be crucial in answering this question. Here goes, then: how to explain propositional content in terms of mental models.

(i) *Conceptual structure*   Consider the following objection to the modelling

[23] For example, Shepard and Metzler, 'Mental Rotation of Three-Dimensional Objects'. Oddly enough, I have yet to see in the psychological literature on imagery any citation of Craik's work, though he seems the clearest possible precursor of the essential ideas of the 'pictorial school'. In particular, Craik has the idea that there are psychological processes that involve the manipulation of analogue structures, where this manipulation is itself analogous to actually manipulating the imaged object; this is, indeed, precisely his notion of internal experiments performed on models in the head.

theory: 'Since thoughts are propositional, the structure of a thought is the structure of its defining proposition. But, by your own admission, models do not have propositional structure. So how can models function as the basis of thought? They can give no account of conceptual structure.' This objection has already been answered, in all essentials. It depends for its apparent cogency on a conflation of ground and object, mechanism and proposition. Tectonic theories are not, I repeat, intended as logical theories. To account for the structure of thoughts – construing this now as an engineering question – we need to produce some underlying mechanism with the right *degree* of structure to realize content; we do not need to find a mechanism with the exact same *kind* of structure as propositions. Then we can say that the proposition appropriately indexes the mechanism, though it does not mirror it (the mechanism does not share its propositional form). Numbers index the motion of molecules, but aggregates of molecules do not literally have the structure of the numbers that do the indexing. And maps can be correlated with indexing propositions, their analogue structure warranting this correlation, without themselves having propositional structure. Similarly, all that is required of mental models for a tectonic account of conceptual structure is an appropriate degree of complexity in the models – it does not have to be the same kind of complexity as the indexing propositions exhibit. In fact, other theories of content must take the same line too. A pure functionalist theory, which construes the basis of content in terms of causal roles or conditional dispositions, must also acknowledge that its preferred basis lacks propositional structure, since no complex of dispositions can itself *have* the form of a proposition – causal structure is not logical structure. Only the sentential theory finds something like genuine propositional structure lodged in the basis, but this is not something we are obliged to emulate. The right picture here is this: when the basis attains the right degree of structure (of the kind appropriate to its elements) it then becomes legitimate to map this structure onto a structure of propositions, thus taking psychological space into logical space; thereafter we can say that the organism in question possesses states with propositional content. We do not need to wait patiently until we can *see* propositional structure lurking within the subject's head; neither do we need to discover reasons for postulating such structure in the brain. Indeed, this idea seems to me dubiously coherent, a kind of metaphysical illusion: logical structures inhabit Fregean logical space (if they live anywhere), not the human cranium.[24] Perhaps the illicit drive to locate

---

[24] I suspect a lingering psychologism about logic may lie behind the insistence that logical structures be located within the head. Only propositions can be said properly to instantiate logical forms; neural architecture cannot. Indeed, public inscriptions or utterances of sentences do not *strictly* (directly) instantiate logical forms; rather, they are mappable onto entities (viz. propositions) that do. The idea that the brain could literally instantiate logical forms, so that we could learn logic by doing

logic in the head comes from a fear that unless it is so located it will be impossible to explain how minds latch onto logically structured propositions. But I think this fear is misplaced – and an injection of indexing is its antidote. Mental models can explain the necessary latching without themselves having logical form. For they supply a richly enough structured ground to give the individual conceptual constituents of propositional contents a causal basis, a firm tectonic underpinning – and that is all that needs to be asked of them. We do not need – and we should not want – to have *senses* in the head. Cerebral propositions are not theoretically necessary, and they would appear to be metaphysically suspect, if not incoherent. The original objection, then, traded on an ambiguity or equivocation in the notion of 'the structure of thought': did it mean the structure of the *object* of thought, or did it mean the structural *ground* of thought? Distinguish these two questions and the worry pretty soon evaporates.

(ii) *Truth and falsehood*   Now listen to this objection: 'Thoughts can be true or false, but models cannot be either, since they are not propositional. So how can models explain the truth-evaluability of thoughts?' What we just said about conceptual structure carries over to this matter of truth-value. True, the propositional content of thoughts renders them truth-evaluable; and true, models cannot be bearers of truth and falsehood: but false, models cannot provide the basis of truth-evaluable contents. What is required of the ground of content is not that it has the *same* properties as what it grounds, but rather that it has *suitable* properties to do the required grounding. Again, consider functionalism: holistic causal roles cannot literally *be* bearers of truth-value either, but that does not eo ipso disqualify them from mapping onto propositions which are truth-bearers.[25] Similarly, mental models can be so mapped without having to share the

neuroscience, seems to me a straight category mistake. The relation neural structures have to logical structures is indexing, not instantiation (though we may allow ourselves to speak loosely of a mental model as, say, conjunctive or atomic or existentially qualified). What we must on no account think is that logical relations can somehow be explained in terms of natural causal relations between cerebral structures which themselves have logical forms (directly and literally): that would be blatantly psychologistic in the classical sense. Beliefs have causal relations with each other, and they also have logical relations, but it is quite wrong to assimilate these relations to each other. The indexing conception helps in resisting this mistake, which I think contaminates a good deal of the usual talk of the 'inferential role' of beliefs. Always sharply distinguish the logical from the causal, entailment from causal consequence. (I know this sounds obvious, but it is surprisingly easy to find oneself indulging in the conflation when considering mental states with content: cf. distinguishing use and mention.)

[25] The mapping is warranted by a certain kind of harmony between the logical and the causal (*not* an identity): roughly, a belief *b* gets assigned a proposition *p* as its content because the entailments of *p* are 'tracked' by the causal powers of *b* – the subject tends to believe the propositions that are entailed by *p*. This mapping, which joins the logical to the natural, is what enables beliefs to have both causal and logical properties – though not in virtue of the same things. Loar discusses mapping the logical to the functional in *Mind and Meaning*.

properties of what they are mapped onto. In fact, they have a property which perfectly suits them for such a mapping: they can be accurate or inaccurate, good simulations or bad, have verisimilitude or its opposite. The basis of a true thought thus consists in an accurate model, one that simulates an actual state of affairs; a false thought is underlain by a model that simulates a state of affairs that does not obtain. We index accurate models with true propositions, inaccurate models with false ones. Thus it is that states of mind come to be truth-evaluable. To build a truth-evaluable machine you first install a model-constructing facility, then you index the models with propositions according to their verisimilitude: now you can go ahead and start awarding truth-values.

It may be allowed that models can deliver the bipolarity of truth and falsehood but objected that they cannot account for the normative force of the distinction. For why should accurate simulation be a good thing and inaccurate simulation a bad thing? How can this property of models explain why beliefs *aim* at (and *ought* to aim at) truth and shun falsity? Mere identity or nonidentity of relation-structure surely does not capture this normativity. This complaint would be justified if our project was to account for *all* aspects of content in terms of models, but that is not our project. Our project, remember, is to solve an engineering problem. We can therefore happily appeal to other notions to explain the normativity of truth. And we have already appealed to such other notions in the previous chapter: teleology, we said there, is the root of normativity. Let us then marry models with functions to yield norms. A model not only replicates things in the world more or less accurately; it is *supposed* to replicate accurately and supposed *not* to replicate inaccurately. The model-constructing system is biologically designed to produce accurate simulations and eschew inaccurate ones. Identity of relation-structure is thus the goal of a model, what it lives for, its allotted function, the reason it exists in the first place. Accordingly, a model is behaving as it ought to when it matches something in the external world, and it is misbehaving when it fails to match. So if truth is underlain by proper functioning of a model, then it inherits this virtue; and if falsity is underlain by improper functioning of a model, then it inherits that vice. The contrast between accurate and inaccurate modelling thus enjoys a normative significance, that derived from the notion of well-functioning. (In fact, of course, such normativity has been implicit all along. We have simply been assuming, with Craik, that the *purpose* of models is to match the world. We have been tacitly presupposing a teleological *background* for the models.[26] I shall say more about this background below.)

---

[26] I am using 'background' here in somewhat the sense Searle gives to it in *Intentionality*: it is the idea that the bearers of intentionality need to be embedded in a wider system of purposes, abilities, and so forth. The idea is, of course, Wittgensteinian ('forms of life' and all that).

(iii) *Logical relations*   Thoughts enter into a network of logical and epistemic relations in virtue of their content; each thought occupies a unique place in (better, with respect to) logical space. This network needs a basis in the structure of the system of mental models. For reasons that have become familiar by now, this basis will not consist in a network of propositional structures which are themselves logically related to each other. The basis of entailment is not itself a species of entailment. Propositions entail one another; models do no such thing. Again, the ground need not recapitulate the object. The propositional indices are the proper bearers of logical relations; mental models just select these logically related indices from logical space. Models enter into causal and combinatorial relations with each other, but not relations of entailment. These nonlogical relations *underlie* the production of thoughts which do stand in entailment relations to other thoughts, but they are not to be confused with those logical relations. That would indeed be a form of psychologism; or, conversely, an illicit logicizing of causal psychological mechanisms. A psychotectonic theory of reasoning based on the notion of mental models will explain how transitions between thoughts are realized in operations on models – how drawing conclusions rests upon appropriate combinations and transformations of models. It will not seek to explain the *validity* or otherwise of such reasoning; for, considered merely as a causal theory of mental transitions, it will simply not have the resources to answer such questions of logic.[27] These questions belong to the theory proper to the objects of the attitudes, not to the theory proper to their grounds. (Sorry to keep repeating this, but it is important.) And it is, of course, an empirical question what the details of such a theory of the grounds of reasoning would look like. Presumably the introduction and elimination rules of logic (if we think of logical consequence in that way) will correspond to various kinds of association and detachment of models.[28] My present point is just that the lack of logical relations among models themselves is not in itself a reason to reject the possibility of such an empirical theory.

(iv) *Modes of presentation*   Any account of the mechanism of content must explain how it is that contents can be individuated more finely than what they are .about. The opacity of embedded 'that'-clauses needs tectonic explication. How, for example, can a pair of contents both be about Venus – one expressed with 'Hesperus', the other with 'Phosphorus' – and yet it not be the case that both are

---

[27] Similarly with functionalism: functionalism describes beliefs in terms of their causal roles, but this mode of description is inappropriate to characterizing the logical properties of beliefs. The relata of logical relations cannot *be* causal roles. But this is no criticism of functionalism; it would only seem so if one conflated questions about the ground of the belief with questions about its object.

[28] It would be interesting to pursue this project further, but I won't attempt it here; it is probably beyond my technical expertise, and anyway would require some developed canonical notation for representing models.

attributable to any subject to whom either one of them is? What, that is, is the engineering solution to Frege's problem about informative identities? How do mental models account for fine-grain modes of presentation?

Sentential theories have a neat (*too* neat) solution: underlying any given mode of presentation of an object (individual concept) there is a cerebral word whose sense incorporates that mode, and differences of word sense are guaranteed to be fine enough to capture distinctions of conceptual content. (The solution is too neat, at least as it stands, because it glaringly leaves unanswered the question what the basis of this difference of internal word sense itself consists in: it thus effectively helps itself to what needs to be explained. I shall say more about this explanatory poverty later.) But how do mental models account for the needed distinctions? No great ingenuity is required to see how the answer to this question might go. We simply appeal to the partiality of models, the fact that they are typically (perhaps necessarily) incomplete. No model m of an object x simulates every aspect of x; m will always select certain features of x to model. Models are not omniscient with respect to the things they model. Modelling, we might say, is always 'under a description', aspect-specific. Thus my mental model of Venus will simulate only certain of its properties, not the totality of them. Accordingly, I might come to have two distinct models of that one object, one of them associated with my use of 'Hesperus', the other with my use of 'Phosphorus'; and so it might come as a big surprise to me to learn that they are both models of the same thing. Just as two photographs of Venus, one taken in the morning, the other in the evening, might differ in how they depict the planet, so that it is informative to be told that they are pictures of the same thing, so two mental models might simulate different aspects of an object and hence differ in their manner of representing it.[29] Analogue representations of the same thing can easily be different representations of that thing. Again, this is not to say that distinctness of individual concepts *consists in* differences in the underlying models; rather, this is how the engineering work gets done. Logical analysis is

---

[29] Interestingly enough, Frege himself compares a sense to the image formed in the lens of a telescope: see 'On Sense and Reference'. Different such optical images might correspond to the same object. So in one of his few attempts to say what kind of thing a sense is Frege finds himself comparing a sense with (essentially) an analogue representation, a model. Still, I *suppose* we should not read too much into this, Craikian as it sounds (apart from Frege's objectivism about senses). If we took the comparison literally, then Frege's view would be that thoughts have as their constituent senses analogue representations of what they refer to: senses would in effect be (abstract) models of references. Frege also compares 'ideas' (subjective states of thinkers) with the several retinal images produced by the single public optical image, these again having an analogue relation both to the optical image and to what it is an image of. But I *suppose* we are only intended to take the comparison as an apt simile, not as an actual *theory* about the nature of senses and ideas and how they relate to references. . .

what determines the identity or difference of concepts; mental models merely allow you to *grasp* one concept rather than another.

This account implies that there is something inevitable about opacity, since models *have* to pick up on only a subset of an object's properties – partiality is their natural lot. Models are constitutionally more finely individuated than what they model, on account of their selectivity. So there is nothing adventitious about opacity; it is not merely an optional feature of thought. Models inevitably breed opacity. I think this is an advantage of the theory. We want any theory of modes of presentation to exhibit them as naturally or ineluctably cut more finely than what they present; we want this to flow visibly from their essential nature. The mechanism should ensure this result. Mental models have the kind of nature from which this consequence can be seen to flow smoothly. They generate a naturally opaque psychology. The idea of 'direct intentionality', i.e. an unmediated apprehension of objects of thought, finds no home within mental model theory; indeed, it comes out looking impossible.[30]

Modes of presentation can be more finely individuated than the objects they present, but they can also be (at least on one interpretation of the notion) *less* finely individuated than these objects. Distinct objects can be presented to a subject (or pair of subjects) in the same way. This is simply because distinct objects can be viewed or apprehended under the same aspect(s). Such is the case in twin earth stories: both water and retaw can present the very same appearance to subjects. What is 'in the head' is therefore the same while what is thought about is different. How do mental models account for this? In essentially the same way they account for the converse possibility – by appealing to inherent partiality. The properties of the two substances that are modelled are the same properties in the two cases; the models themselves thus do not contain enough to distinguish the two substances, since they fail to simulate the chemical compositions of what they model. I and my twin earth double have the same models running through our heads, but these models have different aetiologies and operate in different contexts. They model distinct entities in virtue of these extrinsic relations, but there is no choosing between them on the score of internal structure. They are like a pair of indiscriminable photographs of identical twins. The modelling relation in such cases is therefore not fixed solely by what is in the head, but also by aetiology and context; and this explains how mental contents can represent different objects in the same way.[31]

[30] If the modelling theory is correct, then unmediated intentionality would require representation without an enabling mechanism, since any mechanism would have to consist in a (partial) model. But I take it that intentionality cannot spring from a cerebral vacuum. The aspect-involving character of mental representation thus seems guaranteed by the nature of the enabling mechanism.

[31] Going back to the concerns of chapter 1, the upshot is that the internal mechanisms are mental

(v) *Holism*   Let me distinguish two kinds of holism, which I shall call *integral* and *circumstantial* holism. Consider the totality T of concepts possessed by a subject S, and single out a particular concept C from this totality. Suppose it is now claimed that C is holistically related to the other members of T. This claim can be taken to mean (at least) either or both of the following: (a) it is necessary in order for S to *possess* C that he possess some (possibly improper) subset of T; (b) the employment of C in S's thought is potentially *governable* by the employment of any other concept drawn from T. The former kind of holism is integral in the sense that it makes C and the relevant subset of T necessarily co-possessed; S simply could not *have* C unless he also had these other integrally related concepts. The latter kind of holism is circumstantial in the sense that *if* S has a certain range of concepts R in addition to C, then C and R will necessarily interact (at least potentially) when C figures in S's reasoning – but S *need* not have this other range in order to *have* C. Circumstantial holism says (roughly) that sets of possessed concepts necessarily operate as a totality, not in isolation from each other; integral holism says' that certain sets of concepts *can* only be possessed in clusters, not singly.[32] Putting the two sorts of holism together, we arrive at the following image: a total set of concepts possessed by a subject can be partitioned into integrally related clusters, these clusters interacting circumstantially in episodes of reasoning or decision making. For example, it is very plausible to regard *male* as integrally related to *bachelor*, so that to possess the latter concept you need a grip on the former. But it would not (presumably) be very plausible to link *bachelor* with *car* in this integral way; yet it might well be held that thoughts about bachelors are potentially influenceable by thoughts concerning cars, *if* you are capable of both kinds of thought – that there are 'epistemic liaisons' between these two concepts if you have both. Or again, *tree* is plausibly integrally related to *leaf* but not to *bird*; yet thoughts about trees may necessarily interact circumstantially with thoughts about birds *if* both concepts are possessed.

models, these being literally in the head; but content itself extends beyond these internal structures and scoops up things in the world. The internal models are thus indexed by propositionally embedded worldly entities. You cannot hope to reconstruct the intentional relation from intrinsic features of models, but models do serve to make that relation (tectonically) possible.

[32] A strong form of holism says that if C is governable by T then C is integrally related to T. That is, if the occurrence of C in a judgement can be epistemically connected with arbitrarily many other judgements of which the subject is capable, then the content of C is contaminated with the concepts occurring in those other judgements: that very concept could then only be possessed by a subject in possession of the concepts with which it has epistemic links. See Fodor, *Psychosemantics*, for a discussion of this kind of runaway holism. The two holisms I am concerned with are nothing like as extreme as this kind of holism. Integral holism claims only pockets of inextricably linked concepts; while circumstantial holism is not a claim about content individuation at all but a claim about the way concepts set up a field of epistemic force that controls their occurrence in judgements and their effects on action (rather like the multiply interacting gravitational forces of massive bodies).

Integral holism imposes certain constraints on the stepwise acquisition of concepts; circumstantial holism does not – it tells how concepts behave once they have been acquired (they have a special kind of mutual affinity).

Now clearly this distinction, and its implications, could be discussed at greater length, but I hope I have said enough to communicate a sense of the basic idea – and enough to set the stage for explaining how the modelling theory might account for the two sorts of holism. Recall, again, that we are asking how to build a psychological system that exhibits holism; we want to know what the wiring diagram will look like. The question then is whether installing mental models is a good way of providing for holism of the two sorts we have distinguished. Are models suitable components to yield these two kinds of holism, assuming that we want them yielded? Will a cognitive system constructed from mental models turn out to be holistic in the desired ways? I think that mental model theory does indeed give a rather natural account of the mechanism behind these holisms. Take integral holism first. The conceptual clustering it envisages is neatly explained by the fact that models are inherently *composite*: they represent a multiplicity of features simultaneously. Pictures do this most obviously: to picture one thing or feature you have to picture others (a picture of a bachelor must depict a male), so that pictorial representation involves representational clustering. It is the same with the engineer's models. This is a direct consequence of their needing to match what they model, since properties of objects themselves come in clusters – there is a kind of integral holism of property instantiation.[33] To model a complex object instantiating a range of properties you need a model that replicates that complexity (or at least some sizeable chunk of it). Integral holism is thus predictable from the very nature of models. As we might put it: simulation is itself holistic. The sentential theory, for its part, offers to explain conceptual holism by appeal to semantic holism in the language of thought: thought is holistic because it is underlain by linguistic meaning and *it* is holistic. Again, the explanatory charge of this suggestion is minimal, since it does not tell us how to make a system that exhibits *semantic* integral holism – it simply takes the explanation of this for granted. Mental model theory, by contrast, preens itself on providing a genuine foundational explanation of the holism of content, both conceptual and semantic. What the sentential theory takes as given, the modelling theory tells you how to get.

[33] All I mean here is that instantiating one property involves instantiating others that are necessarily connected with that property: e.g. instantiating bachelorhood involves instantiating maleness. Also, of course, objects only instantiate properties in clusters, even if the clusters are not themselves indissoluble. Is there any connection between the holism latent in the relation of instantiating a property and the holism latent in the relation of representing a property (having a concept)? Does the fact that properties cannot be instantiated singly have anything to do with the (alleged) fact that concepts cannot be possessed singly? I shall leave this as a homework question.

Turning to circumstantial holism, the way to design a system that incorporates this feature is to ensure that the models can freely interact with each other – we need to build smooth causal channels between them. Think of your total world-view – your entire system of beliefs – as your overall model of the world, itself made up of a huge number of submodels. This big world-model is a bit like a toy city, composed of a large number of variously connected submodels – of houses, bridges, roads, parks, people, etc. This toy city is not such that any given part of it could not exist without the other parts, though it has some parts of which this condition holds (no model buildings without model bricks and mortar, for example); but it may yet be true that the several parts of the city operate in concert, as a sort of complex unity, so that what happens in one part of the city may be affected by what happens in other parts.[34] There is local clustering and global interaction. The elements of your world-model are likewise circumstantially related to other elements by dint of having a place in the whole system, but it is not as if the big model can only be bought and installed as a package. In constructing a total model of the world the mind must keep track, as it were, of where each element fits, thus allowing for circumstantial holism; and it must also build into each submodel whatever structure is necessary to make it rich enough to match its worldly prototype, thus delivering integral holism. It therefore seems to me that the modelling theory offers a smooth and attractive account of the tectonics of holism. The two sorts of holism seem to flow naturally from the nature of the postulated mechanism. No doubt a good deal more needs to be said here, but I think it is clear even from this brief sketch that the modelling theory has resources of the right general shape to provide a basis for integral and circumstantial holism.

(vi) *Predictiveness* This is a feature of thought upon which Craik himself lays particular stress (he says nothing about the features mentioned so far). As the quotation above makes clear, he regards it as a cardinal merit of the modelling theory that it can explain the capacity of thought to predict. He first points out the great adaptive advantage conferred by the predictive capacity: it enables us to discover the likely results of our actions without actually performing them. Then he asks how you might actually make a prediction machine, suggesting that a device for experimenting on models would have the desired properties. A thinker predicts what would happen in the real world if he were to do such-and-such by constructing a parallel 'model world' in which simulations of those things do actually happen. This is held to explain the predictiveness of thought because it

[34] I mean here to recall Quine's discussion of holism in 'Two Dogmas of Empiricism', but I would not construe the potentially ramifying impact of belief revision as a kind of integral holism with respect to the interlinked beliefs: that is, I would not construe holism about verification as entailing holism about content itself (not myself being a verificationist about meaning).

specifies a mechanism for conferring it. The capacity to think is essentially a problem-solving capacity for Craik ('only in the context of a problem does a thought have content'), and solving problems typically requires prediction; so we will have explained the essence of thinking if we can say how a prediction machine might be engineered. And working models are, according to Craik, the ideal devices from which useful predictions can be made; they are the right components to put in the prediction machine. The modelling theory thus vaults an explanatory hurdle that the sentential theory fails even to address. For there is nothing in the sentential theory that tells us how to make a prediction machine, nothing that specifies the underlying mechanism that makes prediction possible. To be sure, it will claim that covert sentences figure in predictive thinking; it does not *deny* that predictiveness is an essential feature of thought. But it does not explain it either. Words and sentences are not the kinds of structures that constitute an engineering solution to the prediction problem. Told that thinking involves subpersonal linguistic manipulations, we do not say 'Oh, so *now* I see how prediction is possible.' Craik's idea was that we do (or should) react in that way when we are told that thinking is experimenting on working models.

I think that Craik is right to stress predictiveness as an adaptive asset, and right too that the modelling theory has the form of an answer to the question what makes prediction possible. Organisms that can run internal experiments thereby acquire a powerful means of coping with what the future might bring; they are relieved of the heavy obligation to 'suck it and see' whenever they want to do anything novel. Simulations are a lot safer than the real thing, and they can be just as informative. Mental models enable organisms to select from among a range of unrealized alternatives by realizing these alternatives in simulated form. (Clearly the genes must have been in a great hurry to get this powerful hi-tec machinery installed: for he who can model best survives longest. The capacity for predictive modelling was one of evolution's smarter moves.[35]) Thought works by modelling because prediction depends on simulation. Thus the mechanism of prediction is also the mechanism of intentionality. Here I think Craik had hold of an important insight.

(vii) *Naturalism*   Any engineer is constrained by the raw materials at his disposal. It is no good coming up with fancy design plans that cannot be embodied in any known materials or which violate the laws of physics. Sensible engineers do not design perpetual motion machines that run on supernatural forces. This elementary point, no doubt urged on all tyro engineers, provides a constraint on the theorist of intentionality: if the manufacturer of intentionality has no supernatural materials to work with, then neither can the theorist of

[35] Cf. Richard Dawkins, *The Selfish Gene*, where the capacity of organisms to simulate future events is stressed.

intentionality avail himself of such materials. If evolution must get by without magic, then so must we. In effect, we must respect the known natural facts about how the brain works, supposing only such mechanisms as it could conceivably harbour. Nothing numinous. This naturalistic constraint brings us up against what has come to be called 'Brentano's problem' – the problem of accounting for intentionality naturalistically.[36] By what natural mechanism or process or relation does the mind get to be 'directed' onto states of affairs, about one thing rather than another, evaluable for truth with respect to particular objects and properties? What is the natural explanation of these 'intentional rays', these invisibly prehensile mental tentacles? What is the correct engineering solution to Brentano's problem?

The sentential theory draws a blank here. It is mute in the face of the problem. For it simply trades one intentional relation for another. Asked to explain the aboutness of thought in naturalistic terms, it offers the reference of internal words – without yet saying how *that* is brought off. Anyone puzzled about the nature of mental intentionality is not going to be unpuzzled by having it reduced to semantic intentionality. The puzzlement will recede when and only when a theory of interpretation (a semantics) for the internal language is provided, and this is where all the hard work will get done.[37] The sentential theory does not solve Brentano's problem; it merely shifts it. But the modelling theory probes deeper – it takes us outside the magic circle of intentional notions. It *explains* the intentional relation as the modelling relation (plus some natural teleology). Craik is quite explicit about the naturalism present in his account: he wants to exhibit thought as relying upon mechanisms already found elsewhere in nature. And mental models do indeed have their primitive ancestors in relations as natural as that between the rings in a tree trunk and the passing of the years, or between a foot and its print in the mud. Mental models take this simple mechanism and sophisticate it into intentionality. Evolution exploited this basic capacity for one thing to parallel another and converted it into the basis of content. The brain is a very clever device for generating such parallel structures. And identity of relation-structure is as natural a relation as you could wish. Any doubts about the

---

[36] I think it was Hartry Field who coined the phrase, as well as insisting on the project.

[37] Some of that work has been undertaken, of course. But my point is that internal words do not themselves do any of the labour; nothing semantical can be read off the shape of a word, no matter where it is located (on paper or in the frontal lobes). By contrast, mental models do incorporate the mechanism of intentionality; they do not loiter impotently waiting for a jolt of semantic life to be delivered to them. True, they need a teleological background if they are to ground intentionality, but they do already contain machinery of the right structure to fit them out for their role. Words, on the other hand, are nothing without outside interpretation. Keys have the right structure to fit them for locks, but the word 'key' cannot open any doors. Keys and 'key' both have shape, yes, but only one of them has the shape for the job. Words in the language of thought are just that – words. It is not always easy to remember that.

mental model theory will not then come from its infringement of the naturalistic constraint; rather, the worry will be whether anything as basic and natural as *that* could really be the basis of content. On the score of naturalism, mental models pass muster smartly enough. Brentano's problem for maps is solved by their analogue relation to what they map, and mental models are just another kind of analogue representation. The brain, as the engine of intentionality, has the wherewithal to construct complex analogue structures, so we are not asking more of it than it could possibly deliver. We may need to add some causation and context to the models to handle content that is not fixed by what is in the head, but this is not to abnegate naturalism – nor is it to jettison models as the basic natural mechanism by which the mind latches onto the world.

I have divided the problem of content into two subproblems: accounting for the *point* of intentionality – what general conception or theory the notion is embedded in; and accounting for the *mechanism* of intentionality – how it is engineered.[38] I addressed the first problem in the previous chapter, locating the point of content in teleological conceptions of the organism. The second problem I am dealing with now, trying out the hypothesis of mental models. However successful these efforts may (or may not) be, they are both resolutely naturalistic, in any sense of that term that is not impossibly and unreasonably restrictive (I have certainly not shown how to translate intentional talk into the terms of basic physics!). That the skin contains a pigment whose function is to protect the organism from the sun is a natural fact, as is the pigment itself. That a perceptual state has the function of indicating a particular state of affairs (occurring in the mind when and only when it is caused by that state of affairs) is also a natural fact, as is the mechanism of modelling which constitutes the machinery of this function. There is nothing numinous here. I think therefore that the engineer of content who proposes to ground intentionality in mental models (which have a specific teleology) is not in the position of a crank telephone engineer who promises to connect you up by means of wire-free telepathic links. Models

---

[38] Notice that neither of these tasks involves trying to analyse or reduce intentionality to something else. I want to obtain some philosophical illumination by asking why intentionality matters and what its supporting basis might be, not by asking how it might be reductively analysed. The best of luck to those who are out to produce such an analysis, but let us not suppose that theirs is the only project worth undertaking. Some philosophers, despairing of reductionist approaches to meaning, have advocated an indirect method: thus Davidson asks how we might construct a formal theory of meaning for a language and how that theory might be empirically tested in application to a particular speech community. I am also in effect suggesting that we adopt an 'indirect' approach, in which we seek the wider point of attributions of content and the type of mechanism that could subserve it. Or again, I am asking what more basic properties of organisms intentionality might intelligibly emerge from, without assuming that the emergent properties can be exhaustively explained in terms of the properties they emerge out of.

connect you to the world by means of entirely natural relations. So you need not worry that there is something spooky going on in your head when you think.

5   It would be an error to suppose that models are intended to do all the work of intentionality unaided. As I keep saying, they figure only as the underlying machinery. The machinery needs a purpose if it is to subserve content. Considered merely in themselves, in isolated abstraction, modelling structures cannot realize intentionality. What has to be recognized is that models realize content only in as much as they are embedded in a certain background of goals, behavioural propensities and a network of causally related states. Mental models are located within living organisms which act upon the world and are acted upon by it, which instantiate certain kinds of complex input/output links, which deploy their models to achieve various ends. Shorn of this background mental models are apt to appear inert and inutile; equipped with it they become bearers of significance, imbued with semantic life.[39] There is more to a functioning mental model, then, than mere identity of relation-structure with some external state of affairs; there is the entire psychological and biological context in which the modelling process takes place. I can sum up the character of this necessary embedding by reverting to Ramsey's pithy formulation: a belief, he said, is a map *by which we steer*. The realizing model, in other words, has a certain kind of teleologically significant causal role − to navigate the organism through life. Without this role a model in the head would be like a map without a use: a map only really *represents* because it is employed in a certain way − otherwise it is a mere adventitious small-scale replica of something else. A map needs to have a steering function if it is really to represent; but, equally, there can be no successful steering without the map to go by. Similarly, models in the head need a function in order really to represent; but, equally, the function cannot be discharged without an appropriate mechanism, viz. the models. *Both* elements − mapping and steering − need to be present and properly coordinated if mental models are to underlie representation. To paraphrase Ramsey: a representational content is a model by which we function.[40]

[39] We might say: in order for models to have representational significance for the world they need to have functional significance for the organism; they can only point beyond the organism if there is a point *for* the organism in their so pointing. Having intentionality needs to have some *value* for the organism.
[40] I think this captures the element of truth in functionalism: internal structures need to have functional roles if they are to subserve mental states. But the functionalism I favour is specifically teleological in character − it stresses the biological function of internal states, where this notion cannot be defined simply in terms of causal dispositions. Many disparate doctrines jostle together under the label 'functionalism' and we need to be very clear about exactly which doctrine we are

Appreciating this point helps dissolve a worry that might be nagging at some readers: namely, that mental model theory makes covert use of a representational homunculus. The worrying thought here is that, just as maps need map readers in order to represent anything, so mental models need internal homuncular model builders and interpreters in order to have representational significance; they need a little engineer in the head, himself already equipped with contentful states. That is to say, models have their intentionality *conferred* upon them by an homunculus conceived as antecedently endowed with intentional properties, so that the models cannot possibly *explain* the possession of intentionality. This worry goes away, however, when we remember that the models are situated in a causal-teleological context: *this* is what their steering function consists in, not the actions of a little helmsman in the head. Compare the sentential theory. Presumably it would be equally misguided to insist that the internal sentences need a cerebral interpreter himself already possessed of language and propositional attitudes; no, the sentences would perform their 'steering' function by having certain causal roles, a place in the life of the organism. There is no need for internal gazing at the cerebral language, just as there is no need for such gazing at mental models. Rather, the organism's cognitive (and conative) system is simply wired up in such a way that the models operate according to certain laws or principles.[41] What breathes semantic life into the models is not some cranial incubus squatting up there thinking its own dubious thoughts, but rather the pattern of causal-teleological relations by which the models are surrounded. Ramsey was clearly not supposing that the believing agent needs a miniature cartographer in his head to tell the homuncular helmsman what to do; rather, the map does the steering off its own bat, as it were, by dint of its causal embedding. If you make a machine that has functionally active models in it, then you have made a system with content; you do not need to install an homunculus in the mechanism too (if you did you would not yet have arrived at an adequate design). So we do not need to presuppose beliefs *about* mental models in order for mental models to act as the machinery of belief. Mental models do not need to be *interpreted* – they just need to be used.[42] But, equally, they can have the use they

endorsing from among this motley. My version of 'functionalism' says only that the biological function of a mental state constrains its content. This is utterly different from claiming, for example, that content can be reductively defined by reference to the actual causal role of the state that has that content. (I think myself that the indiscriminate use of the label 'functionalism' has muddied the waters enormously.)

[41] It might be easier to rest easy on this point if one thinks first of lowly intentional systems such as frogs or bats or rhinoceri. For they seem sufficiently tightly wired (highly strung) to render an homunculus redundant. The internal machinery clicks away without the necessity for outside intervention.

[42] Wittgenstein argued against the idea, which seems perennially tempting, that all meaning

have only because they have the structure they have. Neither use nor structure is dispensable. The two aspects are complementary in accounting for content.

6   The modelling theory imposes strong requirements on the structures and operations employed by the brain (or its subpersonal cognitive architecture) – stronger, apparently, than those imposed by the sentential theory. The sentential theory calls for a fixed and bounded alphabet (or some such) capable of generating a finite lexicon, and then a limited range of symbol-manipulating operations that assemble and transform whole sentences, these latter being potentially infinite. The symbolic powers of a language – overt or covert – are constrained only by its capacity to combine simple symbols into complex strings of symbols; and this is a matter solely of the intrinsic features of the language – how *it* is structured. A word-crunching machine pays heed only to the 'shapes' of the symbols it handles; it does not need to pay attention to the properties of what those symbols stand for. Living in a purely syntactic world, such a device is not compelled to be sensitive to what goes on in the reality semantically represented. A sentential engine can be propelled by its own inner laws. But a simulation engine has heavier obligations to the outside world: since its models must actually replicate the reality simulated, it needs to have the resources to match the complexities of what it represents. The structures and operations it employs must therefore measure up to the reality represented (at least in respect of the aspects of reality that get simulated in the model). Of course, complex models will be generated by a finite stock of combinatorial processes from simpler models, but still the generative richness of the system must in some way match that of the represented world. In short, the sentential theory seems to be able to do a lot with a little, whereas the modelling theory needs a lot to do a lot – as much indeed as what it does. The brain has, apparently, to work much harder on the modelling theory; it needs more tricks up its sleeve.[43] Is this difference a reason to prefer the sentential theory to the modelling theory?

I do not think so. It would be a reason only if we knew that the tricks required of the brain by the modelling theory simply could not fit up its sleeve, that it just wasn't up to handling the sort of complexity needed. Yes, *if* the brain were operationally too feeble to manage what the modelling theory asks of it, and yet it

depends upon an act of interpretation. He suggested instead that the root of meaning is naturally based use. (See my *Wittgenstein on Meaning* for a defence of this interpretation.) I am saying something similar, at least in this respect: content can come to rest upon natural facts about the way internal structures function. (Of course, Wittgenstein would have deplored the idea of mental models in the head, at least in his later work.)

[43] Something like this point was put to me by Jerry Fodor in conversation.

could comfortably handle the demands of the sentential theory, *then* we would have a convincing objection to the modelling theory. But what reason is there to believe this? Who says that the brain is too simple an organ to construct models of whatever the mind can represent? Surely the legendary and stupendous complexity of the brain will not be strained beyond capacity by the need to make myriad models of the world. If anything, the sentential theory might be thought to *underestimate* the capacity of the brain, asking too little of it: do we really need all that fancy neural hardware just to combine a few hundred simple symbols into strings according to a bunch of syntactic rules? And besides, there is in fact some empirical evidence to suggest that the brain is organized rather as the modelling theory predicts: the neural projections from receptor fields in the retinae to central banks of neurons, for example, are known to preserve cell neighbourhood relations – they are topological mappings.[44] Of course, we are here flailing in the realm of speculative neurophysiology, but it does not seem to me that what is known of the brain *precludes* the modelling hypothesis as a general theory of mental representation. The brain appears to have complexity enough. The modelling theory does not overestimate its powers.

But there is another point to be made against the sentential theory. This is that it purchases the relative simplicity of its operating principles at the cost of poverty of explanatory power. By making those principles syntactic in nature it leaves all the semantic questions unanswered. The richness will then have to come from the semantic department. The bare idea of a sentential engine does not, as I have said, explain the nature of intentionality; it shunts that question into a mysterious shed labelled 'semantics for the language of thought'. It is not that no proposals have been made about what goes on in that shed; the point is rather that sentence manipulation *by itself* does not do the necessary explanatory work, since sentences qua syntactic items do not have their semantics written into them. This makes for a stark contrast with the modelling theory, since models are *already* intrinsically semantically significant – they have the mechanism of intentionality engraved right on them.[45] The sentential theory will have explained the distinctive features of content when it has given a semantic theory for the internal

---

[44] See Patricia Churchland, *Neurophilosophy*, esp. part III, for a discussion of this and allied neurophysiological findings.

[45] In the same way, they have the mechanism of predictiveness built into them. Mental models are expressly cut out to do what any mechanism of content must be able to do. They have the right 'shape' to do the job. But the 'shape' of bits of syntax is not ready-made to do what needs to be done: for why should the shape of a word have anything to do with its semantic features? Words have shapes, to be sure, but it is hard to see how their shapes fit them out to be the basis of intentionality (*pace* Fodor). What has the intrinsic shape of a word got to do with the worldly item it refers to – or with its inferential links with other words? Building a device with word-shaped components is not the way to construct an intentional system. It is like trying to string a piano with lengths of spaghetti.

symbols it postulates; but the modelling theory explains these features just as it is, without supplementation from a substantive semantics. The modelling theory goes one level deeper than the sentential theory; it tells you how things look at the foundations. Associating internal sentences with mental models would suffice to interpret the sentences — thus demonstrating the superior explanatory power of the models — but then, of course, the sentences would drop out as theoretically otiose. The modelling theory *requires* more of the brain because it *explains* more about the brain's capacities. So the greater economy of the sentential theory is, from this point of view, somewhat spurious, the result of doing less theoretical work.

And this relative unambitiousness is liable to have two further results. The first is that the sentential theory is apt to seem safer than the modelling theory, less adventurous, less open to objection (by attempting less it risks less). This relative security should now seem suspect, in view of the explanatory lacunae left gaping by the theory.[46] The second result is that there will be a perpetual threat that the sentential theory is incapable of finding a solid theoretical place for semantic content; it will be liable to degenerate into a wholly syntactic theory. This is because it finds no role for properly semantic machinery in its account of mental processing; so far as processing goes, the internal symbols might just as well be uninterpreted.[47] There is no such threat in respect of the modelling

---

[46] It can seem, momentarily, that the sentential theory has the resources — the flexibility — to deal with any kind of content, since you can always find a word for anything that is mentally represented. So, it might be thought, the theory can deal as smoothly with representations of minds themselves or mathematics or ethics as it can with representations of the world of material objects. The modelling theory, by contrast, looks to have substantive problems to overcome in these domains (how, for example, does it deal with the infinite?). But this apparent advantage should now seem spurious, since the sentential theory has said nothing about how these various things are represented until it has provided a semantics for the mental language: and we can expect precisely the same kinds of problems (or similar ones) to arise in extending this theory beyond the case of ordinary objects as arise for the modelling theory. Since the modelling theory is a real *theory*, it has to shoulder the burdens consequent on its status. But the sentential 'theory' is not a theory of intentionality until it is supplemented with a substantive semantics, e.g. a causal semantics, and then the problems will start to emerge. Without such a semantics the 'theory' has (to quote Russell in another connection) all the advantages of theft over honest toil. It can be a merit of a theory that it highlight what are in fact substantive problems: that is a sure sign that the theory is not vacuous.

[47] This is essentially Stich's complaint against what he calls the Weak Representational Theory of Mind: see *From Folk Psychology to Cognitive Science*. If nothing semantic plays any role in one's account of mental processes, e.g. belief formation, then it looks as if a psychology that describes mental processes has to be a completely syntactic psychology; and then we have to ask what *other* useful purpose appeal to content might serve. It seems to me that we do want our account of mental causation to interlock at some point with our account of what determines intentionality: the mechanism of the one should coincide (or at least overlap) with the mechanism of the other. Mental models seem to satisfy this requirement: their intrinsic structure is the basis of mental causation, and this structure is also the basis for their representational relations. Thus the basis of their interactions with other models is the same as the basis of their intentionality. To see this, think of a tankful of model ships (a)

theory, since the structures it postulates have the semantic mechanism carved right into them, ready to serve as input to the relevant mental processes.

If the modelling theory is superior to the sentential theory in point of explanatory depth, it is also superior in respect of explanatory breadth. What we seek is a general theory of representational content, applicable to any creature capable of bearing content. Now some content-bearing creatures have a public language with which they talk to each other (and to themselves), but some do not – or so it seems. Anyone who believes that there can be content without public language will want a theory of content that allows for this possibility. The sentential theory has to claim that those who lack public communicative language are nevertheless blessed with a language of thought: they do not overtly speak, but they nevertheless operate with language covertly. Thus, assuming we want to attribute contentful states to frogs and dogs and human infants, the sentential theory has to credit these apparently infralinguistic creatures with a rich internal language; as it were, their brains can do what they cannot do. Now while this does not seem a priori impossible (to me anyway), I think it is a consequence to be avoided if we can: for if they deploy a rich internal language, what is there to stop them from going public? Would not evolution seize upon the presence of an internal language and quickly convert it into a useful public language, this being such a seemingly small and simple step? And is it really *plausible* to suppose that dumb creatures possess ceaselessly chattering brains?[48] Does it (be frank now) *look* to you as if your pet cat has actual *sentences* going through its silent little furry head (it is not as if it constantly seems to have words on the tip of its tongue!)? If all this linguistic imputation strikes you as just a bit far-fetched, then you will favour a theory of the basis of content that does not commit you to it. And the modelling theory does not invite you to swallow such consequences; it asks merely that you to accept that the brains of these speechless creatures contain structures

---

interacting with each other and (b) simulating a real fleet: the features that govern the causal interactions are the very features that make the models simulations of real ships. So the modelling theory gives us an account of mental causation that does not leave out the mechanism of intentionality altogether (though it does, of course, leave out the relation of intentionality itself).

[48] The case looks appreciably worse for dumb perceivers than for dumb thinkers, I think. You might persuade yourself that the capacity to think contains a capacity to chatter silently, but does the capacity to perceive – to see, hear, smell – contain such a linguistic faculty? Experiences have content, it seems, even if they are not accompanied by thought or speech (most reptiles, I would have thought, are in this position); but it stretches credulity to suppose that there has to be a language involved in having such experiences – a grammatical structure with nouns and verbs and connectives. Internal representations, yes; systematically interrelated, yes: but an actual language structurally like English or Japanese – no! Frogs don't need predicates like 'bug' in their brains in order to be able to have experiences that detect the presence of bugs, i.e. experiences as of a bug within striking distance. They really don't need to be that sophisticated. Frogs do not 'see in words', no matter where the words are or how monosyllabic frog language is. Yet they visually represent.

that parallel states of affairs in the world. These cannot be readily transformed into public language, since they are not linguistic at all; and they require nothing *like* internal speaking. Models range from the very primitive to the impressively sophisticated, but sentences do not have this kind of flexibility – to have them at all is already to have something pretty fancy. Mental models thus seem more able to capture the gradations of sophistication we observe in content-endowed creatures. In particular, they do not force us to find more sophistication in the mental lives of certain creatures than they appear to have.

A connected point concerns developmental saltationism, evolutionary or individual. At some stage in species or individual development representational states come to be instantiated: before there were no such states, now here they are. What explains this transition? A reasonable principle here is that saltationist explanations are to be avoided where possible: we want to be able to see the new capacity as an intelligible outgrowth of what existed previously – we do not want to posit sudden and unforeshadowed leaps into the unknown. Building on what was already around is the preferred way of moving forward. Developmental continuities should be sought where possible. By this principle the modelling theory clearly abides, while the sentential theory must struggle to come to terms with it. For, if content comes into the world on the back of sentences, then it is hard to see how it could have been prefigured in what was there already: either sentences were already there but they had no content; or they were not and then they sprang into existence, already fully equipped with meaning, without prior warning – neither alternative being very attractive. But mental models exploit principles already present in the nonintentional world: similarity of structure is not the prerogative of the already content-endowed, as Craik stressed. Shadows have it, as do tree rings, as do the images in the lens of a mollusc's eye – all the way up to visual images and beyond. To build a basis for content, then, the developmental mechanisms have simply to exploit these pre-existing structures in the right way – complicating them, giving them a function, locating them against a background of other such structures, hooking them up systematically to sensory input and motor output. The mechanisms of development thus have something available to work with in making the ascent to content. But for the sentential theory it looks as if all they can do is wait about until language comes newly on the scene: for we do not find intelligible prefigurements of internal sentences in the nonintentional world – sentences seem essentially to be creatures of the mind.[49] The anti-saltationist principle thus favours mental models over mental sentences (though not, of course, with the force of deductive logic).

---

[49] There is, of course, the story about how prelinguistic 'communicative' noises among animals – shrieks, purrs, barks – become transformed into genuine language by a series of intelligible steps. But (a) these are not *internal* presentences and (b) I do not believe that there is in fact a real continuity

I have been recommending the model theory on the score of overall explanatory strength. But I have said nothing about the strictly empirical merits (or demerits) of the theory; indeed, I have said nothing about how the theory might even be empirically tested – in particular, how it might be experimentally verified as against the sentential theory. There does in fact exist a body of experimental work that purports to favour mental model theory over 'mental logic' theory in the empirical explanation of actual syllogistic reasoning.[50] This work must, of course, be evaluated according to the usual canons of empirical psychological research – which is not something that I, as a philosopher, am especially competent to do (though it looks pretty convincing to me). What I can do, though, is indicate in a schematic way how empirical evidence *might* in principle bear on the two theories – thus showing that the two theories are by no means empirically equivalent. I shall thus offer a philosopher's view of what an experimental psychologist might do to convince herself that mental processing operates on models and not on sentences; I am not intending to suggest a fruitful research programme for which it would be sensible to apply for a government grant. I am concerned simply with the question of principle.

Introspection is unlikely to be of much help, of course, since the relevant processing undoubtedly takes place subconsciously. What we need then is some kind of reasoning task whose observable characteristics show up the difference of underlying processing principles – one theory claiming that these involve sentential manipulations, the other imputing operations on models. Suppose, then, that we can match two reasoning tasks for complexity of the underlying sentential processing but mismatch them for complexity of model processing; suppose, that is, that we have some workable criterion for complexity in the hypothesized hidden machinery, sentential or simulatory. Then the sentential theory will predict that subjects will find the tasks equally difficult (other things being equal), while the modelling theory will predict a difference of difficulty. Assuming that task difficulty can be measured by the time taken to complete the task, the theories will make different predictions about how long subjects will take to perform the two tasks. Conversely, we could match for difficulty on the modelling hypothesis and mismatch on the sentential hypothesis. If it takes the same time to perform the tasks matched for sentential complexity but mismatched for model complexity (or matched for model complexity and mismatched for sentential complexity), then the sentential theory is confirmed and the model

---

here. Animal noises are qualitatively different from speech. Both have effects on other creatures in virtue of their acoustic properties, but the kinds of noise are really very different. In particular, the grammatical structure of language is not prefigured in these instinctive vocalizations. I won't go on about this now, however.

[50] See Johnson-Laird, *Mental Models*.

theory disconfirmed (or the model theory confirmed and the sentential theory disconfirmed). In effect, we plot response time as a function of tectonic complexity, according to the two theories, by finding tasks that call for different degrees of complexity in the hypothesised mechanisms. All we need, then, is some way to make these comparisons of complexity; some way to read off complexity differentially from the nature of the task. A simple example will illustrate how this might be done. In task 1 we get subjects to solve a problem in which the concept *triangle* occurs; in task 2 we match the problem except that the concept *square* is involved. Now if the sentential theory is correct, then some mental synonym of 'triangle' is involved in the processing underlying task 1 and some mental synonym of 'square' in task 2. It seems reasonable to take this as an equal degree of linguistic complexity, thus yielding a prediction of comparable response time. But if the modelling theory is correct, then some model of a triangle is involved in the underlying processing needed in task 1 and some model of a square in task 2. It seems reasonable to take this as a *different* degree of model complexity, thus yielding a prediction of unequal response time. The reason this seems a reasonable assumption is that squares are more complex than triangles with respect to what they demand of a model – what with squares having that extra side. So when we run the experiment we can decide between the two hypotheses on the basis of response times. I hasten to add that this illustration is not intended as serious science; it bristles, indeed, with methodological problems and questionable assumptions. It is intended only to illustrate in a simple way the general truth upon which the experimental strategy I have sketched relies: namely, that model complexity is in general a function of the complexity of the represented object, whereas linguistic complexity is not. This is of course a direct consequence of the analogue character of models, in contrast to the digital character of words. It is because of this difference in how models and words relate to what they represent that we can pull apart the two sorts of complexity and conduct the type of experimental test just outlined. The two theories are not empirically equivalent precisely because they generate different hypotheses about the degree of complexity of the processing machinery; and these differences are in principle open to empirical detection.[51] I will leave it to the experts to devise and conduct realistic experiments that trade on this fact.

Philosophers, being a verbal breed, have become accustomed to conceiving mental intentionality in linguistic terms, as a kind of inward-directed ventriloquism – a displaced echo of the human voice. In thinking we speak

---

[51] Methodologically, this is like testing the psychological reality of different grammatical theories by taking response latencies on various psycholinguistic tasks. If one theory postulates more transformations than the other, then this ought to show up in the time taken to perform the task, assuming the transformations to be psychologically real.

quietly to ourselves; or something (our brain) speaks quietly to us. Thus it is that representational content gets into the mind; it is the visible symptom of all that hidden verbal activity. The basis of thinking is conceived as *describing* the world in an unheard language. The modelling theory abandons this picture entirely. It represents thinking as (sometimes) expressed by language, but not as resting on it, not as issuing from it. The basis of content is more like an engineer's workshop in which no one speaks. There are no volleys of verbal activity occurring in the recesses of your brain, only the production of vastly many practical models. You are not a secret speaker of some hitherto undeciphered language; you are more like the maker of a very sophisticated atlas that covers much more than ordinary geography. This contrasting picture may at first sound implausible, naive, even wildly outlandish. But I hope I have shown that it is more defensible than one might initially suppose. It may not, on a first hearing, strike the right chords in our linguistically tuned minds, but it stands up remarkably well as an explanatory theory of the basis of content. Verbal people do not make the best engineers.

Summary Conclusion: a Diagram of Content

It may be helpful at this point to present a diagrammatic synthesis of the main conclusions I have reached during the course of this book. The diagram below is intended to depict the various relations between relations that I have been working with heretofore. A prose gloss follows. It should be observed that such diagrams are seldom perfect, and this one is of course not supposed to substitute for discursive understanding. I intend it only as a useful mnemonic.[1]

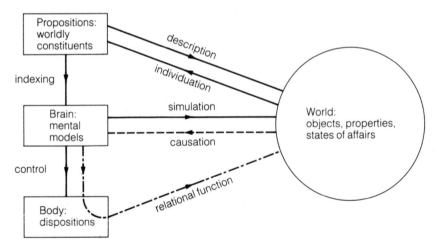

The diagram should be fairly self-explanatory (at least to those who have slogged through the whole book), but let me just offer a brief commentary on it to clear up any unclarities it may leave. Up at the top there we have propositions made up of worldly entities – objects, properties, logical operators, etc. These propositions describe the world and are individuated by reference to the world. The

---

[1] I have also found it useful as a pedagogic aid (this is a hint).

propositions, which inhabit 'logical space', index states of the head, shown in the
middle box. These states of the head, which realize propositional mental states,
are mental models. The propositions that index these models are not themselves
in the head. Because the propositions are individuated by worldly entities, the
mental models are indirectly indexed by such worldly entities. The mental
models thus indexed stand in the relation of simulation to the worldly entities that
individuate the propositions that index them; this relation of simulation is not like
the relation of description, which the propositional indices stand in to the world.
The models are typically, but not invariably, caused by the simulated entities
(hence the dashed line); there is also cognitive generativity in the aetiology of
mental models. The models are then the causal basis for motor control of the
body – they underlie behavioural dispositions. These dispositions admit of
teleological descriptions which link them to things in the world: they have
relational proper functions in respect of things in the world. Thus the causal
grounds of these dispositions, viz. the models, have relational functions – to
cause the body to behave in such a way with respect to the world as to fulfil the
organism's needs.[2] (I have drawn this relation with a broken line to indicate that
it is not a relation that is *additional* to the relation of control; it is rather another
way of describing that relation.) Accordingly, specifying the relational function
of states of the head will take us back to the very worldly entities that are
simulated by the models and which individuate the propositions – and hence to
the extrinsic content of the mental state in question. There is thus a closing of the
circle that leads from the world to propositions, from propositions to models,
from models to relational functions, and from functions to the world: the entities
we start out with turn out to be the very entities we end up with. The models are
the structures that realize the functions that fix the propositions that index the
models. As for the mind itself, which I have not tried to depict, we might
envisage it as enclosing the upper two boxes and stretching out to the worldly
circle. Unlike mental models the mind is not itself located in the head, though it
has its mechanical basis there. It should be drawn in a faint line so as to indicate
its want of substancehood. The person, I suppose, would take in the lower two
boxes and not include either the upper box or the worldly circle – since persons
are not externally individuated. The person line should be drawn bold and
substantial. A belief, say, would be constituted by the whole system of relations
linking the person to the world: a belief is (realized by) a modelling state of the
head that is indexed by an externally individuated proposition, which state has a

---

[2] Of course the underlying models are not the only causal factors involved; there are also the
particular propositional attitude relations towards the contents that the models realize – as well as the
causal apparatus proper to the motor system itself. The aetiology of behaviour is no doubt multiple,
and mental models are just one (central) component in the complex of causal factors operative.

relational function with respect to the entities that individuate the proposition. In the first chapter of this book I investigated some questions about the individuation relation attached to the top box; in the second chapter I brought the teleological relation attached to the bottom two boxes to bear; and in the third chapter I urged the virtues of the simulation relation attached to the middle box. Now I have tried to explain how these three relations relate.

I hope all that is perfectly clear.

Bibliography

Armstrong, David: *Belief, Truth and Knowledge*. Cambridge University Press, 1973.

Block, Ned: *Imagery*. Cambridge, Mass.: MIT Press, 1981.

Burge, Tyler: 'Individualism and the Mental'. *Studies in Metaphysics*, ed. P. French, T. Vehling and H. Wettstein, Minneapolis: University of Minnesota Press, 1979.

Burge, Tyler: 'Other Bodies'. *Thought and Object*, ed. A. Woodfield, Oxford: Clarendon Press, 1982.

Burge, Tyler: 'Individualism and Psychology'. *Philosophical Review* 95, January 1986.

Chomsky, Noam: 'Review of B. F. Skinner's *Verbal Behaviour*'. *Language* 35, 1959.

Churchland, Patricia: 'A Perspective on Mind–Brain Research'. *Journal of Philosophy* 78, 1980.

Churchland, Patricia: *Neurophilosophy*. Cambridge, Mass.: MIT Press, 1986.

Churchland, Paul: 'Eliminative Materialism and Propositional Attitudes'. *Journal of Philosophy* 78, 1981.

Collins, Arthur: 'Action, Causality, and Teleological Explanation'. *Causation and Causal Theories*, ed. P. French, T. Vehling, and H. Wettstein, Minneapolis: University of Minnesota Press, 1984.

Craik, Kenneth: *The Nature of Explanation*. Cambridge University Press, 1967.

Davidson, Donald: 'Mental Events'. *Essays on Actions and Events*, Oxford University Press, 1980.

Davidson, Donald: 'The Individuation of Events'. *Essays on Actions and Events*.

Davidson, Donald: 'On Saying That'. *Inquiries into Truth and Interpretation*, Oxford University Press, 1984.

Davidson, Donald: 'Radical Interpretation'. *Inquiries into Truth and Interpretation*.

Davidson, Donald: 'Reality without Reference'. *Inquiries into Truth and Interpretation*.

Davidson, Donald: 'A Coherence Theory of Truth and Knowledge'. *Truth and Interpretation*, ed. E. Lepore, Oxford: Basil Blackwell, 1986.

Davidson, Donald: 'Knowing One's Own Mind'. *Proceedings and Addresses of the American Philosophical Association*, 1987.

Dawkins, Richard: *The Selfish Gene*. Oxford University Press, 1976.

Dennett, Daniel: 'Three Kinds of Intentional Psychology'. *Reduction, Time and Reality*, ed. R. Healey, Cambridge University Press, 1981.

Descartes, René: 'Principles of Philosophy'. *Philosophical Works of Descartes*, ed. E. Haldane and G. Ross, Cambridge University Press, 1911.

Dretske, Fred: *Knowledge and the Flow of Information*. Cambridge, Mass.: MIT Press, 1981.

Dretske, Fred: 'Misrepresentation'. *Belief*, ed. R. Bogdan, Oxford: Clarendon Press, 1986.

Evans, Gareth: *The Varieties of Reference*. Oxford: Clarendon Press, 1982.

Field, Hartry: 'Logic, Meaning, and Conceptual Role'. *Journal of Philosophy* 69, 1977.

Field, Hartry: *Science Without Numbers*. Oxford: Basil Blackwell, 1980.

Field, Hartry: 'Mental Representation'. *Readings in Philosophy of Psychology*, Vol. II, ed. N. Block, Harvard University Press, 1981.

Field, Hartry: 'The Deflationary Conception of Truth'. *Fact, Science and Morality*, ed. G. MacDonald and C. Wright, Oxford: Basil Blackwell, 1986.

Fodor, Jerry: *The Language of Thought*. New York: Crowell, 1975.

Fodor, Jerry: 'Methodological Solipsism Considered as a Research Strategy is Cognitive Psychology'. *Representations*, Cambridge, Mass.: MIT Press, 1981.

Fodor, Jerry: *The Modularity of Mind*. Cambridge, Mass.: MIT Press, 1983.

Fodor, Jerry: 'Semantics, Wisconsin Style'. *Synthese* 59, 1984.

Fodor, Jerry: *Psychosemantics*. Cambridge, Mass.: MIT Press, 1987.

Frege, Gottlob: 'On Sense and Reference'. *Translations from the Philosophical Writings of Gottlob Frege*, ed. P. Geach and M. Black, Oxford: Basil Blackwell, 1952.

Johnson-Laird, Philip: *Mental Models*. Cambridge University Press, 1983.

Kaplan, David: 'Quantifying In'. *Words and Objections*, ed. D. Davidson and J. Hintikka, Dordrecht: Reidel, 1969.

Kaplan, David: 'Dthat'. *Syntax and Semantics 9: Pragmatics*, ed. P. Cole, New York: Academic Press, 1978.

Kripke, Saul: *Naming and Necessity*. Oxford: Basil Blackwell, 1980.

Kripke, Saul: *Wittgenstein on Rules and Private Language*. Oxford: Basil Blackwell, 1982.

Loar, Brian: *Mind and Meaning*. Cambridge University Press, 1981.

Locke, John: *Essay Concerning Human Understanding*. Ed. A. Fraser, Oxford University Press, 1984.

Marr, David: *Vision*. San Francisco: W. H. Freeman, 1982.

McDowell, John: 'Singular Thought and the Extent of Inner Space'. *Subject, Thought, and Context*, ed. P. Pettit and J. McDowell, Oxford: Clarendon Press, 1986.

McGinn, Colin: 'On the Necessity of Origin'. *Journal of Philosophy* 73, 1976.

McGinn, Colin: 'Charity, Interpretation and Belief'. *Journal of Philosophy* 74, 1977.

McGinn, Colin: 'Philosophical Materialism'. *Synthese* 44, 1980.

McGinn, Colin: 'The Structure of Content'. *Thought and Object*, ed. A. Woodfield, Oxford: Clarendon Press, 1982.

McGinn, Colin: *The Subjective View*. Oxford University Press, 1983.

McGinn, Colin: *Wittgenstein on Meaning*. Oxford: Basil Blackwell, 1984.

McGinn, Colin: 'Radical Interpretation and Epistemology'. *Truth and Interpretation*, ed. E. Lepore, Oxford: Basil Blackwell, 1986.

Millikan, Ruth: *Language, Thought and Other Biological Categories*, Cambridge, Mass.: MIT Press, 1984.

Millikan, Ruth: 'Thought without Laws: Cognitive Science without Content'. *Philosophical Review* 95, January 1986.

Nagel, Thomas: 'Physicalism'. *Philosophical Review* 74, 1965.

Nagel, Thomas: 'What is it Like to be a Bat?'. *Mortal Questions*, Cambridge University Press, 1979.

Nagel, Thomas: *The View From Nowhere*. Oxford University Press, 1986.

Papineau, David: *Reality and Representation*. Oxford: Basil Blackwell, 1987.

Peacocke, Christopher: *Sense and Content*. Oxford: Clarendon Press, 1983.

Putnam, Hilary: 'The Meaning of "Meaning"'. *Mind, Language and Reality*, Cambridge University Press, 1975.

Putnam, Hilary: *Reason, Truth and History*. Cambridge University Press, 1981.

Putnam, Hilary: 'Computational Psychology and Interpretation Theory'. *Realism and Reason*, Cambridge University Press, 1983.

Pylyshyn, Zenon: *Computation and Cognition*. Cambridge, Mass.: MIT Press, 1984.

Quine, Willard: 'Two Dogmas of Empiricism'. *From a Logical Point of View*, Cambridge, Mass.: Harvard University Press, 1953.

Quine, Willard: *Word and Object*. Cambridge, Mass.: MIT Press, 1960.

Ramsey, Frank: *Foundations of Mathematics and Other Essays*. London: Routledge & Kegan Paul, 1931.

Russell, Bertrand: 'The Philosophy of Logical Atomism'. *Logic and Knowledge*, ed. R. Marsh, London: Allen & Unwin, 1956.

Russell, Bertrand: *The Problems of Philosophy*. Oxford University Press, 1968.

Sartre, Jean-Paul: *Being and Nothingness*. London: Methuen, 1969.

Schiffer, Stephen: *Remnants of Meaning*. Cambridge, Mass.: MIT Press, 1987.

Searle, John: 'Minds, Brains and Programs'. *The Behavioural and Brain Sciences* 3, 1980.

Searle, John: *Intentionality*. Cambridge University Press, 1983.

Segal, Gabriel: 'Seeing What is not There'. Unpublished typescript.

Shepard, Roger and S. Chipman: 'Second-Order Isomorphism of Internal Representations: Shapes of States'. *Cognitive Psychology* 1, 1970.

Shepard, Roger and J. Metzler: 'Mental Rotation of Three-Dimensional Objects'. *Science* 171, 1971.

Shoemaker, Sydney: 'Causality and Properties'. *Identity, Cause, and Mind.* Cambridge University Press, 1984.

Sklar, Lawrence: *Space, Time and Spacetime*. Berkeley: University of California Press, 1974.

Stalnaker, Robert: *Inquiry*. Cambridge, Mass.: MIT Press, 1984.

Stampe, Dennis: 'Toward a Causal Theory of Linguistic Representation'. *Midwest Studies in Philosophy*, Vol. 2, Minneapolis: University of Minnesota Press, 1977.

Stich, Stephen: *From Folk Psychology to Cognitive Science*. Cambridge, Mass.: MIT Press, 1983.

Strawson, Peter: *Individuals*. London: Methuen, 1959.

Strawson, Peter: 'On Referring'. *Logico-Linguistic Papers*, London: Methuen, 1971.

Strawson, Peter: *Subject and Predicate in Logic and Grammar*. London: Methuen, 1974.

Stroud, Barry: *The Significance of Philosophical Scepticism*. Oxford: Clarendon Press, 1984.

Wittgenstein, Ludwig: *Tractatus Logico-Philosophicus*. London: Routledge & Kegan Paul, 1961.

Wittgenstein, Ludwig: *Philosophical Investigations*. Oxford: Basil Blackwell, 1974.

Index